THE HISTORY OF THE NEW DEAL 1933-1938

BY
BASIL RAUCH

CAPRICORN BOOKS

NEW YORK

CONTENTS

COPYRIGHT 1944, © 1963 BY BASIL RAUCH

Capricorn Books Edition, 1963

PRINTED IN THE UNITED STATES OF AMERICA

Fourth Impression

PREFACE to the CAPRICORN EDITION

THE New Deal has mightily puzzled many people ever since it burst upon Washington like a cannonade on March 4, 1933. No episode in America's three and a half centuries, except the Civil War, has stirred more passionate disagreement among professional knowers and sayers; and unprofessional ones are even more excitable when the name of Franklin D. Roosevelt or the New Deal comes up. Was it socialism? or colossal governmental bungling? or subordination of citizens to unconstitutional growth of governmental powers? or the traditional kind of American piecemeal reformism? or a good thing for all except the rich, who got properly soaked? or a bad thing for all except power-mad theorists and bureaucrats? or the extension of democracy from political to economic and social spheres? or the collapse of the dream of the Fathers of the Republic that men might wisely govern themselves? and so on and so forth.

The Civil War has kept us tied in a straitjacket of questions: Did the South fight for states rights or for slavery? Did the North fight for conquest or for democracy and Negroes' freedom? Answers have always varied wildly, and not entirely along North-South lines. No agreement is in sight. Like the tides of the hard-fought battles so typical of that terrible War, one side advances a bit, then it is pushed back again.

Disagreements about the New Deal have unfolded in

a pattern that does not repeat itself. During the years of New Deal dynamism which provide the matter of this book, opponents of Roosevelt and the New Deal reached a pitch of outraged emotion which one imagines might have led them into a righteous mood for civil war if they had not begun to win some victories in 1937 and 1938. "Anti-New Dealers" and "hate-Roosevelt" people formed a well-defined category escaping party, sectional, and to some extent class lines. Today's young people learned to love Roosevelt and admire the New Deal either because their parents did or because their parents were so obviously irrational in their anti and hate feelings that adoption of contrary attitudes consoled their children's longing to rebel.

This and the dying out of the older generation are likely to make us forget how powerful the anti and hate feelings of many Americans actually were during and for quite a while after the years of major New Deal activism. Civil commotion was also held in bounds because the antis and the haters failed to find a sectional or a party bastion. In every region and almost every State of the Union, passionate supporters of the New Deal dominated opinion. Politicians of both parties—all except a few wild men—knew this and prevented the pot from boiling over. The 1936 Republican Platform, like that issued by the "conservative" party every presidential-election year since, was a pro-New Deal document. The antis and the haters found neither a substantial doctrine nor leaders endowed with any slight charisma. Herbert Hoover and Alf Landon were the best the opposition could find, and they were politically dreary. Al Smith killed his chances by the immoderation of his anger against Roosevelt. Only the wild men had leaders with some sort of popular appeal: Huey Long and Father Coughlin fascinated millions with their medicine men's imprecations and promises, but at election time almost all these millions refused to buy their snake oil. Wendell Willkie, the Republican candidate for President in 1940, had genuine political appeal, but he was a "Me-too" New Dealer.

Until Roosevelt made his most serious mistake by fighting for his Court Packing plan in 1937, he gave the opposition no moral or Constitutional opening wide enough for effective attack against him and the New Deal. This mistake, the failure of the primaries "purge" campaign of 1938, and the economic Recession of 1937-1938 took much of the shine off the New Deal. With his domestic program incomplete, Roosevelt turned to foreign policy to meet the threats posed by Hitler's Germany, Mussolini's Italy, and Imperial Japan. Many an American who had cursed the New Deal followed Roosevelt's leadership in support of the nations that fought the Axis. Some Americans traveled down the other highway from support of the New Deal to attack against Roosevelt's foreign policy. These were not many, but a few of them, like the editors of the New York *Daily News* and *Chicago Tribune*, and Senator Burton K. Wheeler of Montana, raised a frightful din. The columnist Westbrook Pegler conducted a one-man hate-Roosevelt industry, delivering a daily stab against the President, his family, his friends, and all his domestic and foreign works, as sinuous as if he wrote with a kris.

Delirious hatred of Roosevelt and the New Deal has died out. Only truly logical enemies of the welfare state, a little band who peep from time to time that we ought to repeal the 1913 Income Tax Amendment, maintain a sad revetment against the New Deal. No politician, not even those ultra-conservatives who give rise to doubts about their sanity, openly attack the New Deal or propose to repeal its major statutes. The strongest anti-New Deal argument now capable of kicking up some political dust is the argument against deficit spending; but its champions rarely specify

[v

any New Dealish activity of the Federal Government that should be abolished. Eight years of Republican rule under President Eisenhower brought coolness towards New Deal goals but also a certain amount of expansion of New Deal programs along with the largest budgetary deficits of peace time.

The collapse within half a generation of the fanatical hatred of the New Deal is certainly one of the marvels of American history. It would be easier to raise a regiment to fight for the Confederacy than against the New Deal. Indeed one fancies that the DAR would if they could incite their men-folk to lift a blunderbuss against the UN more militantly than against the New Deal—which is not to say that these eminent descendants of ancestors do not nourish a rich detestation of, for example, Mrs. Roosevelt and her friends among Jews, Negroes, and assorted Americans who do not incur the doubtful benefits of DAR approval. But a political cause that finds its biggest oomph in the bosoms of the DAR is by definition lost. Businessmen and their friends have long ago rejected serious anti-New Dealism as impracticable. In fact they can wax eloquent on the beauties of certain New Deal agencies such as the Federal Deposit Insurance Corporation.

The victory of the New Deal in the arena of opinion is all the more remarkable because controversy continues over what the New Deal actually is and means. It is like a dish whose secrets do not yield themselves even to the most knowing palate. Practically all historians, political scientists, sociologists, and economists like the New Deal, but they cannot agree on what it is or on what to call it. "New Deal" is just a manufactured name on a political menu. The chief argument of this book is that the New Deal was, in general, two things. The labels "First New Deal" and "Second New Deal" caught on with other writers on the subject. Still they do not agree on either the value or the meaning of the two "Deals:" they only agree that important changes occurred in 1934-1935. The rather portentous labels applied to the two New Deals in this book ("pro-big business" and "economic nationalism" for the First New Deal; and "pro-labor" and "economic internationalism" for the Second New Deal) have been refined by the subtle analyses of later writers, most particularly, Arthur Schlesinger, Jr. And it would be a neat trick if someone could establish a means to determine whether the things the two New Deals had in common were more important or less important than the things that differentiated them.

Certainly the New Deal early and late meant a willingness to use Federal powers to the limit in order to rescue the nation's people and economy from the ravages of the Great Depression; a dynamism in inventing and trying out *ad hoc* solutions of problems as varied as the gold standard and the unemployment of dancers; and a spirit of well-doing rooted in the ideas and consciences of social workers. This book emphasizes those other respects in which the New Deal policies of the Hundred Days in 1933 were reversed in the legislation of the great 1935 session of Congress. The temptation to emphasize these was two-fold: the sheer intellectual pleasure of dissecting into differentiated parts what appears to the casual eye to be homogeneous; and curiosity to find an explanation for the great tide of public opinion from virtually unanimous support of Roosevelt and the New Deal in 1933 to sharp polarization by 1935 which made "anti-New Deal" and "pro-New Deal" more potent expressions of political passion than party labels.

Without regret for yielding to the temptation, I think I would be inclined now to underline the unity of the New Deal more than its shift from early to later policies. In the first place, a longer perspective inclines one to emphasize broader outlines and reduces the importance of differences in detail. In the second place, the New Deal one looks back at today is scarcely separable from the leadership of Franklin D. Roosevelt, and Roosevelt imposed a personal stamp on everything important that happened in Washington while he was President. It is easy to over-emphasize the change in character of his most intimate advisers from the early Raymond Moley, a "conservative," to the later Harry Hopkins, standing in the position Roosevelt described (but did not occupy so consistently himself) as "a little to the left of center." The fact is that Moley in 1932 and 1933 helped organize programs which were quite radical enough to suit demands to rescue the country from the disasters it had fallen into under the genuinely conservative President Herbert Hoover.

For quite a while debate about the character of the New Deal was directed by the Amherst College faculty in their pamphlet: *The New Deal: Evolution or Revolution?* This contained analytical passages by many authors who could presumably help the reader arrive at a reasoned answer to the question posed in the title. But this question essentially concerned not facts but the semantic values one may give to the words "evolution" and "revolution." Therefore this debate turned out to be arid.

The most provocative analysis of the character of the New Deal was published in 1955 by Richard Hofstadter as the final chapter, "From Progressivism to the New Deal," of *The Age of Reform: From Bryan to F. D. R.* (Knopf). In this he emphasizes those characteristics which unify the New Deal even while he denies that it amounted to a single, consistent and coherent program. Then he proposes a view of the New Deal that is strikingly original. He views it from the perspective of the pre-First War Progressive Movement. Other writers rather lazily pointed to the con-

viii]

tinuity of Progressivism and the New Deal. Hofstadter vigorously asserts that the New Deal was a "New Departure." He admits that New Dealers shared with Progressives great willingness to use governmental power to "meet the needs of the people and supplement the workings of the national economy;" that the New Deal often seemed to stand squarely in the tradition of the New Nationalism as formulated by Herbert Croly; that New Deal rhetoric was "strongly reminiscent of Progressivism;" and that on a number of particular issues, like the antagonism to holding companies and monopoly and the support of public power, the New Deal took a familiar, Progressive stand. But he nevertheless declares that the New Deal was different from anything that had ever happened in the United States—different in its central problem, in its ideas, spirit, and techniques.

The central problem was restoration of a sick economy, and no reform President before Franklin D. Roosevelt had ever taken power in such circumstances. All earlier protest movements had been organized in the interest of small entrepreneurs or those ambitious to become entrepreneurs. Accordingly, they had all accepted the market economy and competition, and only wished to use government to police and moralize them to make room for new men. Hofstadter minimizes the positive functions of government which earlier reformers had proposed and neglects to mention prior "New Deal" ideas like Theodore Roosevelt's proposal to give the federal government regulatory licensing power over all corporations, or agencies like the Federal Trade Commission, or the authority over credit in the entire economy which was lodged in government by the Federal Reserve Act of 1913. He does not claim that "planning" differentiated the New Deal from the reform tradition. He calls the New Deal "a chaos of experimentation." This would seem to deny that the historian can find any underlying principle in the great series of New Deal laws which included the Wagner Labor Relations Act, the Social Security Act, and the Wages and Hours Act.

At the same time, he notes the New Deal's assumption of responsibility for the condition of the labor market. But he attributes this to a "silent revolution" in public opinion which occurred before Roosevelt took office and passes over Roosevelt's own contribution to the formation of public opinion. He calls federal relief to the unemployed and the federal guarantee of the right of collective bargaining simply matters of political necessity. It may be sound to say that the success of the New Deal is attributable to the coincidence of "good politics" and the urgencies of social conscience. Then we might find that Roosevelt did indeed have a great deal in common with his reformist predecessors among Presidents of the United States. When he does mention social security, unemployment insurance, wages and hours, and housing, Hofstadter pictures the New Deal as "fated" to take on the social-democratic tinge because of the demands of the newly powerful labor movement and the unemployed. He gives the New Deal no credit for helping to clear the road to large-scale labor organization or for overturning Hoover's denial of federal responsibility for the needs of the unemployed.

After so much is shorn away from the New Deal, what the "New Departure" may be becomes a question. The term can be justified in this way: the sheer quantity of governmental reformist activity launched by the New Deal produced a qualitative change in American government. This view becomes all the more useful because the Second World War and the Cold War have reinforced the New Deal by using its agencies for the overwhelming necessities of foreign policy. Defense and space exploration contracts and the enlarged armed forces serve—and over-serve—the

x]

functions of New Deal agencies which were intended to be temporary, such as the PWA and the WPA. So the welfare state by unforeseen and unavoidable permutations has become something like a barracks state.

The necessity for such an evolution is doubtless deplorable, but one may be grateful that this barracks state has at its foundation the social idealism and the institutions of the New Deal. What more fortunate circumstance can we imagine for the modern democratic state when its operations are threatened by the ravages of the business cycle at home and aggression abroad? We can do nothing other than accept the danger that the only possible means of overcoming the diseases of depression and war may injure and possibly destroy the patient—and still fight against all imaginable odds for the preservation of democracy.

BASIL RAUCH

Wickford, Rhode Island
June, 1963

PREFACE

THE purpose of this book is to examine the evolution of the policies of the Roosevelt administration from 1933 to 1938. Historians and commentators have usually assumed that the New Deal is a single body of policies expressive of a single political philosophy, however they may picture it as torn by contradictions and patched by opportunism. Most attempts to organize its history in orderly fashion have divided the vast body of New Deal legislation according to subject matter, banking, relief, tariff, agriculture, and so forth, and have described the laws passed and the administration activities in each field in turn, as if they were accumulations to be understood in terms of mass. The chief clue such a compendium provides to a possible shift in basic policies is the series of Supreme Court decisions which found unconstitutional many of the first batch of New Deal laws.

This neglects the fact that all but one part of one of the invalidated laws were rewritten to meet constitutional objections and repassed without alteration of their essential purposes. The only exception was negative: the Court's invalidation of the NRA codes of fair-trade practice probably encouraged the administration to abandon the code system for industry as a whole after many administration leaders and supporters had already turned against it. The net influence of the Supreme Court on New Deal legislation was slight.

A fundamental change in the political philosophy and policies of the Roosevelt administration did occur during 1934. It divides the six years covered in this book into two distinct periods, and its importance justifies the designations First New Deal and Second New Deal. The reorientation was undertaken deliberately, and it fulfilled the President's campaign promise that his method would be experimental. Only two policies were pursued consistently through both periods: political foreign policy, and the extension of government regulation of the kind first imposed on railroads by the Interstate Commerce Act of 1887 to further selected fields, such as aircraft and motor carriers, public utilities, securities, and banks. In the broad fields of agricultural, industrial, labor, tariff, money, and unemployment relief legislation the policies of the First New Deal were fundamentally altered and in some cases reversed to create a Second New Deal.

These changes may be described in general terms of purpose and political philosophy. The primary aim of the First New Deal was recovery, while that of the Second was reform. Higher prices for industry and agriculture were the immediate objective during the first period; increased purchasing power and social security for the population as a whole were the immediate objectives during the second period. The policies of the first period were expressions of the philosophy of economic nationalism and scarcity, while those of the second illustrated the philosophy of international economic coöperation and economic abundance. The First New Deal was chiefly beneficial to big business and large farmers. The Second New Deal was chiefly beneficial to labor and smaller farmers.

The administration did not during either period attempt to revive the laissez-faire economic liberalism of the mid-nineteenth century, which in this country had been undermined steadily since the Lincoln administration by interventions of the state and federal governments in ways variously favorable to business, farmers, and labor. The federal government during the Hoover administration and the First New Deal developed new interventions which were desired by and favorable to businessmen, and large farmers, and were likened to corporativism by some observers. By this time terminology was confused by the advocates of government intervention favorable to dominant interests claiming that "freedom of enterprise" was still their objective and that "liberalism" was still their philosophy. For the contrary program of government intervention desired by and favorable to labor and smaller farmers, which became the characteristic policy of the Second New Deal, as for the program of all pro-labor administrations during the twentieth century, the term "new liberalism" has been favored by historians. The American term "progressivism" aptly labels the policies of the Second New Deal; in this book the term "liberal" is used to designate policies favorable to labor, and "conservative" those favorable to business. In this broad sense, the First New Deal was conservative and the Second New Deal liberal.

By 1936, the transition to the Second New Deal was complete. The President appealed to the country for re-election as the leader of a liberal reform administration carrying out the program of farmers and laborers. His victory was the most overwhelming in party-election history, and it was a victory for the Second New Deal. In 1937, the administration undertook to complete the structure of the Second New Deal with measures designed to benefit particularly the less well-organized groups of farmers and workers. By the end of 1938, this process had stopped, and the creative period of the New Deal ended: no important new reform law has been passed since that year. But the structure of the Second New Deal was by no means complete. The South had been called the country's economic problem Number One in August,

1938, and one-third of the nation was still ill-clothed, ill-fed, and ill-housed. Passage of legislation to meet these problems was prevented by rising opposition in Congress.

The reasons for the failure of administration support in Congress were many. Conservatives had become alarmed by the rights and privileges given to groups formerly submerged and by the expansion of the federal debt and administrative agencies. Southern Democratic Congressmen especially feared that the administration was intent upon raising the status of the Negroes and poorer whites of their section and disturbing social and economic relationships in ways dangerous to their own control. And the administration embarked upon three enterprises in 1937 and 1938 which failed, and in the process strengthened the opposition within as well as outside the Democratic Party. These were the bitter fight for the Supreme Court "packing" bill, the reduction of WPA relief and credit inflation which led to the economic recession of 1937, and the attempted "purge" of conservative Democratic Congressmen in the elections of 1938.

At the same time that opposition to further domestic reforms grew powerful, the administration was faced with the need to consolidate national unity against the rise of aggression by the Axis powers. A vigorous pursuit of further domestic reforms would alienate the Southern Democratic leaders, who, on the other hand, were willing to support a strong foreign policy against aggression. Western Congressmen who were progressive on domestic issues were largely isolationist in temper. The decision was made to minimize domestic reform for the sake of Southern support on foreign policy.

The permanent changes in the country's domestic institutions established by the Roosevelt administration were chiefly the product of the Second New Deal. The administration has defended these reforms against conservative attack since 1938 with almost complete success, while primary attention has been concentrated on foreign affairs. A second volume is planned to study the evolution of policy of the Roosevelt administration since 1938 during the periods of "National Defense" and "Global War."

The two volumes are not intended to uncover more than the main outlines of development with enough detail to support the hypothesis that experimental evolution is the key to understanding the history of the New Deal. The complexities of interrelationships among various New Deal policies, the multiplicity of detail, the scope of the economic, social, and political areas touched, and the storms of personal and partisan conflict have until now militated against the attempt to discover the interpretive pattern which best explains the meaning of even the first six years of the Roosevelt administration. The present war is rapidly filling up a vast foreground behind which those years withdraw into perspective. It is not imagined that the historical interpretation which is presented in the present volume will be accepted as "final," or "definitive." But that is no reason for not attempting an interpretation of a period which is acquiring some of the perspective indispensable to the historian, and is at the same time so full of meaning for the immediate future of the American people and the world. Besides, finality and definitiveness have not been achieved by the historians even of ancient Egypt.

*　　*　　*

The encouragement and comment of Professor Allan Nevins of Columbia University were especially valuable to the author. He gratefully acknowledges the assistance of three of his former students, graduates in History of Barnard College, Columbia University: Miss Lucille Osmer, Miss Joan M. Brown, and Mrs. Fanny Brett de Bary. Mr. Louis H. Bolander of the Mahan Library was particularly generous with his time and valuable suggestions. Permissions to quote copyrighted material have been granted by Random House, *Public Papers and Addresses of Franklin D. Roosevelt*, Volumes I-V; The Macmillan Company, *Public Papers and Addresses of Franklin D. Roosevelt*, Volumes 1937–1939, and Stuart Chase, *A New Deal;* Charles Scribner's Sons, W. S. Myers and W. H. Newton, *The Hoover Administration: A Documented Narrative;* Harper and Brothers, Raymond Moley, *After Seven Years;* Harcourt, Brace and Company, James A. Farley, *Behind the Ballots;* and Doubleday, Doran and Company, H. S. Johnson, *The Blue Eagle from Egg to Earth* and W. S. Myers, editor, *The State Papers and Other Public Writings of Herbert Hoover.*

* * *

No attempt has been made to survey all of even the printed material on the New Deal, the volume of which is already awesome, hence a formal bibliography was not deemed useful. The reference notes at the end of this book indicate the materials on which the work is directly dependent. The author has not had access to the stores of private papers of President Roosevelt, which are accumulating in the Hyde Park Memorial Library and will provide compendious materials for an army of historians and biographers in future. The generous collections of public papers which the President has already published, the *Congressional Record* and printed reports of committee hearings, the *Statistical Abstract of the United States*, the Supreme Court *Reports,* and published accounts of several early leaders of the administration are the chief sources which have been used. The *New York Times* and *Current History* provided the best running accounts of political events. The author is indebted to

an article published by a journalist in about 1937, which de-
fies present efforts to locate it, for the original suggestion that
there were *two* New Deals.

BASIL RAUCH
Lieutenant, USNR

Annapolis, Maryland
July 1, 1944

CHAPTER I

THE OLD DEAL

FIVE times in American history peaceful revolutions have been made by voting into power new administrations which abandoned the policies of their predecessors and turned the nation towards new goals. The New Deal of President Franklin Delano Roosevelt was the fifth of these main turnings on the American political road. To understand it, which is the purpose of this book, it will be useful first to notice what antecedents it had in the comparable revolutions of Presidents Washington, Jefferson, Lincoln, and Wilson.

Each of these Presidents' administrations signified the coming to power of a new coalition of two or more sectional-class interest groups in revolt against a preceding administration which represented only one such group.

Both the sole piece of constructive legislation and the general impotence of the Confederation Congress which preceded Washington's administration had served the interests of Western debtor farmers at the expense of Eastern creditors. The Northwest Ordinance of 1787 encouraged farmers to move west, while the inability of the government to provide a sound currency permitted them to scale down the value of their debts by measures ranging from violent interference with judicial process to inflationary money schemes. A coalition of Southern planters and Northern businessmen wrote the new Federal Constitution to create a government strong enough to achieve their immediate purpose

[3

of securing creditor interests as well as other more general national purposes, and the same coalition came to power when Washington was inaugurated in 1789.

Under Hamilton's brilliant leadership, the Federalist administration not only implemented the strict letter of the new Constitution, but stretched its meaning by interpretation in order to enact funding, tariff, banking, and monetary legislation which sacrificed the interests of Southern planters as well as Western farmers. When the Federalist administration of John Adams showed by its enforcement of the Alien and Sedition Acts of 1798 that it was willing to suppress civil liberties in order to ensure the continued rule of Northern businessmen, Southern planters finally abandoned the party and united with Western farmers and the small beginnings of the Northern laboring class to expel the Federalists from office.

The new coalition which came to power with Jefferson's inauguration in 1801 was the only one of the five great revolutions which proposed states' rights and the devolution of federal power as its program. Nevertheless, from Jefferson's purchase of Louisiana, without benefit of the constitutional amendment which he admitted was necessary, to Jackson's high-handed destruction of the United States Bank, this coalition expanded federal authority as much as any other, and changed only the interest groups which were served. By 1860 the Jeffersonian coalition had broken down, and the Democratic Party had come under the exclusive control of Southern slave-owning cotton planters. The refusal to throw open the west to farmers for free homesteads, and the aggressive expansion of slavery, threats to Northern free laborers as well as farmers, alienated these two groups and caused them to unite with Northern businessmen in a new coalition.

When Lincoln came to power as the leader of this coalition, the South seceded rather than lose control of the national government. But the Republican Party organized supporters of the Union for its successful restoration by force, at the same time that it enacted the homestead, banking, tariff, and railroad subsidy legislation for which its supporters had voted it into office. Then it abolished slave ownership to destroy the only sectional interest which has ever refused to accept peacefully its defeat at the polls. After the Civil War, Republican administrations came increasingly under the control of Eastern businessmen, until—after the defeat of the farmers' revolt under Bryan in 1896—raising the tariff rates, preserving the gold standard, and imperialism became their chief concern. Theodore Roosevelt attempted to restore farmers and laborers to equality in the coalition, but Taft failed to maintain the balance. In 1913 Woodrow Wilson, aided by the split in the Republican Party which Roosevelt precipitated, was able to come to power as the leader of a restored Jeffersonian coalition of Southern planters, Western farmers, and Eastern laborers.

Not states' rights but strong federal action against the abuses of big business was the essence of the Wilsonian New Freedom. Lower tariffs, the Federal Reserve Bank system, a graduated income tax, federal loans to farmers at low interest, restrictions on business monopoly, federal sanction of the right of labor to organize unions, the eight-hour day for railroad workers, and woman suffrage were the most important reforms achieved. In 1920, the Democratic Party staked everything on the League of Nations, an issue on which Western farmers offered little support, and it was defeated. The Republican Party returned to power with no new program calculated to satisfy a broad coalition of interest groups. It merely revived the policies favorable to business, chiefly high tariffs, low taxes on large incomes, and subsidies to business, which had led to its defeat in 1912. Through the twenties, so long as industrial expansion and prosperity continued, it was able to win elections.

It is clear that certain factors in the four revolutions described above were constants. They justify generalizations on the process by which basic changes occur in American political history, and they may perhaps be termed the laws which govern such change: when an administration comes to represent the interests of only one major sectional-class group, its tenure of power is limited; the groups whose needs have been neglected by such an administration will sooner or later unite to form a new coalition capable of winning electoral majorities; the policies of an administration representing a coalition of interest groups will be the sum of the requirements of each group, whether arrived at by simple addition, or by compromise between conflicting needs, or both; strict interpretation of the Constitution is rejected when it interferes with the realization of the program of a new coalition; within a coalition the most powerful single interest tends in the course of time to dominate the others, and to abandon their policies in favor of exclusive devotion to its own. Therewith the cycle is complete, and the stage is set for its repetition.

That this cycle is the fulfillment of the hope and the deliberate design of the authors of the Federal Constitution is evidenced by James Madison in his prophetic *Federalist*, Number 10. The Father of the Constitution assumed that the chief cause of political faction is economic interest. A balance of political power shared by at least two major economic classes, he believed, would be the best guaranty of the liberty of all. In the new Republic each major economic interest was localized in its own geographic section. The Constitution established an electoral system which gave power to majorities of states rather than mere majorities of population, and thereby ensured that only an administration which won and held the support of more than one sectional-class interest could win and hold power. Any attempt of one interest to injure all other interests could easily be defeated at the polls by a more representative coalition of interests.

The degree to which the events of 1929 to 1933, comprising the fifth great revolution in our political history, conformed to the process which the Founding Fathers ordained, and obeyed the laws which governed the four previous comparable revolutions, will be clear from an examination of those events.

The economic depression which began with the Wall Street panic of October, 1929, was the most important event of the years from 1929 to 1932. News of it seldom appeared on the front pages of the newspapers unless a story reduced the disaster of society to personal terms. But such stories abounded: suicides of speculators, flights from justice of utilities magnates and bank presidents, a farmer's use of wheat instead of coal to heat his house, the murder of his starving family by an unemployed workman—in endless variation. And the sociologist could no doubt also read the meaning of the depression in the "ordinary" crime news, which covered expanding acres of newsprint and produced galleries of new American types, including the gun-moll, the finger-man, the racketeer, and the gangster.

Only the back pages of the better newspapers summarized in dry statistics, shorn of all personality, the complete story of the nation's troubles. The most important statistical expression of the course of the depression was the one which was most disputed. The estimates of unemployment which were offered by respectable authorities differed by as much as five million. None denied that in 1932 at least ten million wage-earners were out of work. Expressed in index numbers adjusted for seasonal variation, employment in manufacturing industries fell from 108 in August, 1929, to 61 in July, 1932, or over 40 per cent.[1] Workers who still had jobs in 1932 had taken reductions in pay and hours until their average weekly earnings had fallen from $28 in 1929 to $17. However, prices had fallen during the same period so that the decline in real wages was only from 104 to 88.

The fall of farm prices was more severe than any other aspect of the depression except the collapse of stocks. Farm prices were considered to be the most serious domestic problem of the nation in 1925 when their index stood at 156 as compared with an average of 100 during the years 1909 to 1914. But by 1932 they had fallen to 65. The cash income of all farmers fell from seven billion dollars in 1929 to two billion in 1932. This disastrous loss of over 70 per cent of his cash income was compensated by a drop of only 30 per cent in the prices of the manufactured goods the farmer bought, and the interest and principal of farm mortgages did not decline at all. The inadequate share of the farmers in 1929 of less than 12 per cent of the national income, as compared with the fact that they composed almost 50 per cent of the population, fell to 5 per cent in 1932.

The total income of all individuals fell during the years 1929 to 1932 from eighty-two billion dollars to forty billion. The income of corporations, as reported for taxes, fell from eleven billion to two. Commercial and industrial failures increased from an average of about 20,000 per year prior to 1929 to 31,000 in 1932. The *New York Times* estimated the loss of value by industrial and railroad stocks during the four years to have been almost 80 per cent. The index of industrial production fell from 119 to 64 in the same period. Foreign trade fell over 60 per cent. Despite the frantic search of professional optimists, no "bright spots" could be found; the national economy functioned as a unit: nothing was exempt.

[1] Reference notes begin on p. 341.

However slightly aware the average citizen might be of the statistical definition of the depression, a day arrived when its meaning was brought home to him. The time had passed when a considerable group of Americans was isolated from the tides of national economic events. Whether he was thrown out of work, or his broker told him his account was liquidated, or his wages were cut, or the bank refused to renew his mortgage, or customers stopped buying in his store, whatever guise it took, no one entirely escaped the depression.

The immediate doctrinal resource which was as available to an American who suffered economic mishap as his next breath of air was the individualism according to which he had only himself to blame. This doctrine presumably sustained and guided the private citizen while those who had the nation's welfare in charge assured him that the depression was a natural phenomenon which would automatically adjust certain ill-defined minor imbalances of the economic system. Immediately after the crash of October, 1929, the Hoover administration announced that the business structure was fundamentally sound, and that the stock market would presently recover. Later, when these expectations were not fulfilled, and decline spread from Wall Street to Main Street, administration leaders spoke of necessary and healthful deflation of unnatural values to a level where the sound basis of the business structure would provide support for a new and more secure return of prosperity. This meant that wage-cuts, which the President had at first strived to prevent, were now considered to be justified by the need to find a profit margin below the falling price level, for the prospect of such profit opportunities was the only motive which would encourage industry to expand production—as well as the only hope for recovery.

Rugged individualism now seemed to require of millions

of unemployed docile waiting for the bottom to be reached and the upturn to begin, as well as self-blame if they did not find or make for themselves the economic opportunities which were equally free to all. But the official analysis that deflation and its attendant ills were natural phenomena, and repeated statements that prosperity was "just around the corner," gradually lost their popular appeal, particularly as it appeared that the President's utterances were invariably followed by plunges of the indices to new depths. With the waning of faith in the old gods came a search for new doctrines which should more adequately explain the cause of the depression and suggest a less painful cure—a search which resulted in one of the great public debates of American history.

Radical doctrines ranging from orthodox Marxism to native cure-alls like the old single-tax scheme of Henry George and new share-the-wealth and funny-money plans all won converts, but none ever acquired large popular support. Curiously, academic economists who were expected to know all about the "facts," ordinarily had no dogmas on the cause or cure of the depression to offer. Rather, a hybrid type, to be found in the area bounded by journalism, the universities, the churches, minority political parties, and the publicity and research branches of business, farm, and labor organizations came forward as the most influential leader in the formulation of diagnoses and prescriptions for dealing with the depression. His variety of mildly unorthodox economic thought came to the American people like rain to dry earth, and within three years it created a climate of opinion in which even businessmen were ready for unconventional experiments.

A series of Congressional investigations into the nation's economy provided ample material for the publicists of unorthodox doctrine. They divided into two more or less distinct groups, according to whether they were slightly more conservative or liberal, that is, more interested in achieving the recovery of the capitalist system as a means of providing for the human needs of the population, or in providing for those needs by reforming capitalism. The policies of the former group were to dominate the First New Deal, while the policies of the latter dominated the Second New Deal. John T. Flynn may be taken as an outstanding spokesman of the first approach, and Stuart Chase of the second. Between them, they comprehended most of the new doctrines which undermined the official philosophy of the Hoover administration.

In his book, *Graft in Business*,[2] Flynn argued that businessmen were their own worst enemies and could hardly be trusted to pursue intelligently even their own interests. They had fastened on the business structure a parasitic system of graft which had sapped its vitality until their own main interest in efficient, profitable enterprise was defeated. Secret profits of directors who manipulated holding companies, dummy corporations, executive bonuses, rebates, reorganizations, wash sales of stocks, pools, and a host of other devices were commonly used by businessmen to fleece each other as well as the public. While Flynn's implication that the cause of the depression was the inability of business to maintain legitimate profits and at the same time pay off the grafting insiders was hardly profound, his proposed cure was the one accepted by more and more businessmen until the United States Chamber of Commerce and the National Association of Manufacturers began to advocate it publicly. Flynn declared that businessmen must be saved from themselves by government enforcement of rules of fair competition. This was the central idea of the National Industrial Recovery Act which became the keystone of the First New Deal.

Stuart Chase condemned this proposal as the enthronement of monopoly and a step towards fascism: "A temporary, compromise dictatorship forced by the present crisis, in which certain bankers and business men combine with government officials and a labor leader or two, to set up a steering committee whose watchword will be 'normalcy' at the earliest possible moment." [3]

The fundamental cause of the depression, Chase believed, was the inadequate purchasing power of the mass of Americans. Potentially abundant production had been achieved, but distribution lagged because five types of abuses were practiced by business: restriction of output through monopolies, patents, and secret processes; distortion of markets by forced selling of useless and even harmful commodities; gambling in the prime economic essentials of land, raw materials, and securities; economic parisitism by racketeering, political and business graft, and sweating of labor; and needless duplication of production facilities. These abuses could be abolished only by a series of stringent reform laws. The restoration of purchasing power could be achieved by devaluation of the dollar, high taxes on large incomes, lower tariffs, high wages, shorter hours, unemployment insurance, vast public works programs, public housing, rural electrification, and national and regional planning boards. As late as the summer of 1932, Chase had no hope that his program would be accepted by the Democratic Party, much less by the Republican Party, but within a year the Roosevelt administration was attempting to combine it with the Flynn program, and in succeeding years the Chase program was fully installed as a Second New Deal.

The ideas of Flynn and Chase represented the demand for new methods of dealing with the depression, particularly in respect to industry and labor. The farm problem was in a special case because agriculture had suffered virtually continuous depression since 1921, and the formulation of unorthodox new methods of dealing with it was already far advanced when President Hoover entered the White House. In fact, the first "new deal" legislation was passed by his administration before the industrial depression began in an effort to solve the problem of farm surpluses.

The Agricultural Marketing Act of June, 1929, was the chief accomplishment of the Hoover administration during its "honeymoon." This law was intended to do for the farmer what business was doing for itself: control the marketing of its products so that overproduction and competition should not ruin prices. The Coolidge vetoes of the McNary-Haugen Bills had been directed against the fixing of farm prices by the government. Under Hoover as Secretary of Commerce from 1921 to 1929, methods had been worked out whereby the government did not fix prices for industry, but it encouraged corporations to exchange information and to observe voluntary codes of fair-trade practice, and competition was minimized. The result was that, until the industrial depression revived competition and made the codes dead letters, business, through the agency of its trade associations and seconded by government, was largely successful in controlling marketing and fixing prices for itself. The Republican administrations had gone so far as to prosecute violations of the codes under the antitrust laws, while largely ignoring monopoly practices.

Hoover believed that the farmer should be encouraged by the government to imitate the practices of business. Voluntary farmers' coöperatives should be organized to do for them what trade associations did for businessmen, and more: they should buy up surplus crops during harvest time to prevent them from ruining prices, and market them through the rest of the year as demand justified. Since farmers could hardly finance such operations, the government would lend money at interest to their coöperatives. Stabilization corporations using federal money would buy any surpluses from coöperatives which had to be held off the market for longer than a year, and a central farm board would supervise the whole. The government would not initiate price-fixing—rather the farmer himself would voluntarily act to prevent disorderly marketing from causing prices to fall when he had something to sell, and to rise when he had nothing to sell. The government would merely provide the machinery and capital to second the farmers' efforts. This scheme was launched with the passage of the Agriculture Marketing Act, only a few months before the Wall Street crash.

Even without the decline of domestic purchasing power and the drying up of foreign markets which began late in 1929, the Agriculture Marketing Act would have failed. Farmers proved to be unaware that voluntary coöperation was the most useful definition of Hoover's rugged individualism. They expanded production in hope of profiting from the high prices which the Farm Board promised, and thereby swamped it with greater surpluses than ever. These redoubled the effects of the depression on farm prices and the Farm Board was totally incapable of managing them. Within two years it gave up and sought to make a gift of its holdings of wheat and cotton to the Red Cross, while farm prices dissolved to foreclosure levels.

The flaw in Hoover's strict logic was that if only the very largest industrial corporations, firmly organized in trade associations, could achieve production limitation, controlled marketing, and price understandings without direct government enforcement—and this, as the event proved, only during a period of rising prices and prosperity—it was hopeless to expect that the millions of small farm units, only partially organized in coöperatives, could achieve even comparable results. The depression broke down the most highly developed codes of the trade associations, so that businessmen

14]

began to demand that the government enforce them, in the manner finally achieved under NRA. The farmer required even more drastic government controls if limitation of production were to be achieved, and leading farm spokesmen and organizations began to demand such a scheme as was adopted in the Agricultural Adjustment Act of 1933. The measure of President Hoover's stubborn adherence to principle is that he refused to countenance direct government regulation of industry or agriculture even after his own programs of self-regulation seconded by government had failed —and even after businessmen and farmers begged to be saved from themselves and the evils of competition.

The high hopes which the administration had entertained for its farm policy were dashed, and it became a specter threatening revenge in the very tangible form of farmers voting for the Democratic Party in the critical Western states.

Inevitably the depression placed the problems of industry in the center of the political stage. Shortly after the stock market crash a conference of business and labor leaders resulted in promises to maintain wages and production. A special inducement was granted to business in the form of a 1 per cent reduction in income taxes. Unemployment was relieved by expanding the government's public-works program. The administration urged that confidence was the key to the situation.

The response of business to this first attempt to deal with the depression was disquieting. Corporations increased their dividend rates, and new fixed-investment trusts and pool managers worked up a partial restoration of the bull market. But production failed to gain. Consequently, in May, 1930, the stock market crashed again, and a two-year downward spiral of prices and production began. Industry ignored its promises to maintain wages and employment in a desperate effort to cut them faster than prices fell.

For over a year the President accepted the collapse as an inevitable liquidation of inflated values which should be allowed to run its course. In June, 1930, he signed the Hawley-Smoot Tariff Act, which raised the rates to the highest level in history. Economists had warned him that the new law would deepen the world depression and benefit the protected American interests very little if at all. The President himself had promised to lower the rates, but by 1930 he had decided that the danger of foreign dumping in American markets justified violation of his promise.

In October of that year the President's Emergency Committee on Employment was appointed, with Colonel Arthur Woods, a business leader, as its chairman. The Committee, launched two weeks before the Congressional elections, was widely interpreted as a bid for the labor vote which should commit the administration to nothing more than recognition of the problem. It failed to turn the electoral tide in favor of the administration, and within a few months its chairman had resigned. One labor paper declared that the resignation of Colonel Woods made the "futility" of Hoover's interest in the unemployed "sort of official." [4]

Democratic gains in Congress in the elections of November, 1930, left the Republicans only a minority of members of the House, but did not result in repudiation of the administration's policies. The dominant leadership of the Democrats was in the hands of Eastern conservatives, and they worked with the President's party to pass every important measure for which he asked. Shortly after the November elections, the leaders of the National Democratic Committee, Jouett Shouse and John J. Raskob, assured the President that they would not be partisan, but would stand by even the Hawley-Smoot Tariff.

Only a minority of liberal Democrats in Congress worked with the Western insurgent wing of the Republicans to fight

16]

for more thorough-going action by the administration to deal with the depression. They joined in a conference which passed resolutions in favor of unemployment insurance, lower tariff rates, and other liberal measures. Governor Franklin D. Roosevelt sent the conference a message of approval, thus early displaying his support of the liberal rather than the conservative wing of his party, and of the Republican insurgents besides. In Congress this bi-partisan group succeeded in passing a resolution in favor of government operation of the power plant at Muscle Shoals, site of the future Tennessee Valley Authority, but Hoover vetoed it in March, 1931.

The argument which was to be most potent in turning the 1932 election against Hoover—that his administration was interested only in protecting businessmen from the worst effects of the depression—was developed in a debate over drought-relief. Farmers of the plains country were suffering in 1931 from the first of a series of severe droughts which were to turn great areas into a dust bowl. The President proposed that the government lend money to the drought-ridden farmers inasmuch as they were in the position of businessmen who needed credit. The loans were to be made only when secured by property, and were to be used only to restore property values by feeding livestock, buying implements, and otherwise increasing the capital value and money-making potential of farmers' enterprises. It was pointed out by such Western Senators as Caraway and Robinson, however, that farmers were going hungry, and that they could not feed livestock unless they themselves were fed first. The administration countered that it was no part of the duties of the federal government to provide direct relief as gifts in order to relieve human suffering. Such relief should be provided by local private and public agencies. The limit of the federal government's obligation was the provision of loans to relieve credit stringencies in productive enterprises.

It was well understood by both sides that not merely relief for a relatively few farmers, but the administration's policy on relief for the ever-swelling millions of unemployed was being debated. Private charity in even the richest districts was unable to meet the need, and local and state governments were exhausting their credit. The drought-ridden farmers merely presented the problem in the most acute form: local relief was unable to save them from starvation. Nevertheless the administration clung stubbornly to its principle.

Threatened with an extra session of Congress, the President signed a Drought-Relief Bill which appropriated $20,-000,000 for loans for seed and for "further agricultural rehabilitation"—a loophole which Secretary of Agriculture Hyde admitted, when pressed by Senator Borah, might possibly be used to provide food for the starving farmers. But the administration did not admit that it was violating its relief policy, and the President promptly vetoed the Wagner Bill to extend the work of federal employment agencies to states which sponsored no agencies of their own, on the ground that it would interfere with state control over unemployment problems.

In 1931, bank failures emphasized the new depths to which the country's economy was descending. The President's efforts to restore confidence by making optimistic statements began to be treated as comic diversions from the realities of life. In a speech at Indianapolis he made a strenuous effort to present his policies in a constructive light. He promised an American "Twenty-Year Plan" for the development of the country's prosperity by judicious federal encouragement of private enterprise through public support of airways, river transport, and land reclamation. But the twenty-year scope of this plan seemed to indicate not so much far-sightedness as timidity in the use of federal power to solve immediate problems. Little more was heard of the plan. Similarly, the President's appeals to Wall Street and the commodity exchanges to stop the short-selling which was depressing prices to unnaturally low levels, appeals to the voluntary good will of operators, seemed timid to the point of absurdity when the President of the New York Stock Exchange, Richard Whitney, told the House Judiciary Committee that the very existence of exchanges depended on short-selling.

In September, 1931, Great Britain went off the gold standard. The President was convinced that deflation had gone far enough. Believing that lack of confidence was driving the process to the point where the banking and money systems were endangered, he determined to act in defense of these last bulwarks.

His first action merely encouraged bankers to help themselves. On October 8, after conferences among the President, Congressmen, and bankers, it was announced that the latter would form a $500,000,000 National Credit Corporation, which would rediscount frozen assets unacceptable to the Federal Reserve Banks and a wide range of assets of banks which were not members of the Federal Reserve. The Corporation was opened for business on November 10. During the interval the President's new Organization on Unemployment Relief had reported that such relaxation of bank credit was the main solution of the unemployment problem.

Less than a month after the National Credit Corporation had been established, the President decided that self-help would not save the banking system. He asked the new Congress to establish the Reconstruction Finance Corporation to lend federal money to banks, insurance companies, railroads, and other key enterprises. Congress complied, and the RFC was set up early in 1932 with capital of $500,000,000 provided by the government and $1,500,000,000 obtained by the sale of notes guaranteed by the government. Many banks and corporations were undoubtedly saved by RFC loans, but deflation was not halted, and within a year a new wave of bank failures could not be prevented.

Meanwhile the RFC was attacked as the final proof that the administration favored bankers and businessmen above other citizens, and great corporations over small businesses. The latter contention seemed valid when the President vetoed the Wagner-Garner Relief Bill which would have extended RFC loans to small businesses and to individuals. This veto was the only administration action which did not square with its principle that loans were within the limits of the government's obligation to any economic group. The administration showed, however, that it was willing to extend the benefits of its credit policy to certain other groups by passing a measure to expand the capitalization of Federal Land Banks, and by establishing Home Loan Banks to lend money on home mortgages. The facts remained that federal action to limit agricultural production was the most pressing need of the farmers, federal action to stop competitive wage-cutting was the most pressing need of employed workers, and direct federal relief was the only means of preventing extreme hardship for the unemployed. And the opinion grew bitter among farmers and laborers that not constitutional rectitude but class favoritism dictated the administration's refusal to meet the most pressing need of any group except big business.

This opinion was increasingly reflected in Congress during the spring of 1932. Liberal Democrats and insurgent Republicans did not deny the administration's duty to combat the depression in the areas it had selected; rather they demanded that similar action be taken in all areas. The Glass-Steagall Bill to broaden acceptability of commercial paper by the Federal Reserve Banks and to release gold formerly held to support currency was passed unanimously, taxes were increased, executive agencies reorganized, and government payrolls cut. After the veto of the Wagner-Garner Relief Bill, it was amended to meet the President's objections, and a provision added for loans to the states for relief, after which it was passed and signed. But a bill to give Congress the President's existing right to make emergency changes in tariff rates and authorizing reciprocity tariff treaties was vetoed. Measures which passed the House but not the Senate to provide expansion of the currency and direct federal unemployment relief were blamed by the President for the failure of business to regain "confidence."

Politically the more significant fact was that revelations by Congressional investigations of malpractices of bankers, utility magnates, and brokers, and the President's failure to adopt any counter-measures, resulted in a rapid ebb of public confidence in both business and the President. While the Chief Executive seemed to lose no measure of his respect for big business, he harried out of Washington with tear gas and fire the war veterans who petitioned for a cash bonus.

A slight upturn in business which began in July offered the President his chief argument for re-election. He and the leaders of his party relied heavily on statistical proofs that the worst was over when active campaigning began in September. The argument failed to still the demands of laborers and farmers for government aid, or to overcome the general impression of the administration's favoritism to big business and its political incompetence.

For months before the presidential election of 1932, the traditional danger signal for an American administration had been flying: the only major sectional-class interest which was

[21]

united in support of the Hoover administration and the Republican Party was Eastern business, and it was apathetic as well as outnumbered in its own section by laborers and unemployed who wanted a change. The natural beneficiary of the failure of the Hoover administration to hold the loyalty of at least two major sectional-class groups was the Democratic Party. By adding to the votes of the Solid South those of Eastern laborers and unemployed and Western farmers, that party could recreate the great coalition which had elected Jefferson and Wilson. It remained to be seen whether a leader of their stature could be found who would make his election another main turning on the road of American history.

CHAPTER II

THE PROMISE OF A NEW DEAL: 1932

A COMMONPLACE of political exegesis in 1932, which has been widely accepted by historians since then, was that Franklin D. Roosevelt campaigned for the Presidency without a program, or even a record of accomplishments in public office which would provide clues to what his program as President might be. The classic statement of this view was Walter Lippmann's description of the Democratic candidate as an amiable gentleman who would like very much to be President.

Some justification for this viewpoint may be that Roosevelt had not as yet been the center of any stormy controversy involving a main issue of twentieth-century politics. Nevertheless, he had clearly identified himself with the philosophy and practice of liberalism on most important issues. He had been one of the inner group of President Wilson's supporters when he held the post of Assistant Secretary of the Navy during the First World War, and this evidenced faith in liberal reform at home and collective security abroad. His unsuccessful campaign for the Vice Presidency in 1920 had been based on advocacy of the League of Nations. As Governor of New York since 1928, he had carried forward the reform program, inherited from Governor Alfred E. Smith, which put New York in the ranks of the most progressive states in the nation. It remains true that in none of these rôles did he originate policies. His public character did not yet suggest the future boldness and originality of his leadership.

[23

Born to privilege as the son of an ancient Dutch family of New York merchants and Hudson Valley landowners, Franklin Roosevelt became that rarity of modern America, a gentleman politician. He chose the less genteel of the great American parties, in a state where its traditional emphasis on the common touch automatically shunted "respectables" as like him as his cousin Theodore into the Republican Party. The peculiarities of the position of the Democratic Party in New York State could teach valuable lessons to a young practitioner. In general, the party stood for the common man of the great urban centers of the state, and in Albany it therefore advocated those economic and social reforms which might humanize the industrial system. But in New York City the power of the party's affiliate, Tammany Hall, was such that businessmen who depended upon the city administration for tolerance if not favors found it expedient to come to terms with the dominant politicians, and this arrangement vitiated when it did not corrupt any reformist tendencies of the city leaders. Repulsion for the methods of Tammany and fear of becoming a political and economic annex of New York City pushed most of the farmers of the state into the Republican Party, which also embraced the great majority of the business and financial leaders of the cities. The result was that a Democratic leader who wished to develop liberal policies in the state government found himself flanked on one side by Tammany men of dubious motives within his own party, and on the other by suspicious farmers and conservative businessmen in the Republican Party. The difficulties of such a position may help to explain the cautious quality of Roosevelt's leadership before he became President, but they also explain the superb schooling he acquired, first as Assemblyman and then as Governor, in the nature and management of political interest groups.

Liberal critics might argue that Governor Roosevelt's

popular support, both rural and urban, as evidenced by his election in 1928 when the state voted for a Republican President, and by his re-election with an unprecedented plurality in 1930, would have justified him in defying the politicians and striking out with all boldness to achieve the full liberal program without compromise or delay. But this ignores the fact that Roosevelt accepted the two-party system and believed that progress could be made, however slowly, only by working within the framework of a major party, with due respect for the profound roots of party factions in group interest and for the weight which the electoral systems of the states as well as the nation give to geographic sections. Stated negatively, he refused to risk the defeat at the polls which has been the invariable fate of leaders who founded third parties on single interests or who tried to establish control over a major party by a single interest.

Political corruption was a pressing issue for liberals during Roosevelt's terms as Governor, and his manner of dealing with it among the Tammany leaders of his own party did not arouse enthusiasm. When official investigations revealed the malfeasance of Tammany officials, the Governor moved cautiously and with extreme regard for the rights of the accused. He removed Sheriff Thomas M. Farley from office as justice required, but in a way which permitted no party leader to accuse him of "persecution." On the other hand, the demand for repeal of the Eighteenth Amendment, in which liberals and Tammany were united, Roosevelt made his own. He advocated repeal personally, and he approved a bill which petitioned Congress to repeal the Amendment.

These two issues tended to steal the newspaper headlines from the Governor's efforts to achieve other liberal reforms. Public ownership of hydroelectric power resources was the most significant cause for which he fought. The question whether the great power potential of the Saint Lawrence

[25

River should be privately or publicly owned had divided Republicans and Democrats for years, and was inherited by Roosevelt after previous administrations had prevented both outright sale and long-term lease of rights to private companies. He insisted that ownership and control of natural water-power sites be inalienably vested in the people of the state, and that a state agency should produce and transmit the electricity, while only distribution should be entrusted to private companies, their rates to be controlled by the state. The net achievement was the passage of the Water Power Law of 1930, which established the public ownership principle and provided for a commission to prepare a plan for the development of Saint Lawrence power. This was not much, but in the course of unending and complex struggles with conservatives, chiefly Republicans, in the legislature, and with the Hoover administration over the question of the state's rights in the negotiations with Canada, the Governor had made his position in favor of public ownership very clear, and he had shown that he could wage a campaign for a key demand of liberals with consistency and skill to the limit of his political support.[1]

Governor Roosevelt's record in the field of labor legislation left no room for doubt that he favored "as matters of an absolute right"[2] the demands of organized labor for statutes to improve its position. He pressed a series of bills upon the recalcitrant Republican legislators, and won laws limiting the hours of labor of women and children and a mutilated Old-Age Security Law providing gratuities instead of the insurance pensions for which he had asked. In other fields, farm relief, regulation of public utilities, court reform, housing, public health and welfare, accomplishment was no more spectacular, but the net gain of social democracy in New York State during his terms as Governor was the product of his leadership, and it no less than his clear and persistent presentation of the liberal argument identified him as an heir of the tradition of Woodrow Wilson. By 1932, a thoughtful student of his career could not but conclude that if he were elected President he would carry to the White House an integrated philosophy and program of liberalism, as well as proven skill in handling the fractious politicians of the Empire State. In foreign affairs Roosevelt had been unable to play an active part since the 1920 campaign, but in a significant essay published in 1928 he had reaffirmed his faith in international coöperation and his disbelief in the possibility or desirability of isolated national existence, and he had specifically anticipated the Good Neighbor policy of non-intervention in the affairs of the Latin American Republics.[3]

If Governor Roosevelt failed to capture the public imagination as a crusader for liberalism, it was because the crusading work had been done by his immediate predecessor. And if he failed to achieve in his state the sweeping reforms he was to achieve as President, it was because Republican majorities in the state legislature frustrated him while the corruption of Tammany prevented harmonious relations with a powerful section of his own party.

The event which more than any other made Roosevelt a candidate for the Presidency was his re-election as Governor in 1930 by the great plurality of 725,000 votes. The Governor's capable organizer, James A. Farley, declared that the magic of this figure "turned it from a mere state event into a political happening of nationwide importance. The men and women who make politics their business started to cast their eyes toward Albany."[4] Immediately the spadework was begun to win the Democratic nomination in 1932 for the phenomenal vote-getter.

It is notable that long before the "brains trust" was organized, a corps of keen politicians who had small interest in programs and policies set to work to make Governor Roosevelt President. James A. Farley was a Tammany leader who had not lost his reputation for personal integrity in the course of developing extraordinary skill as a political organizer. An ardent supporter of Alfred E. Smith in the 1928 campaign, after the latter's defeat he turned easily to support of Roosevelt on the assumptions that religion was an immovable obstacle to Smith's success and that Smith had meant it when he had announced that he would not again be a candidate. Farley became Roosevelt's chief organizer of support among the local and state officials of the Democratic Party. Most Tammany leaders were prevented from abandoning Smith with Farley's ease by loyalty to their greatest leader, resentment at the unfairness of the religious prejudice against him, and suspicion of the squire of Hyde Park. The leaders of most of the Democratic machines in the Eastern cities shared these sentiments. It therefore became Farley's strategy to build up support for Roosevelt's candidacy in the South and West where New York aspirants were usually weak, until he had assembled a bloc of convention delegates so formidable that the Eastern city leaders should become amenable.

His first step was to send out as a "feeler" to all party officials a booklet containing nothing more controversial than a description of the Democratic organization and its activities in New York State. The response was a great many suggestions that Governor Roosevelt be nominated for President in 1932. The next step was a "follow-up" booklet presenting unadorned statistics which compared Roosevelt's vote-getting record with that of other Democratic candidates for Governor of New York since 1916. The figures were eloquent proof of Roosevelt's attraction for rural as well as urban voters.

Farley's specialty was the personal touch. He undertook a

vast letter-writing campaign. "We went on the theory that people ... delight in believing there is a close link between them and the folk who run the show and, above all, they want the knowledge that their efforts are being appreciated by the 'higher-ups' in the organization. ... We attempted in every way possible to be obliging." [5] Louis McHenry Howe, the Governor's personal secretary, worked closely with Farley. They gave lists of party leaders throughout the country to Roosevelt who called them personally by telephone. This "pleased their pride" and built up a corps of last-ditch supporters at the party convention. Scouts were sent to the Western states, and interest was enlarged into conviction and loyalty. Soon, in the spring of 1931, campaign headquarters were established at 331 Madison Avenue, New York City. Success warranted the public commitment which this implied, and it brought a first challenge.

Not only the groundswell of Roosevelt's popularity, but the increasing difficulties of the Hoover administration which made a Democratic victory in the next election seem probable, led to the first inner-party struggle precipitated by Roosevelt. The sources of this struggle were fundamental issues. The leadership of the Democratic National Committee, headed by the banker, John J. Raskob, was conservative. In ordinary times it could hold in line on a conservative platform the Southern wing of the party and the city machines, if not the Westerners. By 1931 many signs indicated that Democrats everywhere were moving rapidly towards a liberal reform policy on economic issues. This movement was adopting Roosevelt as its candidate, and together they threatened to overwhelm the conservatives and capture the party. Raskob determined to split Roosevelt's support before it should grow too strong by distracting attention from economic questions and centering it on the issue of prohibition repeal. Southern drys and Northern wets were deeply divided on this issue, which had almost torn the party in two during the 1928 Convention. The Southern wing of the party could easily be turned against Roosevelt, who stood for outright repeal, and, under the rule of the Democratic Convention that nomination required a two-thirds majority, without the support of Southern delegates his candidacy would be stopped. Raskob called a meeting of the Democratic National Committee for March, 1931. In a preliminary letter he declared that he wanted a resolution passed for repeal of the Eighteenth Amendment as a plank in the 1932 platform of the party.

Roosevelt and Farley determined to use this unprecedented anticipation of an explosive question fifteen months before it was due to test the strength of their new organization. The strategy was determined at a bedroom conference in the Executive Mansion at Albany. The Democratic State Committee, which was amenable to Roosevelt influence, was encouraged to pass a resolution that the National Committee had no authority to pledge or advise the party on controversial issues. Armed with this resolution, Farley went to Washington and pointed out the shoal waters to party leaders. The substance of his argument is suggested in his statement: "I found Southern Senators and Representatives felt that if the Prohibition question was permitted to take precedence over the economic situation, the party was bound to suffer." [6] Senators Hull of Tennessee and Byrd of Virginia became friendly, and a telephone campaign brought local leaders to Washington to urge their representatives on the National Committee to coöperate with Farley. When the Committee met, Senator Joseph T. Robinson performed the first of many tasks of leadership for Roosevelt by heading the counter-attack on Raskob. Two-thirds of the National Committee were found to be oppossed to discussing the question of Repeal, and Raskob was unable to obtain even a vote.

This victory may well be designated as the turning point in the Roosevelt campaign for the nomination. It prevented party disunity on the issue which could defeat him, and ensured that the economic issues on which he could unify the sections within the party and ultimately among the voters would be in the forefront. More broadly, it marked the turnaway of the Democratic Party from the conservatism and the squabbles over secondary issues which had bedeviled it during a decade of defeats, and opened the way for its emergence once more as the party of the most liberal groups in all sections. Not least among its meanings was the proof that in Farley Roosevelt had a political technician of superb ability.

Alfred E. Smith, although not a member of the National Committee, had been given consent to speak at the March meeting, and he had supported the Raskob resolution, thus indicating his opposition to Roosevelt's candidacy. A moment came when he decided to try once more for the Presidency, this time in rivalry with the man who had long been his intimate friend and supporter. Entering the race late, after Roosevelt had effectively become the leader of the liberals in the party, Smith found his candidacy looked upon with great favor by the conservatives. They were working to build up state-wide, favorite-son candidacies in the South and West which, after a few ballots at the Convention, could be united with Smith's loyal following among the leaders of the Eastern city machines to form a two-thirds majority for someone other than Roosevelt. To counter the favorite-son campaign, Farley and Howe in the summer of 1931 embarked on their famous excursion "to the Elks Convention in Seattle." First they went to the Roosevelt home at Hyde Park "equipped with a Rand-McNally map of the United

States, a flock of train schedules, and the latest available list of Democratic National Committee members and state chairmen."[7]

Farley met over 1,100 party leaders on the trip. The "political drummer," "making Democratic medicine," received a typical response from National Committeeman William W. Howes of North Dakota: " 'Farley, I'm damned tired of backing losers. In my opinion, Roosevelt can sweep the country, and I'm going to support him.' "[8] Back home again, Farley did not neglect to send every one of his new friends a personal letter, signed with the green ink he was making famous.

In January, 1932, Governor Roosevelt formally announced his candidacy for the Presidential nomination. He warned his opponents that he would campaign as a political liberal, and he invited attention to the "progressive laws" he was working to secure in New York State.[9] Within the next few weeks the pre-Convention lines within the party became fixed. The race was one of Roosevelt against the field. Smith was strongest in Massachusetts, New York, New Jersey, and Pennsylvania, Speaker John Nance Garner in Texas, California, and Georgia, and Governor "Alfalfa Bill" Murray in Oklahoma and North Dakota. Other opponents had support in one state at most. Only a coalition of all his opponents could defeat Roosevelt.

The Hearst press, the most important group of Democratic newspapers in the country, was supporting Garner chiefly because he was strongly opposed to the United States joining the League of Nations. Roosevelt had come to believe that the League had evolved from Wilson's original plan into an organization which it was no longer to the interest of the United States to join. He made this clear now in a statement which was possibly intended to attract the support of William Randolph Hearst.[10] Whether or not this was its only object, the move probably made easier Hearst's widely-reported abandonment of Garner and shift to Roosevelt at a critical moment during the Convention.

Meanwhile, three months before the Convention met, Roosevelt decided that the time had come to present his policies to the party and the nation in specific form. To assist him in organizing the details of his program, he had assembled a corps of experts, chiefly academicians, which became famous as the Brains Trust. These organizers of policies came to match in efficiency of technique Farley and his staff of organizers of political support, and the two groups complemented each other to form a victorious combination unprecedented in American history. Progressive political leaders had used academic experts before Roosevelt, beginning probably with the senior LaFollette's use of the professors of Wisconsin University as advisers and administrators while he was Governor of that state early in the century; political organizers like Farley were as old as political parties; and conservative leaders had combined masters of machine politics with experts on policy usually drawn from the ranks of journalists, trade-association publicists, and corporation lawyers; but never before had a liberal leader succeeded in using both professors and politicians, "idealists" and "realists," as did Roosevelt.

As Governor, Roosevelt had already used academic experts in official as well as private capacities. Thus Professor Raymond Moley of Columbia University, a specialist on penal administration, had been appointed to a committee to draft a plan for a model state-parole system and as a commissioner to improve the administration of justice in the state. He became the first leader of the Brains Trust. Moley was a liberal only in the limited sense that he favored experiment with new types of government supervision over areas of economic life which were moving through disorganization to disaster. He believed in such controls as should appeal primarily to businessmen rather than to labor and liberals. On such issues as the tariff he was conservative, and he was the chief advocate among Roosevelt's advisers of the policy of economic nationalism which prevailed during the First New Deal. He was extremely useful as an organizer of material for speeches, and this function he performed for a time after his opinions on policy no longer coincided with Roosevelt's, but by the 1936 election he had broken this tie also. In the meantime, he had gathered together a number of experts whose more liberal views enabled them to outlast his own usefulness.

Rexford Guy Tugwell was brought into the group as an expert on agriculture. He was an economist of originality who was to be the chief target of those who accused the Brains Trust of being "red." His interest was in improving the condition of sharecroppers, tenants, and small farmers, and his brain was fertile in devices to benefit them, but the power of the large staple farmers in Congress forced the administration to subordinate Tugwell's plans, particularly during the period of the First New Deal. Adolph A. Berle, Jr., an authority on business corporations, whose opinions were not particularly unorthodox, was the third leading member of the original Brains Trust.

That these and the other experts who were called in from time to time did not "advise" Roosevelt, but only worked out the details and assembled material for a political program which Roosevelt originated has been stated authoritatively by Raymond Moley.[11]

The first product which was developed with the help of his Brains Trust was Roosevelt's speech of April 7, 1932. It was the overture of his campaign, announcing in a few striking phrases the main themes of his program: "The Nation faces today a more grave emergency than in 1917"; it calls for "plans like those of 1917 that build from the bottom up and not from the top down, that put their faith once more in the forgotten man at the bottom of the economic pyramid"; "a national program of restoration" calls for "restoring farmers' buying power, relief to the small banks and homeowners, and a reconstructed tariff policy." The remainder of a dozen such "closely related objectives . . . of a planned program" was promised for future disclosure.[12]

The "forgotten man" caught the public imagination. He became a focus for a people bewildered and groping for causes and cures. He was the common man who had been the hero of earlier American dramas, and he accused a people who had run after idols. Everyone could identify the forgotten man with a neighbor out of work, an apple-seller on the street corner, a man in the breadline, or a farmer who had lost his homestead. Roosevelt's phrase entered the language, and awoke a profound response.

Only two more addresses of national importance were made by Roosevelt prior to the Democratic Convention. At a Jefferson Day dinner in Saint Paul he invoked the vision and policy not only of the party founder, but of the central leaders of liberal democracy, Benjamin Franklin, Jackson, Lincoln, Theodore Roosevelt, and Wilson, as his guides in replacing business standards with moral standards, and narrow, Eastern, "crusty conservative" views with a multi-class and -sectional outlook in order to achieve a "concert of action, based on a fair and just concert of interests." The Hoover administration was damagingly associated with Federalism, the philosophy that government owes protection only to the strong. Two specific objectives were presented: public control of electric power and reciprocity tariff agreements.[13]

In an address at Oglethorpe University when it gave him an honorary degree, Roosevelt reviewed in realistic terms the economic ills and ironies which faced his "fellow classmates," and he offered "bold, persistent experimentation" as the technique for their cure. "It is common sense to take a method and try it: If it fails, admit it frankly and try another. But above all, try something. The millions who are in want will not stand by silently forever while the things to satisfy their needs are within easy reach."[14] To take the method of experiment out of the laboratory and offer it as a policy of government was revolutionary. Such an approach, always attractive to liberal intellectuals and to youth, now met a receptive mood among all those who had been shaken by the depression out of their confidence in traditionalism. That this last category should come to include not only farmers and laborers but, for a few months in 1933, many conservative businessmen, indicates that Roosevelt had given expression to a growing current in public opinion.

As the time for the party conventions approached, it was apparent that Roosevelt was winning the interest and enthusiasm of voters in all sections. The Republican Convention met first. As an eleventh-hour gesture, President Hoover proposed on June 5 that the Reconstruction Finance Corporation double its funds and make loans to farmers on crop securities and to states for public works to create employment. But this news hardly took a headline away from such items as the march of the "Bonus Expeditionary Force" of war veterans on the capital, the Senate Banking Committee's revelations that officers of great corporations were profiting from the country's distress by shady manipulations of securities, and the most sustained and severe decline of industrial production of the entire depression. Amid such portents, the Republican Convention met in Chicago and wrote a platform on the theme of the administration's success in dealing with the depression. Repeal of Prohibition, an issue the simplicity of which led to strong convictions by voters, was straddled in the Republican platform. At the insistence of

36]

the President, a proposal was adopted which was promptly labeled "wet-dry" and deplored by even the Republican press. The President also insisted that Vice President Curtis be renominated. The apathetic Convention approved the platform and nominated the Hoover-Curtis ticket on the first ballot. The country turned to the Democratic Convention in the hope that its proposals would be unequivocal, and the conviction that it would name the next President of the United States.

This last expectation made the fight within the Democratic Party all the more sharp. The task of out-generaling the "stop Roosevelt" forces at the Convention was in Farley's hands. His organization had obtained instructed delegations and promises of support from free delegates totaling over half of the membership by the time the Convention opened late in June in Chicago. Roosevelt headquarters were set up in the Congress Hotel, and an atmosphere of complete confidence was cultivated. Behind the scenes Farley and his lieutenants worked assiduously, because three difficult tactics had to be carried out to win the necessary two-thirds majority: delegates committed to Roosevelt must be held in line even if the first few ballots were indecisive; the opposition must not unite on any one of its candidates; and the delegates who were committed to only a first vote for a hopeless favorite-son candidate must be attracted to Roosevelt by a bandwagon movement built up by an increase, no matter how small, of the Roosevelt vote on each ballot.

The first problem was solved by the effective discipline which Farley established among the Roosevelt delegates by exercising his fabulous talent for friendship. The second was solved by the mutual jealousies of the opposition factions, judiciously cultivated by the Roosevelt workers, which prevented unity on any one "stop Roosevelt" candidate. The third brought forth Farley's most brilliant maneuvers. Votes which he could have recruited on the first ballot he held in reserve until the second or third, to ensure the increase in the Roosevelt vote which would bring the all-important bandwagon to him. Then, when only Roosevelt showed increasing strength, and the Convention feared a disastrous deadlock, an alliance suddenly executed by long-distance telephone with the most friendly of the opposition candidates, John Nance Garner, and the future Vice President's release of the large Texas and California delegations to Roosevelt brought victory on the fourth ballot. Smith was the only candidate who refused to make the nomination unanimous, and the Tammany delegation remained loyal to him. It had led the "stop Roosevelt" forces; and its defeat was not less bitter because it had been managed by one of its own graduates. This was one of the many blows by which the reforming spirit of the decade reduced Tammany Hall to a minor rôle in local as well as national politics.

Roosevelt had prepared his acceptance speech before the Convention began. Now he launched his campaign by shattering the tradition that a nominee must wait for official notification in assumed ignorance. The Convention was held in session for another day while the new chief of the party went by airplane to Chicago to deliver his speech of acceptance. The image thus given the country scotched any notion that the attack of infantile paralysis which he had suffered eleven years before would interfere with his new rôle.

The first words of his speech assured his audience that the breaking of traditions had only begun. He promised that if he were elected, government would assume greater responsibility for unemployment relief, many of the unemployed would be put to work on reforestation of marginal and unused land, reduction of agricultural production to raise prices would be undertaken, "publicity" would reveal the "crookedness" and the "lack of honor of some men in high financial places," and economy through consolidation of administrative offices would be achieved. Work and security were offered as what the people of America wanted most, and these would be created by giving the men and women who had been forgotten in the political philosophy of the Republicans a "more equitable opportunity to share in the distribution of national wealth."

> I pledge you, I pledge myself, to a new deal for the American people. Let us all here assembled constitute ourselves prophets of a new order of competence and of courage. This is more than a political campaign; it is a call to arms. Give me your help, not to win votes alone, but to win in this crusade to restore America to its own people.[15]

The Roosevelt campaign was designed to make a distinct appeal to each of the main sectional-class groups in the nation. After a vacation spent on a sailing cruise, the candidate first delivered a general address over the radio on the party platform. He strove for simplicity, common sense, and friendliness. The first quality was found in the platform itself, which he had been influential in preparing. It was one-fifth as long as the Republican platform, and chiefly composed of short, specific proposals. Most obvious was the contrast between the Republican "wet-dry" plank on Prohibition, and the Democratic statement: "We favor the repeal of the Eighteenth Amendment," followed by the proposal of a constitutional amendment and state control of temperance legislation.[16] The qualities of common sense and friendliness Roosevelt achieved by his plain logic and language, and by the warmth and sincerity of his voice.

Through the months of August, September, and October, Roosevelt conducted a strenuous campaign during which he covered over seventeen thousand miles and delivered some thousand speeches. At least one major address was made to every important group of citizens in each of the main sections of the country. In these addresses the policies were adopted which the responsible liberal leaders of each group had worked out. When it was pointed out that his advocacy of both governmental economy and federal unemployment relief was contradictory, he answered: "I am utterly unwilling that economy should be practiced at the expense of starving people." [17]

At Topeka, Kansas, the Voluntary Domestic Allotment Plan for limitation of farm production, which had been devised by farm leaders and became the central part of the Agricultural Adjustment Act of 1933, was offered to the farmers. The plan was not mentioned by name, but outlined "so delicately that the urban voters, editors, and newspapermen accepted its broad propositions as generalities too vague to require examination. It won the Midwest without waking up the dogs of the East." [18]

Federal regulation of public utilities and construction and operation of hydroelectric power plants on the Saint Lawrence, Tennessee, Colorado, and Columbia Rivers to serve as "yardsticks" of equitable rates were promised at Portland, Oregon. Despite controversies behind the scenes over whether the low-tariff policy of Cordell Hull and Southern Democrats or the desires for protection of particular groups of farmers and Eastern businessmen should be given most weight, the compromise of reciprocity agreements which the party platform contained was adhered to by Roosevelt.

To the Commonwealth Club of California, Roosevelt addressed a speech which summed up his philosophy of government, particularly the relations between government and business, and appealed to liberals and progressives for their support. He declared that "the issue of Government has always been whether individual men and women will have to serve some system of Government or economics, or whether a system of Government and economics exists to serve individual men and women." Modern nations originated as havens for the protection of the weak against unruly barons, but soon became the instruments of the powerful few to curb the many. In this country the Jeffersonian movement gave the people control over their government and their economy. As long as the West offered land to all comers, equal opportunity and self-government were best achieved by minimizing governmental control. But economic freedom was used not only by the common people seeking a living, but also by a few men "of tremendous will and tremendous ambition" to industrialize the country and win control over its economy. Government itself assisted them to win control, with tariffs, subsidies, and most recently, the Reconstruction Finance Corporation. "Equality of opportunity as we have known it no longer exists." "As I see it, the task of Government in its relation to business is to assist the development of an economic declaration of rights, an economic constitutional order." Then followed a statement of the policy of the National Industrial Recovery Act, the experiment which was to dominate all others during the First New Deal:

We know, now, that [the great industrial and financial corporations] cannot exist unless prosperity is uniform, that is, unless purchasing power is well distributed throughout every group in the Nation. That is why even the most selfish of corporations for its own interest would be glad to see wages restored and unemployment ended and to bring the Western farmer back to his accustomed level of prosperity and to assure a permanent safety to both groups. That is why some enlightened industries themselves endeavor to limit the freedom of action of each man and business group within the industry in the common interest of all; why business men everywhere are asking a form of organization which will bring the scheme of things into balance, even though it may in some measure qualify the freedom of action of individual units within the business.

Thus far, the new "economic constitutional order" was to be achieved through the voluntary coöperation of businessmen. But if

the lone wolf, the unethical competitor, the reckless promoter, the Ishmael or Insull whose hand is against every man's, declines to join in achieving an end recognized as being for the public welfare, and threatens to drag the industry back to a state of anarchy, the Government may properly be asked to apply restraint. Likewise, should the group ever use its collective power contrary to the public welfare, the Government must be swift to enter and protect the public interest.[19]

In other words, if the NIRA should fail through the refusal of business to coöperate, then government would turn to involuntary regulation of business.

This was plain speaking, an invitation and a threat to business such as the country had not heard from a major candidate for the Presidency since Wilson's first campaign.

The campaign was not all plans and policies. Pulling and hauling of factions within the party and jockeying for position of local leaders increased as victory became more certain. Huey Long, the boss of the Louisiana Democracy, wanted a special train in which to campaign for Roosevelt all over the country and to promise immediate payment of the soldiers' bonus. He was enraged when a schedule was worked out to send him, without a special train, into a few states which were already completely lost or safe. But the results were so good from Huey's "curious hodgepodge of buffoonery and demagogic strutting, cleverly bundled in with a lot of shrewd common sense and an evangelical fervor in discussing the plight of the underprivileged," that he was never again underrated.[20]

Tammany persisted in undercover opposition to the party candidate. The circumstance that both Smith and Roosevelt supported Herbert Lehman for the Governorship of New York provided an occasion at a state political rally for a highly-staged reconciliation with Tammany's hero, who shook hands with Roosevelt to the accompaniment of wild cheers. A journalist probably invented the story that Smith greeted his rival: "Hello, you old potato!" which became a vote-getting incantation, and the city machines were "regular" during the election.[21] Evidence that the Tammany leaders had decided to compromise with their principles to aid Roosevelt came with the resignation of Jimmy Walker as Mayor of New York early in September while the Governor was entertaining charges for his removal. More welcome, if not more necessary support developed in the West, where insurgent Republicans, led by Senator Charles Norris, brought their following over to Roosevelt.

Whether Roosevelt's program, or the solid organizational work of Farley, in which he "nationalized" the methods of personal contact he had used to win the nomination was chiefly responsible for the victory in November, or whether "any Democrat" could have won the election in the given situation of public distress and reaction against the Hoover administration, is an insoluble question. The personal qualities of the candidate were probably as important as any factor. He became the most successful campaigner in the country's modern history. People everywhere received a powerful impression of buoyant confidence, simplicity, and broad human sympathies, of his great energy and his gaiety:

Campaigning, for him, was unadulterated joy. It was broad rivers, green forests, waving corn, and undulating wheat; it was crowds of friends, from the half dozen who, seated on a baggage truck, waved to the cheery face at the speeding window to perspiring thousands at a race track or fairground; it was hands extended in welcome, voices warm with greeting, faces reflecting his smile along the interminable wayside. These are the things that ever and ever renew the life of the troubadour. What has "learning" to do with friendship and happiness? Travel is to make friends and influence people.[22]

The Roosevelt smile, radio voice, and ability to send the most irritable caller away happy, were characteristics which began to make a legend, and they did not lose by contrast with the personal impression made by his opponent.

The campaign did not end without bitter passages with the Republican candidate. The campaign of President Hoover was bound to be defensive because the record of his administration was under heavy attack. Most of his utterances were attempts to refute the contentions of his rival. His most effective argument, that the lowest depths of the depression had been passed in July, and that recovery was underway as a result of administration measures, was blunted by his earlier too-frequent announcements that prosperity was "just around the corner." He expressed his sympathy for the human suffering the depression occasioned, spoke feelingly of his countrymen as "weary, and sore, and tired," and stated his general belief that government should try various methods of achieving recovery.[23] But he failed to offer anything specific beyond the tried program of his administration of strengthening private enterprise, and he objected to all the bright new paths which the Roosevelt program seemed to open up. Above all, the President failed lamentably to radiate that confidence which he himself declared to be the clue to better times. He seemed an unfortunate and beaten man. He was inevitably blamed for the depression, and his arguments that foreign countries and Democrats were to blame for it were not effective.

A few days before the end of the campaign, President Hoover delivered a speech in New York City which was heavy with foreboding and warnings of the disasters which would follow a victory by Roosevelt. His policies would "endanger or destroy our system": expansion of Government expenditure by yielding to sectional and group raids on the public treasury; inflation of the currency; entry of the government into personal banking business; destruction of the protective tariff system; entry of the government into the electric-power business; federal employment of all surplus labor at all times; Executive domination of the Supreme Court: with the New Deal "the grass will grow in streets of a hundred cities, a thousand towns; the weeds will overrun the fields of millions of farms. . . . Their churches and school houses will decay." To the philosophy of Roosevelt's Commonwealth Club address, the President opposed the conception that science and invention offered unlimited frontiers for industrial development, and that government should be decentralized to permit private enterprise to expand freely. In thus opposing the idea of the NIRA, Hoover showed that he refused to move with the current even of business opinion, which was increasingly interested in such a plan. He implied that it would require direct government operation of business to realize the Roosevelt program: "It is a false liberalism that interprets itself into Government operation of business. Every step in that direction poisons the very roots of liberalism. It poisons political equality, free speech, free press, and equality of opportunity. . . . My countrymen, the proposals of our opponents represent a profound change in American life . . . a radical departure from the foundations of 150 years. . . ." [24]

Later on the same evening that this speech was delivered in New York, the Democratic candidate made an important address in Boston. He had heard Hoover's denunciations over the radio, and his friends begged him "to ignore the extravagances of Hoover's remarks," but Roosevelt answered: "'I simply will not let Hoover question my Americanism.'"

Nevertheless, in his speech he did not make the sharp answer which had been prepared.[25] Rather, he deplored the "personalities" which Hoover had injected into the campaign, and contented himself with the assertion that the New Deal would not change the fundamental principles on which the nation was founded, but would "aim to bring those principles into effect." [26]

A few days later Roosevelt won the election by the largest electoral majority since 1864 and a plurality of almost seven million votes. He won the electoral vote of every state south and west of Pennsylvania. Only that state, where the strong Republican machine had won every election since the party was founded, Delaware, the fief of the DuPonts, Connecticut, Vermont, New Hampshire, and Maine were loyal to the old regime.

Unwilling or unable to formulate a program which satisfied any major sectional-class group except Eastern business, President Hoover and the Republican Party suffered defeat in an election whose pattern strikingly recalled the defeats of the Federalists in 1800, the Democrats in 1860, and the Republicans in 1912. In these elections, as in 1932, the party in power was overthrown after it had become conservative in the interest of a single sectional-class group, and a party and a leader came to power who promised to solve new problems with new laws in the interest of broad groups in every section. Farmers and workmen formed the mass base of each of these victories. They came once in every generation to remind "the rich, the well-born, and the able" that the needs and desires of the common people might be neglected only at the cost of defeat at their hands. They set the Republic on new courses more to the liking of its ordinary citizens, however painful they might be to the privileged. They are the American substitute for violent revolution, and they fulfill the grand design of the authors of the Constitution.

CHAPTER III

INTERREGNUM

THE four months between the election and the inauguration of President Roosevelt brought the American economic crisis to a dangerous climax. This demonstration of the dangers of so long an interregnum served the useful purpose of encouraging the ratification of the Twentieth Amendment, which shortened the interval for the future to two and a half months. During this last prolonged American interregnum, crisis and changes of course were world-wide. Hitler became Chancellor of Germany even though his strength at the polls in November had declined, and the Reichstag fire inaugurated the Nazi terror. Most of the powers except Great Britain defaulted on their debts to the United States. Japan withdrew from the League of Nations when it condemned the aggression in Manchuria. The new Spanish Republican Cortes abolished government subsidies to the Catholic clergy. The Soviet Union announced the completion of its first Five Year Plan and inaugurated the second one. In the United States hunger marchers moved on the capital, mobs in the corn belt frustrated the mortgage sale of farms, and Charles T. Mitchell resigned from the chairmanship of the National City Bank of New York and its investment subsidiary, the National City Company, after testifying before the Senate Committee on Banking and Currency. The President's Research Committee on Social Trends reported that a "bewildering variety" of changes was in store for the nation.

From December, 1932, to March, 1933, the index of pro-

duction in the United States fell from 64 to the lowest point
it ever reached: 56.[1] The depression had started with a panic
among traders in Wall Street. For three years it had spread
through the nation's economy like a paralyzing disease. Now
it began to reach the heart of the economic system, the
banks, which the Hoover administration had chiefly tried to
protect and stimulate with government loans. A panic among
bank depositors began late in January.

President Hoover blamed the post-election decline and
the banking crisis on public fear of the next administration's
policies, especially fear that it would inflate the currency.
His solution for the crisis was to ask the President-elect to
make public promises that he would not depart from the
gold standard or install any other "unsound" fiscal policies,
and to win his help to swing the Democratic majority of
Congress behind the Republican legislative program.

Even before the December economic decline set it, President Hoover attempted to win the coöperation of Roosevelt
in making plans for American participation in international
debt negotiations, the Geneva Disarmament Conference,
and the World Economic Conference. Participation of a
President-elect in responsibility for executive functions was
unprecedented and extra-constitutional. Politically, the danger was obvious that the dying administration would transfer some of its unpopularity to its successor by entangling it
in policies and commitments which would make a fresh start
on March 4 impossible. Nevertheless, Roosevelt agreed to
"confer" with the President.

On November 22 they met in the White House with Secretary of the Treasury Mills and Professor Moley present in an
atmosphere which the latter found overpoweringly strained.
The President-elect agreed with Hoover's basic points that
the war debts were not political but business obligations,
negotiations should be conducted with each country sep-

arately, debts and reparations were not related, and the United States must take account of proven inability to pay. But he disagreed with Hoover's proposal that they coöperate to appoint a single body of American delegates which should represent the United States in debt negotiations, the Economic Conference, and the Disarmament Conference. The inner purpose of this proposal was to institute a policy of trading whereby the United States would scale down the debts owed to it in exchange for tariff concessions, monetary stabilization, and disarmament agreements. Since debt payments were due in December, while the economic and disarmament conferences would be held after March 4, and the consent of Congress was necessary to scale down the debts, it was imperative that Roosevelt coöperate immediately and commit his administration to carry on the policy of trading, if it was to succed.

According to Professor Moley's account, which is the only one available written by one of the four present, Roosevelt's opposition to the Hoover proposal was caused by two considerations. The proposal was based on the conceptions that the sources of the American depression were foreign, that American recovery was underway since July, 1932, and that international instability was the only threat to continued recovery. These conceptions Roosevelt rejected, believing that the main sources of the depression were domestic, the chief one being the failure of purchasing power to keep pace with production, and could be corrected only by sweeping domestic measures. These measures would cause a rise in domestic prices, which would then need protection from foreign dumping in the American market by maintenance of tariffs and devaluation of the dollar. Monetary stabilization prior to devaluation of the dollar would freeze a situation highly unfavorable to the United States and dangerous to the domestic recovery program of the Roosevelt administration.

[49

In short, the economic nationalist policies of the First New Deal prevented coöperation with Hoover in matters of foreign policy. The second consideration followed from the first: the Hoover policy was the policy of "the internationalists. . . . League advocates, the pro-sanctionists, and those who desired a revival of foreign lending . . . those who would make us parties to a political and economic alliance with England and France—policing the world, maintaining the international *status quo,* and seeking to enforce peace through threats of war." [2]

It was suggested to Hoover that the ordinary diplomatic channels be used for negotiations on war debts alone. To the President:

This was very disappointing. Obviously, unless there was full coöperation both in debts and stabilization, President Hoover could not proceed. . . .

The importance of this to the later banking crisis was simply that it caused discouragement in the country and apprehension as to delay in stabilization of debts and currencies. . . . [3]

In December, and again in January, Hoover attempted to win coöperation and a commitment to his foreign policy from the incoming administration, but Roosevelt held firm, against the advice of Norman Davis and other "League Democrats." Roosevelt's willingness to coöperate with Hoover on policies which did not conflict with his own was demonstrated by his advice to Democratic Congressmen to vote for the administration's Bankruptcy Bill, which was thereupon passed and signed on March 1.

If Roosevelt's refusal to adopt the Hoover foreign policy caused "discouragement in the country and apprehension," his refusal to assure the public that the dollar would not be devaluated was, in the estimation of the official historians of the Hoover administration, directly responsible for the banking crisis.[4] During the campaign Roosevelt had affirmed his support of the pledge in the party platform: " 'A sound currency to be preserved at all hazards,' "[5] and added: "It is obvious that sound money is an international necessity, not a domestic consideration for one Nation alone."[6] But opinions undoubtedly differed as to what would constitute "sound money." After the election rumors spread that the victor was contemplating devaluation of the dollar and inflation of the currency by one or another method. Western supporters of the Democratic candidate, including the members of the Silver Bloc of Congressmen who represented mining districts and traditionally supported inflation, had campaigned for office on that platform. Professors James Harvey Rogers of Yale University and George F. Warren of Cornell, well-known advocates of managed currency theories, were understood to be in consultation with Roosevelt and the Brains Trust. Senator Carter Glass, leader of the Eastern "gold standard" Democrats, was reported to refuse an invitation to become Secretary of the Treasury in the new administration because he could not obtain assurances that the gold standard would be maintained. And the President-elect had by Moley's account instructed the latter to tell Senator Glass that the new administration would not reject ideas simply because they were labeled "inflation."[7]

The President-elect could not disclose, or even hint, that a "sound money" would require devaluation of the dollar, lest he precipitate an immediate panic and speculation in gold. The general tendencies of the Democratic Party, particularly its powerful Western wing, as well as rumors of specific intentions, probably had some influence in causing withdrawal of deposits from banks, domestic hoarding, and the flight of the dollar abroad which began after the middle of January. Another influence was the revelation of unsound banking practices by the managers of great banks who were giving testimony before the Senate Committee on Banking and Currency. Most important was the weakened condition of even the most conservative banks after three years of falling values, bankruptcies, and foreclosures. Exports of gold increased in February, but they had been far exceeded during the first six months of 1932.[8] Domestic hoarding of currency and gold increased rapidly during the same month. That fear of inflation was not as important in creating runs on banks as fear that the banks were unsound is indicated by the fact that only about one-sixth of the domestic withdrawals were in gold and gold certificates.[9]

Early in February, Louisiana declared a bank holiday to halt all transactions. Banks in the larger cities and national corporations were withdrawing their funds from smaller banks. On February 14 the Governor of Michigan closed the banks of the state. Three days later, having returned from a fishing trip off Florida and narrowly missed assassination, President-elect Roosevelt was sent a letter by President Hoover through the Secret Service. In this letter the Hoover interpretation of the cause and cure of economic crisis was once more set forth:

The major difficulty is the state of the public mind, for there is a steadily degenerating confidence in the future which has reached the height of general alarm. I am convinced that a very early statement by you upon two or three policies of your Administration would serve greatly to restore confidence and cause a resumption of the march of recovery.[10]

Then the President "easily demonstrated" that the history of his own dealing with the depression proved how efficacious would be

prompt assurance that there will be no tampering or inflation of the currency; that the budget will be unquestionably balanced, even if further taxation is necessary; that the Government credit will be maintained by refusal to exhaust it in the issue of securities.[11]

The demand that Roosevelt balance the budget was curious in light of the fact that deficits had increased under Hoover's administration steadily since 1930 until the annual amount by which the budget was unbalanced had reached almost three billion dollars in 1932.[12] The letter as a whole, like the proposals on foreign policy, was more than a request for co-operation. It asked Roosevelt to accept the defeated administration's interpretation of the causes of the crisis, abandon his own policies, and adopt those which had been repudiated by the electorate in November. The possibility of thus retrieving the debacle of his administration and winning an eleventh-hour victory over his successor was not absent from the President's mind when he wrote the letter, as is shown by his confidential memorandum to Senator David A. Reed:

> I realize that if these declarations be made by the President-elect, he will have ratified the whole major program of the Republican Administration; that is, it means the abandonment of 90 per cent of the so-called new deal.[13]

The President-elect refused to abandon the New Deal. He replied only to that part of Hoover's letter which suggested that he make a statement, and declared that the banking crisis could not be cured by "mere statements." And the dispatch of this reply was delayed for eleven days "through an assumption by my secretary that it was only a draft of a letter." [14]

On February 21, the President outlined instructions to Secretary Mills for a meeting between the latter and his successor, William H. Woodin, in which he insisted once more that the new administration adopt his own domestic and foreign policies. During the last days of the month new states declared bank holidays, and wild talk of revolution and dictatorship was being heard. On February 28, another appeal was addressed to Roosevelt for a "declaration even now on the line I suggested," and, possibly as a concession to Roosevelt's views, President Hoover offered "full coöperation . . . in any line of sensible action." [15] On March 2, he finally abandoned his own conception of how the crisis should be met, and proposed that a suggestion by Roosevelt be put into effect.

By that time the members of the new cabinet had been designated, and they were already engaged in hour-to-hour consultation with their predecessors, so that a very practical kind of coöperation was underway. The appointment of Woodin to the Treasury was reassuring to conservatives, for he was a banker and industrialist only mildly interested in New Deal experiments, and opposed to inflation of the currency. Cordell Hull as Secretary of State represented the traditional devotion of the Southern Democracy to low tariffs and conservative agrarianism. If his Assistant Secretary, Raymond Moley, was for six months to enjoy more intimate connection with the President than did the Secretary, and to oppose his own superior's policies, the years beyond that would bring to Hull a full measure of success and power. Henry A. Wallace was a leader of the progressive farmers of the Corn Belt, many of whom had abandoned with him their allegiance to the Republican Party and swung the West for Roosevelt. He was an exponent of the Domestic Allotment Plan, and was ready as Secretary of Agriculture to support inflation to raise the purchasing and mortgage-paying power of the farmer's dollar. Harold Ickes had made a career of fighting political corruption in Chicago, and could be expected to remove from the office of Secretary of the Interior the taint which had been attached to it by the Harding administration. Mrs. Frances Perkins's appointment as Secretary of Labor fulfilled Roosevelt's determination to develop a step farther his party's championship of votes and political office for women, and her experience as a social worker brought into the Cabinet the point of view of a profession which was to be influential in the new administration. Farley as Postmaster General represented a concession to politics in the narrow sense. His frankness rather than any difference in methods distinguished him as a distributor of patronage from his most incorruptible predecessors. Senator Thomas J. Walsh, who had revealed the depravity of the Harding regime, had been designated Attorney General, but his tragic death on his way to Washington to take up his duties caused Homer S. Cummings of Connecticut to be appointed in his place. George H. Dern of Utah as Secretary of War, Claude A. Swanson of Virginia as Secretary of the Navy, and Daniel C. Roper of South Carolina as Secretary of Commerce completed a cabinet which was notable for its violations of the timeworn rule that political debts must be paid with high office.

His Cabinet chosen, and with plans in hand for dealing with the crisis, the President-elect moved to Washington on March 2. Over twenty states had declared bank holidays. The first of many all-night sessions in the Treasury began with incoming and outgoing officials working together.

The President now surrendered a position to his successor's policy. He gave up the belief that optimistic words could cure the crisis. Roosevelt had suggested during the campaign that the Executive war powers might be used in a national emergency. President Hoover proposed that the Trading with the Enemy Act of 1917 be invoked to control foreign exchange and hoarding by proclaiming a national bank holiday. He had been advised by Attorney General Mitchell that the authority was so doubtful that certainty of

Congressional approval was necessary. Believing that only
the President-elect had sufficient influence to ensure such
approval, Hoover invited Roosevelt to join him in the proclamation of a bank holiday. Roosevelt replied that, while he
believed the President had authority to close the banks by
proclamation, he himself could not, as a private citizen, join
in such a proclamation, nor could he answer for Congress.[16]

Thus ended Hoover's hope of "coöperation," while the
bulletins of disaster and the hysteria of bankers, pleading to
be saved, spelled out the last minutes of a dozen years of Republican rule.

CHAPTER IV

LAUNCHING THE FIRST NEW DEAL: 1933

A few hours before the inauguration of the new President, Governor Lehman proclaimed a holiday which closed the banks and stock exchanges of New York. All the states had then declared holidays, but only federal authority could close the Federal Reserve Banks or stop the loading of gold on fast liners for Europe. The vast machinery of the country's economic life ground to a virtual stop. The people of the United States never faced a more dangerous economic crisis or looked more anxiously to a Chief Executive for economic salvation than on March 4, 1933, when Franklin D. Roosevelt, under gray, rainy skies, took the oath of office as the thirty-second President of their country.

The Inaugural Address, which went out over the radio a few minutes after one o'clock, was the first of many dynamic appeals and actions which were to transform the nation's anxiety into hope. "First of all, let me assert my firm belief that the only thing we have to fear is fear itself." This might have differed little from the Hoover pleas for confidence. It was followed by a daring analysis of the source of economic ills such as had not been heard from a President since Andrew Jackson's veto of the Bank Bill:

Plenty is at our doorstep, but a generous use of it languishes in the very sight of the supply. Primarily this is because rulers of the exchange of mankind's goods have failed through their own stubbornness and their own incompetence, have admitted their failure, and have abdicated. Practices of the unscrupulous money changers stand indicted in the court of public opinion, rejected by the hearts and minds of men. . . .

Stripped of the lure of profit by which to induce our people to follow their false leadership, they have resorted to exhortations, pleading tearfully for restored confidence. They know only the rules of a generation of self-seekers. They have no vision, and when there is no vision, the people perish.

The money changers have fled from their high seats in the temple of our civilization. We may now restore that temple to the ancient truths. The measure of the restoration lies in the extent to which we apply social values more noble than mere monetary profit.

Then came the promise of action:

Restoration calls, however, not for changes in ethics alone. This Nation asks for action, and action now.

Our greatest primary task is to put people to work. This is no unsolvable problem if we face it wisely and courageously. It can be accomplished in part by direct recruiting by the Government itself, treating the task as we would treat the emergency of a war. . . .

"Hand in hand with this" was envisaged a redistribution of population from industrial centers to rural areas, a movement which would be helped by raising farm prices, preventing foreclosures, reducing the cost of government, unifying relief activities, and planning for and supervising transportation, communications, and utilities.

The placing of what were to be the civilian conservation corps and farm resettlement activities in the center of his program, to which all else would be merely contributory, was, perhaps, dictated by the President's need to focus on solutions of the main problem of unemployment. The First New Deal was to be dominated by other means to that end. But the National Industrial Recovery Act was not yet formulated, and emphasis on the monetary policy would have created fantastic opportunities for gold speculators. He did promise "strict supervision of all banking and credits and investments, so that there will be an end to speculation with other people's money; and there must be provision for an adequate but sound currency."

A warning was clearly given that the relative importance assigned by the Hoover administration to foreign and domestic policies would be reversed:

Our international trade relations, though vastly important, are in point of time and necessity secondary to the establishment of a sound national economy. I favor as a practical policy the putting of first things first. I shall spare no effort to restore world trade by international economic readjustment, but the emergency at home cannot wait on that accomplishment.

Thus economic nationalism as a temporary expedient for recovery was foretold, and Secretary Hull and the "internationalists" were left to exercise patience while Professor Moley and the "nationalists" had their day. That the policy would be temporary and only economic was suggested by the pregnant statement of political foreign policy:

In the field of world policy, I would dedicate this Nation to the policy of the good neighbor . . . the neighbor who respects his obligations and respects the sanctity of his agreements in and with a world of neighbors.

Liberals were later to profess they found the germs of fascism in the First New Deal. Perhaps they found cause for suspicion in the evocation of the "regimented" moods of wartime:

If we are to go forward, we must move as a trained and loyal army willing to sacrifice for the good of a common discipline. . . . We are, I know, ready and willing to submit our lives and property to such discipline, because it makes possible a leadership which aims at a larger good. This I propose to offer, pledging that the larger purposes will bind upon us all as a sacred obligation with a unity of duty hitherto evoked only in time of armed strife.

But the President found that "action . . . is feasible under the form of government which we have inherited from our ancestors." Changes in emphasis and arrangement are possible without loss of the essential form of the Constitution, and have proved it to be "the most superbly enduring political mechanism the modern world has produced."

The nature of such possible changes was defined. "It is to be hoped that the normal balance of Executive and legislative authority may be wholly adequate," but if Congress fails to act of its own volition or under recommendation:

I shall not evade the clear course of duty that will then confront me. I shall ask the Congress for the one remaining instrument to meet the crisis—broad Executive power to wage a war against the emergency, as great as the power that would be given to me if we were in fact invaded by a foreign foe.[1]

The nation could not doubt that a new spirit had begun to move across the land. That democracy could be weakened by a vigorous attack upon the evils that beset it was a thesis developed by conservatives as well as radicals only after the attack had begun to succeed. Meanwhile, all groups, particularly bankers and Congress, begged to be commanded.

The President immediately summoned the new Congress, which was Democratic by large majorities and ready for strong leadership, to meet in special session on March 9, when Secretary Woodin had promised to have ready an emergency banking bill. Powers of the President were found in the Trading with the Enemy Act of 1917 to issue before the banks opened on Monday, March 6, a proclamation which suspended all transactions in the Federal Reserve and other banks, building and loan associations, and credit unions, and embargoed the export of gold, silver, and currency until March 9. And the leading bankers of the country were called to a meeting with the President and his subordinates.

The bankers were in a chastened mood. They had lost confidence in themselves. Three and a half years of attrition ending in the rout of the previous weeks, the disgrace for malpractices of many of their leaders ending in the collapse of the public prestige of their calling, and the forceful lesson that their power and privileges derived ultimately from the power of the people's government brought them to Washington eager to do its bidding. They had lost the cohesion of a vested group, and could not agree on what should be done. Some wanted a nationwide issue of fiat money or scrip; some wanted currency issued against their banks' frozen assets; some proposed that the state banks be forced into the Federal Reserve system; others proposed that the Federal Reserve Banks become government-owned banks of deposit; still others advocated a government guaranty of all bank deposits; and there was talk of nationalizing all the banks to bring them under government ownership and operation.

The bankers' confusion and willingness to give up responsibility to the government was an extraordinary display of the effects of loss of security on a class ordinarily quite self-reliant. If the administration had been bent upon achieving radical reforms as a condition of recovery, it could have had them. A drive for "socialism" of the kind the Brains Trust was accused of planning would have taken advantage of the discredited position and collapsed morale of the bankers to put through nationalization of the country's banks. As it was, a conservative solution, highly acceptable to bankers and businessmen, and symptomatic of the policies of the First New

Deal, was decided upon. An ironic aspect of the decision was that, in deference to the bankers' sensibilities, the "radicals" of the Brains Trust who had helped draw the plan up were kept out of the bankers' sight.[2]

The Emergency Banking Bill provided only such government controls against export and hoarding of gold, silver, and currency, and against the reopening of unsound banks as would assist private bankers to regain control of the situation. Further panic was forestalled by providing for the issuance of Federal Reserve notes on the security of assets of sound banks, so that the latter could immediately reopen for business. Thus the money changers who had fled from their high seats in the temple were invited to return under government escort. Socialists could deplore the loss of an opportunity by the government to install itself in their seats.

The temper of the new Congress was illustrated by its almost unanimous passage of the Banking Bill within four hours of its introduction on March 9, the Bill having been represented by a newspaper in the House where only the party leaders had read it. The only protest against the Bill was made in the Senate by seven Western progressives led by Senator LaFollette, who voted against it on the ground that it strengthened the great New York bankers' control of the country's economy.[3] The Act had been signed by nine o'clock that evening, and the arduous work began of reviewing the condition and licensing the reopening of banks across the country, work which was said to have condemned Secretary Woodin to his untimely death.

The next morning the President fulfilled the campaign pledge which had most pleased conservatives. He sent to Congress legislation to balance the budget by reducing the normal expenditures of the government, particularly in the fields of veterans' benefits and federal salaries. The businessman's thesis, that extravagance by the Hoover administration was a leading hindrance to recovery, was accepted by the President, and instrumented until in 1934 Congress began to pass appropriations over his veto. Later, when he recommended expenditures for unemployment relief which piled up larger deficits than those of the Hoover administration, he insisted on the distinction between "normal" expenditures, in which economy was pledged and fulfilled until Congress overrode his vetoes, and those which carried out his other pledge that he would not practice economy "at the expense of starving people." [4] The Economy Bill was passed on March 11 over the protests of a small group of progressives against catering to "millionaires." [5]

On Sunday evening, March 12, the President made his first "fireside chat" over the radio to the people of the country. The actions taken to solve the crisis he explained in plain terms in order to help dispel the clouds of public fear. His assurance that unsound banks would not be allowed to open created confidence in the banks which did open. Before another week was out most banks had been allowed to open, deposits and hoarded gold were returned, stock prices rose 15 per cent on Wall Street, and the dollar rose in foreign exchange markets. By the end of the year losses of bank deposits had been reduced to slightly over one billion dollars, owing to the failure of 1,772 banks which the Treasury had refused to license. Practically no licensed banks failed. [6]

The swift and successful solution of the banking crisis, the clearing away of danger and fear as if by magic, launched the administration on a high tide of public enthusiasm and support. The mass of small depositors found that the new administration had suddenly made their banks safe. Newspapers were filled with hopeful portents and plans for general recovery. Within a month, legal beer of 3.2 per cent alcohol content was made to flow where home brew and worse had been before. Within a year, Prohibition was an evil memory. Congressmen were made to understand that their constituents would not tolerate opposition or delay in carrying out the program of the deliverer in the White House. Not the least important cause of the almost universal support which the administration received during the next six months was the assurance which the Emergency Banking Act and the Economy Act gave to creditors, businessmen, and bankers that conservative solutions were acceptable to the President. The confidence for which Hoover had pleaded for three years had been restored within two weeks by Roosevelt. And most remarkable was the fact that Hoover's main purpose had been deliberately maintained:

Those who conceived and executed [the policies of the first week] were intent upon rallying the confidence, first, of the conservative business and banking leaders of the country and, then, through them, of the public generally.[7]

Only a seemingly minor clause in the Emergency Banking Act looked toward developments feared by conservatives. This clause granted to the President authority to take whatever steps he deemed necessary in regard to gold, silver, and foreign exchange. The Executive Order which authorized the reopening of the banks forbade transactions in foreign exchange and the withdrawal from banks or export of gold or gold certificates except as authorized by the Secretary of the Treasury for legitimate and normal requirements. These restrictions on the free operation of the gold standard were intended not only to prevent hoarding and speculation, but to be "a step toward permitting the dollar to become adjusted in an orderly manner to a position with reference to other currencies that would be more in accord with our goal of increasing domestic and foreign trade."[8]

The decision had already been made to devaluate the dollar by reduction of its gold content. The purposes of this policy will be examined hereafter; now it is sufficient to note that the President's course was devised to strike a middle path between those who wanted the gold standard maintained at all costs and the extreme inflationists. The crisis had weakened the former group but strengthened the latter, especially in Congress. At his first press conference, the President read a little lesson on monetary theory which made it clear that the United States would maintain some but not all of the requisites of a gold standard. On the other hand he defined the "unsound" currency against which he was pledged, as "printing press" money. He admitted that the government was moving towards a managed currency, but would not allow correspondents to report his words.* While conservatives feared any "tinkering" with the gold standard which would reduce the purchasing power of money paid by debtors to their creditors, the advocates in Congress of inflation through issuance of money which would be "unsound" even by the President's definition were gathering their strength to force their policy on the administration. The struggle came to a climax during the debate over the Agricultural Adjustment Bill, for the farmers were still, as they had been since colonial times, the chief advocates of inflation.

The President had decided to hold Congress in special session beyond the immediate banking emergency, in order to put through a group of basic recovery measures while the atmosphere of emergency helped to minimize opposition. Unemployment and farm relief were announced as his objectives. Before the legislative mills had ceased to grind at the end of the famous "hundred days" a large number of important laws had been passed.

On March 16 a draft of the Agricultural Adjustment Bill was sent to Congress with a message urging its passage in time to restrict the spring planting of crops in accordance

[65

with its provisions.[10] The Bill was the product of the President's campaign pledge, and of general agreement among farm and administration leaders to experiment with the Voluntary Domestic Allotment Plan, but its provisions were so broad that either one, or both, of two methods might be used. The more conservative and nationalistic scheme, sometimes called the Clair Plan, found its chief advocate in George N. Peek. He had been associated with General Hugh S. Johnson in the Moline Plow Company of Illinois, where both had learned the lesson that farmers who were not prosperous could not make industry prosperous by buying its products. Much thought and search for the solution of the problem had finally brought them to Washington in early spring of 1933 with plans which were incorporated into the First New Deal, Johnson's in the program for industrial, and Peek's in the program for agricultural recovery. The plan which Peek advocated aimed to give the farmers the benefit of tariff protection which their surpluses ordinarily denied them because they had to be sold in foreign markets whose low prices therefore determined prices in the American market. The plan was to allot money received by the government from agricultural import taxes to every farmer in an amount proportionate to the percentage of his crop which would be sold in the domestic market. No curtailment or regulation of the farmer's production would be required except in years and areas of superabundant yield, when farmers would be called upon to destroy a portion of the growing crop in order to qualify for their money allotments. High tariffs would be maintained, and ordinary surpluses would be marketed abroad with the same aggressive help of the government which had supported the export of manufactures during the Republican administrations. Peek claimed that this scheme would minimize bureaucratic control of the

66]

farmer while giving him those benefits of economic nationalist policy which industry already enjoyed.

With the substitution of an excise tax on processors of farm products as the source of money benefits to be paid to farmers, Peek's scheme was incorporated in the Rainey Bill and passed the Senate in 1932. Then it was quietly shelved in the House. He and leaders of the main farm organizations thereupon supported the candidacy of Roosevelt because they had been led to believe that their plan would be adopted by him. According to Peek's account,[11] after the election professors and lawyers led by Rexford G. Tugwell and Jerome Frank, and the "mystical idealist," Henry Wallace, took control of farm legislation for the new administration and wrote a bill which embodied the alternative scheme for carrying out the Domestic Allotment Plan. This scheme was for acreage control by the government and would abolish the farm surplus, even in normal years and before the crop was planted, by paying rentals to farmers on acreage taken out of production. Coöperation by farmers was voluntary, but few were likely to refuse to receive checks for not cultivating a percentage of their acres, and Peek believed the scheme to be "collectivist" because it entailed "regulation" of the farmers, as well as "internationalist" because it would benefit the whole world by removing the American surpluses from the international market and thereby raise the world price of farm commodities. It was linked to low tariff and other internationalist ideals and, Peek was convinced, would not work.

He insisted early in March that the dispute be carried to the President, but the latter sided with the Wallace group and acreage control. Nevertheless, the President was unwilling to abandon the "nationalist" features of the Peek scheme as yet, so the terms of the Agricultural Adjustment

[67

Bill were made broad enough to permit either scheme or both to be carried out, and Peek himself was promised the office of administrator of the law. The dispute was also aired before the Senate Committee on Agriculture and Forestry. The broad terms of the Bill, Peek's announcement that he was opposed to acreage control, and the understanding that he would administer the Bill according to his own plan permitted the problem to be passed over and postponed.[12]

The Domestic Allotment Plan was supported chiefly by larger farmers who produced the staples subject to export, such as wheat and cotton, which would be included in the Plan. These farmers constituted the strength of the Farm Bureau Federation, the National Grange, and several other organizations which wielded great influence on the Congressmen of the bi-partisan Farm Bloc. Peek's statement that these farm organizations had little to do with the Agricultural Adjustment Bill must be taken in the narrow sense of actual participation in its writing, because limitation of farm production by a scheme such as the Domestic Allotment Plan had long been their chief demand, especially since the failure of Hoover's Marketing Act. On the other hand, the National Farmers Union and the Farmers National Holiday Association represented the smaller farmers and tenants who were less dependent on staple crops and therefore less interested in the Domestic Allotment Plan.

These two organizations held conventions to pass unanimous resolutions condemning the Agricultural Adjustment Bill. The homespun President of the Farmers Union, John A. Simpson, conducted a vigorous campaign against it over the radio and before the Senate Committee. He considered both acreage control and tariff equalization to be unworkable, and mere palliatives in any case. The fundamental problem was that

40 or 50 per cent of farmers are sinking out in the middle of Old River Mortgage and the first thing is to throw him a life-saver. . . .

A privileged few now hold the obligations of the great mass of the people to the extent that any time they want to foreclose they can make about 120,000,000 of us propertyless. You have got one way to remedy that thing, and that is to make the dollar cheap enough so that the farmer, the little business man, the professional man, everybody, can pay their debts.[13]

Representative Lemke of North Dakota declared that Simpson correctly expressed the sentiments of 85 per cent of all farmers.[14] Certainly the advocates of the Bill did not explain what it would offer to the smaller, diversified-crop farmers and tenants. Whatever soundness there was in the arguments of Simpson, they were eagerly taken up by inflationist Congressmen, among whom representatives of silver-producing states were important. The former hoped to reduce the value of the money which would be used to pay off farm mortgages, and the latter hoped to find a market at the mints for silver. Thus the descendants of the populist farmers and of the Silver Senators of 1896 reproduced the alliance which had gone down to defeat with William Jennings Bryan in the great free-silver campaign. This time the alliance succeeded in exacting an inflationary amendment as the price of its support of the Agricultural Adjustment Bill.

The administration feared an amendment which would make uncontrolled inflation mandatory and defeat its plan for a managed currency. Senator Wheeler of Montana introduced an amendment providing free coinage of silver at a ratio with gold of sixteen to one, far above the market price. This measure was defeated in the Senate by a vote of 43 to 33 on April 17, but the President knew that more than ten more Senators were prepared to vote for other inflationary devices. The House overwhelmingly favored inflation. The problem became one of limiting and controlling the movement: it could not be stopped. When Senator Thomas of Oklahoma introduced an amendment designed to win the support of all varieties of inflationists, the President had it rewritten and then did not oppose its passage. The Thomas Amendment gave permissive power to the President to inflate or alter the currency by one or more of several devices: free coinage of silver at a ratio to gold fixed by the President, unlimited issuance of paper currency, and devaluation of the gold content of the dollar. None of the devices was mandatory, and it became possible for the President to use the one which was necessary to establish a managed currency while ignoring those which would produce an "unsound" money system. One of the President's conservative advisers, Director of the Budget Lewis A. Douglas, believed that the amendment was "the end of Western civilization," [15] but it possibly saved the country from the uncontrolled inflation upon which many Congressmen were intent. Another amendment provided that compensating duties might be imposed to prevent higher domestic farm prices from leading to increased imports.

While Congress debated the Agricultural Adjustment Bill, unrest in the Corn Belt rose to new heights. The Farm Holiday Association, led by Milo Reno, organized strikes by farmers who refused to sell, or allow anyone else to sell, produce at the prevailing low prices. These measures of desperation accomplished little, because the market was too favorable to buyers for sellers' strikes to succeed. More effective was the frustration of farm mortgage foreclosures. Crowds of farmers forced sheriffs to accept bids of a dollar or two at foreclosure auctions, and then turned the farms back to their original owners. At LeMars, Iowa, on April 27, District Judge Bradley refused to promise a mob of farmers that he would sign no more foreclosures, and was dragged from his courtroom and hung by a rope until he was unconscious. States passed mortgage moratorium laws. On May 4, a conference of farm leaders voted for a national strike, which was postponed only at the request of the President that the new farm legislation be given a chance to create recovery by orderly methods. After a special message by the President to Congress another amendment was added to the farm bill, under which farm mortgages would be refinanced at low interest rates by the federal government.

When it was finally passed as an administration measure and signed on May 12, the Agricultural Adjustment Act was an omnibus which gave the farmers of the country their three main demands of the preceding half-century and longer: protection against the ruinous effect on prices of their surplus crops, inflated currency with which to pay their debts, and cheap credit. No law had promised the farmer so much since the Homestead Act of 1863. If the law did not introduce Utopia, it was not for lack of willingness by the administration to heed the farmer's voice in the spring of 1933.

Unemployment relief was the second immediate objective of the administration. On March 21, the President sent a message to Congress asking for three types of legislation, none of which departed far in principle from the relief policies of the Hoover administration. Two of the requests were quickly met by establishment of the Civilian Conservation Corps which provided 250,000 unemployed young men with little more than subsistence wages as workers in the national forests, and the Federal Emergency Relief Administration which made grants to the states for direct relief. The CCC was a type of public works activity which the Hoover administration had not developed, while the FERA grants were gifts as contrasted with the loans to the states for direct relief which Hoover had inaugurated in June, 1932.

The third request was met in Title II of the National Industrial Recovery Act passed in June. This Title established the Public Works Administration and was a simple expansion of the Hoover policy of providing employment by the construction of public buildings, roads, and other traditional federal works. The appropriations for the CCC, FERA, and PWA exceeded the outlays for relief by the preceding administration, but they did not approximate the great expenditures which began in 1935, when, for the period of the Second New Deal, a fundamentally new relief policy was inaugurated to provide federal employment at security wage scales to all employables. Meanwhile a relief policy acceptable to conservatives was intended to mitigate the worst suffering without solving the unemployment problem.

Title I of the National Industrial Recovery Act was intended to solve the broad problem of industrial depression and unemployment. Contrary to general impression, this most significant experiment of the First New Deal was not improvised by the President or the Brains Trust. The occasion of its passage may be called fortuitous, but its policies are traceable to theories and practices of organized industry and labor during the preceding decades, and it was only one more experiment in the world-wide movement by advanced industrial countries in the twentieth century away from *laissez-faire* individualism.

Over the years both of the main groups dependent upon factory production had worked out programs for the improvement of their own position in the industrial system. The depression was an incentive to each group to work more aggressively for its own program as a cure for the ills which afflicted the system, and they both demanded that the government adopt and enforce their programs. Before the depression, labor had chiefly depended on non-political union activity to achieve its aims of shortening the hours of work and raising wages. The depression created a great surplus in the labor market which was unfavorable to the bargaining power of unions. They lost membership and became virtually useless in achieving benefits for labor. In this situation workers looked increasingly to state and federal legislation as the only practicable means of achieving the labor program. Laws to improve labor's position were presented as being in the public interest because they would increase employment and production by increasing the purchasing power of the mass of the population. Manufacturers, on the other hand, had since the First World War developed to a high level the use of trade associations to formulate codes of fair trade practice which should minimize competition, support prices, limit production, and divide markets. These codes suffered from two weaknesses: their legality under the antitrust laws was doubtful, and the courts had not clarified the issue; and agreements by corporations to observe the provisions of a code were voluntary and unenforceable. The latter weakness permitted the collapse of the codes during the depression when the search for vanishing markets led manufacturers to revive the whole arsenal of savage competition. The opinion grew among businessmen that the codes of the trade associations must be exempted from the antitrust laws and enforced by government authority. Since this would raise prices and restore profits, production would be expanded and employment restored, wherefore the scheme was held to be thoroughly justified by the public interest.

The two programs were incompatible to the degree that each group intended to win the lion's share of advantage from an industrial revival. They could be reconciled only by a mutual determination to share the benefits of recovery. Until President Roosevelt came to power there was little hope of obtaining such an agreement.

Meanwhile the two groups worked separately. An important victory in the labor campaign for state legislation was won with the New York minimum-wage law of April, 1933. By that time the fight for a federal maximum hours-law was well underway. In December, 1932, Senator Black of Alabama introduced a bill which would limit the hours of work in factories to thirty per week. Early in January, President Green of the American Federation of Labor told a Senate Committee that labor would resort to a general strike if necessary to compel adoption of the thirty-hour week: "A lot of employers understand only one thing—force, and this change can only be brought about either by legislation or force." [16]

The Black Bill attracted little attention until a committee of the Chamber of Commerce issued a "Report on Working Hours" recommending that a forty-hour week be adopted by industry, that it be only temporary and voluntary, and vigorously opposing any legislation on the subject.[17] As if in defiance of the Chamber, the Senate suddenly passed the Black Bill on April 6. Chairman Connery of the House Committee on Labor added a provision for a boycott of imports produced by foreign industries whose laborers worked more than thirty hours per week. This he considered necessary to prevent dumping of foreign goods in the United States when domestic labor costs were suddenly raised by the thirty-hour rule. Such a boycott would wreck at one blow Secretary Hull's plans to reduce tariff rates and the London Economic Conference which was scheduled to meet in June. Nevertheless, there were signs that the House would pass the Black-Connery Bill with a large majority.

This precipitated in a form unwelcome to the administration the whole question of its industrial recovery program. On April 4 the President had decided, after considering many conflicting plans offered by industrialists and others, to postpone the question because "thinking in business and government circles on the subject had not yet crystallized sufficiently." Now he immediately appointed a Cabinet committee headed by Secretary Perkins to "work out a substitute for the Black Bill." [18]

Secretary Perkins carried the findings of her cabinet committee to the hearings on the Black-Connery Bill, and proposed them as "suggestions" of the administration. She declared that the Bill, while not an administration measure, represented a general policy which had the sympathy of the President.[19] The suggestions were that a minimum-wage provision be added to the Bill to prevent employers from cutting wages when they reduced the hours of work, and to bring substandard wages up to a minimum level; that some flexibility be permitted in the hours provision to suit the needs of seasonal industries; and that power be vested in the government to restrict production to prevent it from again outrunning consuming power and forcing the cut-throat competition and low prices which would make obedience to the hours and wages provisions impossible. The whole should be administered by the Department of Labor.[20]

Organized labor heartily endorsed the plan, although it was inclined to fear that minimum wages would become maximum wages unless an amendment guaranteed the right of collective bargaining.[21] But the Perkins suggestions were a shock to employers. The President was "aghast at the commotion" they caused.[22] A hundred leading industrialists met in Philadelphia on April 11 to protest against the Bill, and similar meetings were held in other cities.[23] Manufacturers were accused of coercing their employers to oppose the Bill.[24] Leaders of the main organizations of business, including President Henry I. Harriman of the Chamber of Commerce, President James A. Emery of the National Association of Manufacturers, and Robert Lamont of the Iron and Steel Institute, appeared before the House Committee to register their protest.[25] Immediately when the aggressive opposition of business began to be felt, the President directed Moley to obtain plans from business groups which they would favor as substitutes for the Black-Connery-Perkins Bill.[26] On May 1, the administration leader Senator Robinson announced that the Bill was no longer supported by the administration.[27] The House Committee continued its hearings nevertheless, indicating that it might be impossible to divert the movement for a recovery plan based exclusively on the labor program.

The business plan for recovery which was formulated by the administration under these circumstances had been officially adopted by the Chamber of Commerce as early as April, 1931, when its annual convention urged that the government modify the antitrust laws to permit industry to limit competition, raise prices, and restrict production. This would provide the guaranty of profitable operation of factories which was indispensable to recovery.[28] The trade associations were the instruments best fitted for the organization of the proposed controls, but their inability to enforce their own codes of fair-trade practices demonstrated the need to find stronger sanctions than they possessed. In December, 1931, the Chamber announced that it favored a national economic council, not under government supervision, to enforce codes drawn up by the trade associations.[29]

The specter of government regulation of business was being fought valiantly, but the deepening depression and further collapse of the trade associations' codes brought businessmen to admit in desperation the need for governmental authority to bring order out of the chaos created by destructive competition. In June, 1932, after another convention, the Chamber of Commerce launched a nation-wide drive to win support for relaxation of the antitrust laws and "government approval" of trade association codes.[30] At this stage businessmen hoped that the power of government could be used in their favor without submitting to government regulation or even supervision.

At about the same time, Roosevelt and the Brains Trust began to collect plans for the organization of new relations between government and industry. Many variations on the theme of government authority behind trade agreements were gathered together and filed. To these Moley turned when the President suddenly needed to placate business fears of the Black-Connery-Perkins Bill. Moley handed over to General Hugh S. Johnson the task of integrating them in one plan. At the same time the President authorized Senator Wagner of New York, Secretary Perkins, Assistant Secretary of Commerce John Dickinson, Donald Richberg, Rexford Tugwell, and others to work independently on the same problem.[31]

While all were at work, business leaders who were appearing before the House Committee on Labor complemented their protests against the Black-Connery-Perkins Bill with proposals which finally added to the business program for suspension of the antitrust laws and codes of "fair competition" the admission of the need for government supervision.[32] On May 3, two days after the administration had ended its support of the pro-labor Bill, the Chamber of Commerce convention met in Washington and voiced further strong protests against it. But it became clear to the convention that the administration was struggling to avoid passage of the Bill and needed support. Speakers explained that the government might be forced to regulate industry directly unless business coöperated with it to make concessions to labor under a system of self-government by industry with government supervision.[33] The President himself addressed the convention to appeal for concessions to labor in return for government aid in the suppression of cut-throat competition.[34] The convention promptly resolved in favor of the President's plan.[35]

After these developments it remained for the framers of the new Bill to work out details such as the degree of government control which "supervision" would require, and the exact nature of the concessions to labor which would be demanded of employers in return for the suspension of the antitrust laws. In the end, the President ordered all those whom he had assigned to draw up plans to shut themselves in a room until they could agree on a single draft of a bill.[36]

Their product was the National Industrial Recovery Bill. It was based on the assumption that labor and industry would share the benefits of recovery, and to this end both interests were granted government support in the achievement of their programs. In the famous Section 7A, labor was promised the inclusion in industrial codes of unspecified minimum-wages and maximum-hours rules, and was guaranteed the right of collective bargaining with employers through representatives freely chosen by employees. For businessmen, limitation of production and exemption of codes from the antitrust laws were provided. The question of the degree of government control in the drawing up of codes was left to a tug-of-war between the trade associations which were given the right to formulate them, and the government which could reject them and promulgate codes on its own motion. Violators of code agreements could be prosecuted before the federal courts and punished. The President was left free to establish whatever administrative agencies he deemed necessary. The Bill was considered by the President to be a deliberate step away from the philosophy of "equalitarianism and *laissez faire*" which Hoover's failure and his own election had proven to be "bankrupt." [37] Ideally, the system envisaged would consist of separate institutions of self-government for both labor and industry, with the government requiring them to coöperate and preventing either one from injuring the other or the public.

The draft was sent to Congress on May 15. The Black-Connery-Perkins Bill was dropped, and hearings were held on the substitute by both houses. Senator Wagner sponsored the new Bill, and he and Donald Richberg represented the administration at both hearings. In the Committee on Finance hearing Senator King of Utah asked Senator Wagner whether the Bill was "drawn largely from the philosophy of Mussolini or the old German cartel system," and Senator Wagner denied it,[38] but to the House Committee on Ways and Means Donald Richberg admitted that the Bill encouraged manufacturers to fix prices immune from prosecution, and thus to achieve the same ends as cartels did in Europe. He stated that the trade associations wanted the antitrust laws suspended in order to legalize codes of fair competition chiefly to end unfair competition in the use of labor.[39] However, since labor unions and labor contracts had already been exempted from the antitrust laws by the Clayton Act of 1914, Congressmen questioned whether the proposed law was motivated by a desire to raise wages as much as by a desire to raise prices. Answering this, President Harriman of the Chamber of Commerce, who had been in close consultation with the authors of the Bill, admitted that a price rise was the primary motive.[40] Some business leaders believed that Section 7A made too great concessions to labor. President James A. Emery of the National Association of Manufacturers and R. P. Lamont of the Iron and Steel Institute frankly spoke their fear that Section 7A would cause labor unions and collective bargaining to thrive and "individual bargaining" to perish.[41] That the Bill left the way open for the building of company unions and thus avoidance of collective bargaining presently became apparent to businessmen and lessened their opposition to Section 7A.

The most important amendment made by Congress provided that the President might limit, prohibit, or make conditions governing imports when the new law caused rises in prices which invited foreign goods into the American market. In this way the economic nationalist implications of the Bill were recognized, and tariff provisions made which matched the compensating duties of the AAA. Businessmen had advocated a manufacturers' sales tax as the source of new revenue needed to service the borrowing of $3,300,-000,000 for the public works program which was authorized in Title II of the Bill, but the administration's recommendation to increase income, corporation, excess profits, and gasoline taxes was carried out by Congress.

The National Industrial Recovery Act was passed by large majorities and signed on June 16. The President said that history would probably record it as "the most important and far-reaching legislation ever enacted by the American Congress. . . . Its goal is the assurance of a reasonable profit to industry and living wages for labor." [42] Thus were added to the farmers the second and third main interest groups to whom the administration during the First New Deal tried strenuously to grant their main demands.

The chief purpose of the AAA and NIRA was recovery. They dominated the First New Deal, and the administration's first crusades were organized around them. Three other laws were passed during the Hundred Days the chief purpose of which was reform rather than recovery. These attracted less attention at the time, but their greater permanence and their capacity for organic growth make them significant. Each of the three laws had been promised in the Democratic platform, and was a specific application of the reform traditions which had been interrupted when Woodrow Wilson left the White House.

The Tennessee Valley Authority Act of May 18 was a victory for those who, without discussing socialist theory, insisted that the government own and operate for the benefit of the people hydro-electric plants on the great waterways of the nation in order to prevent private corporations from exploiting these vast resources for private profit. Republican administrations had nowhere shown themselves more ineffective than in their inability to find any solution other than shutting down the government's great wartime power and munitions plant at Muscle Shoals. Senator George W. Norris of Nebraska had conducted a relentless struggle to end the waste of power on the Tennessee River and to place it at the service of the people of the region. The TVA was a personal victory for him as well as for the public policy which Roosevelt had painstakingly developed while Governor of New York.

The law created a corporation with a board of three directors appointed by the President with the consent of the Senate. This body was vested with the power of eminent domain to build dams and power plants with the purpose of developing the Valley economically and socially. It was empowered to produce, distribute, and sell electric power and nitrogen fertilizers to the people of the region and to industry, and to sell explosives to the United States government. Flood control, navigation, proper use of marginal lands, reforestation, and the general welfare of the region were within its sphere. Direct competition with private power companies was authorized by the erection of transmission lines to farms and villages not otherwise supplied with electricity "at reasonable rates." [43] The widespread opposition which the latter feature of TVA might have aroused in normal times was distracted by the dramatic events of the Hundred Days on other fronts, and also by the cloud which had passed over the private utility companies with the collapse of the Insull holding company pyramid and the revelations of widespread abuses. As it was,

[81

the full development of opposition was postponed until the success of TVA was assured, when the only question which remained was whether the costs of a federal corporation on which TVA power rates were based constituted fair competition with private companies, or even a fair yardstick by which the rates of private companies might be measured. To the people of the Valley and the manufacturers who moved in to use the cheap power, the question was fairly academic. Wendell Willkie was to attract his first admiring attention from the business world when, as President of the Commonwealth and Southern Power Company, he drove a particularly sharp bargain in the sale of facilities to the TVA. His victory might well be called Pyrrhic. The general success of TVA encouraged federal development of similar sites in other regions. When war came again, the nation did not lack vast power facilities for munitions, aluminum, and a thousand other purposes.

The Securities Act of May 27 originated in the conviction of liberals over many years that a federal "blue-sky" law was needed to protect the public from fraud and misrepresentation in the issuance, manipulation, and sale of stocks and other securities. The depression had thrown glaring light on the unscrupulous purposes behind many securities issues, the devious methods by which insiders rigged the stock market, and the deceptions practiced by high-pressure salesmen who gulled the small investor. Correction of these abuses was a part of the Democratic platform. Confusion of counsel separated regulation of securities issues and sales from the allied problem of stock-exchange regulation, postponed action on the latter until 1934, and resulted in a bill drawn chiefly by Felix Frankfurter and hastily passed without hearings by Congress. Its main provisions were that new issues of securities be registered with the Federal Trade Commission along with a statement of the financial position of the company, and that the same information be given to all purchasers of the issue. "Let the seller beware!" was substituted for the older slogan: misrepresentation was made subject to prosecution. Whether or not this Truth-in-Securities Act was cumbersome, as its revision in 1934 argues, and hindered the flotation of new issues in 1933, it was of less pressing importance than the regulation of stock exchanges. In the absence of the latter reform, a speculative Wall Street boom, garnished by all the abuses of the pre-depression era, threatened to discount recovery before the administration's program could be put into effect and purchasing power be increased to keep pace with rising prices.

The Glass-Steagall Banking Act of June 16 established three reforms which most bankers as well as liberals had come to believe were necessary to prevent repetition of the abuses which had aggravated the boom, the depression, and the banking crisis. Investment banking was separated from commercial banking so that affiliates could no longer be used by bankers for speculation with their depositors' money. The Federal Deposit Insurance Corporation was established to afford a government guaranty of bank deposits under $5,000, and thus remove the motive for runs on banks by small depositors such as had occurred prior to March 4. The Federal Reserve Board was given powers over interest rates and other factors which would enable it to prevent excessive speculation with borrowed money.

The TVA, the Securities Act, and the Banking Act were all sustained by the Supreme Court, while the chief recovery laws, AAA and NIRA were invalidated. This remarkable fact, usually forgotten at the time of the struggle over the President's court reorganization plan, made the reform legislation of the First New Deal more important for the future than the recovery legislation which was at the time the administration's chief concern.

The three reform laws which were passed during the Hundred Days were also distinguished by their compatibility with the purposes of the recovery program. On the other hand, reforms which had been promised in the sphere of economic foreign policy, especially tariffs, were not reconcilable with the domestic recovery measures. How this conflict was resolved will be the subject of a separate chapter.

CHAPTER V

THE BOMBSHELL MESSAGE

THE development of irreconcilable domestic and foreign economic policies by the administration led to crisis when the London Economic Conference met in June, 1933, and to solution by the President in favor of his domestic policy.

The AAA and NIRA were intended to raise the prices of farm and factory products in the American market. A faster rise in American prices than in world prices would invite foreign products into the American market and exclude American products from foreign markets. By themselves the two Acts were self-defeating, for imports would swamp the United States the moment its price level rose and thereby largely prevent it from rising. The American price level had to be protected and insulated from the rest of the world. This might be done by raising the tariff rates higher than the Hawley-Smoot levels, and provisions were accordingly made in the AAA and NIRA.

But raising tariff rates would not increase, and might decrease the ability of foreign countries to buy American products, the increased export of which was an important requirement of American recovery. A method of providing foreign purchasing power and at the same time providing further protection of American price levels was to devaluate the dollar. A sufficient decrease in the amount of gold for which a dollar could be bought would cause a fall in the gold value of American prices even while their dollar value rose, with consequent protection against foreign competition in the American market; and the same decrease in the amount of gold for which a dollar could be exchanged would, on the other hand, make it easier to sell American products abroad because low gold prices could be accepted for them insofar as the dollar value of gold increased. These effects had been realized to some extent after the dollar had been divorced from gold in March, 1933. The dollar had fallen in gold value on foreign exchanges. Since Britain and the sterling bloc of nations had gone off gold previously, and reaped advantages thereby in international trade, the fall of the American dollar was looked upon by the President as merely putting us "in the same position with nearly all the other Nations of the world." [1] The remaining countries of the gold bloc, led by France, had from time to time reduced the gold content of their monetary units even before the depression. Thus the United States by allowing the dollar to fall to its "natural" level was only eliminating the advantages which virtually all countries had enjoyed in trade with this country.

The President evidently expected that the dollar would fall sufficiently so that when the London Economic Conference met in June the United States could start on the same footing with the other nations, "and because we are such a large Nation, it ought to emphasize the necessity for all Nations getting together on a more stable basis." [2] The various actions on gold which were taken by the administration during the Hundred Days were all calculated to free the dollar from gold so that it might fall far enough to justify stabilization with other currencies, while at the same time the gold reserve backing the country's currency was preserved. Hoarding and export of gold were forbidden, and all gold was called into the Federal Reserve Banks where it was "nationalized" by the federal government taking title to it in exchange for certificates. Congress passed a resolution which abrogated the gold payment clause in private and public obligations, including federal gold bonds and certificates. It remained to be seen whether foreign buyers of the American dollar would now bid its gold value down sufficiently to encourage the administration to stabilize the dollar with other currencies.

Besides monetary stabilization, lower tariffs were a leading object of the London Economic Conference. The import tax clauses of the AAA and NIRA did not hold out much hope for American coöperation to lower rates. As a gesture of good will preliminary to the meeting of the Conference, Norman Davis for the United States had agreed to an international tariff truce. On May 13 the President announced that in observance of this truce he had forbidden AAA officials to undertake acreage control and compensatory duties without his consent. But two days later the President removed the ban.

The possibility of new increases in American tariffs cast a strange light on the conversations which the President was holding with foreign statesmen preliminary to the Conference. A procession of foreign leaders, including Prime Minister MacDonald, Edouard Herriot, and Hjalmar Schacht, passed through the White House, and optimistic statements were issued. On May 7, in his second fireside chat, the President affirmed that the United States was seeking "a cutting down of the trade barriers," as well as "the setting up of a stabilization of currencies. . . . The international conference that lies before us must succeed. The future of the world demands it and we have each of us pledged ourselves to the best joint efforts to this end." [3] A few sentences earlier he had said that domestic recovery was the first concern of Americans.

On May 16, a day before Hitler was scheduled to make an announcement of his foreign policy to the Reichstag, the President issued a dramatic "Appeal to the Nations," in which he urged upon the nations the purposes of the Economic Conference and of the Geneva Disarmament Conference. He declared that the cause of economic peace was closely linked with that of political peace, and urged that no nation take responsibility for failure in either sphere. The threat of new American tariffs in the AAA and NIRA seemingly set a poor example of economic pacifism to other nations. But the President had probably ceased to think of lower tariffs and monetary stabilization as the main objects of the London Conference. Its original agenda had included, and the President in his "Appeal" now added to his own list of the objects of the Conference "international action to raise price levels." [4] Such action would make unnecessary protection by tariffs and dollar devaluation of the price rises in the United States which AAA and NIRA were intended to effect.

Meanwhile the President decided not to send to Congress a bill prepared by an interdepartmental committee which would have given him the power to carry out the campaign promise of lower tariffs through reciprocity agreements.[5] And his decision to postpone monetary stabilization was made when the dollar began to fall in May on the international exchange, and was accompanied by a sensational rise in American prices. Moley later wrote:

F.D.R. suddenly took the position (in private, of course) that the dollar might sink to lows that the experts hadn't conceived of. He was in no hurry to stabilize until he was sure he was going to get the best bargain there was to be got. With the dollar falling as it was in the exchange markets, our stock and bond prices were leaping upward and our commodity prices soaring. New purchasing power was being created in this country, he held. This stimulating movement must not be stopped. This was recovery—not a dangerous speculative spree! [6]

The tragi-comedy of the London Economic Conference was the result of the American delegates' ignorance of the President's determination not to enter into tariff or monetary stabilization agreements which might compromise domestic recovery, and of the determination of France and the gold bloc nations to achieve monetary stabilization before any other part of the agenda was considered.

In the absence of strong control by the President, the various American delegates pursued each his own conception of correct policy. Secretary Hull, the head of the delegation, believed that business recovery must be preceded by the restoration of international commerce and monetary stability. He told newspapermen that he hoped joint action to lower tariffs would be given priority over all other matters. But the majority of the delegates favored high tariffs and continued devaluation of the dollar. Dissension within the delegation reached such a pitch by the time it arrived in London that the Secretary of State threatened to resign until the President sent him an encouraging cable. Hull's first draft of his opening speech of the Conference condemned the high tariff and depreciated currency policies which the President was determined to pursue. On instructions from the latter, the tenor of the speech was changed, but not its essential meaning. Premier Daladier of France in his opening address declared that an end to the currency war and stabilization were the first steps. Montagu Norman of the Bank of England and Clement Moret of the Bank of France negotiated with anti-devaluation members of the American delegation a "temporary" stabilization agreement to hold the dollar at the level it had then reached: $0.85 in gold value and $4.00 in relation to the English pound. The President rejected this agreement, suggested that further devaluation, until the pound should be worth $4.25, was more desirable, and warned that he would not approve "close" stabilization in any case. Then a proposal by Hull, that a 10 per cent tariff cut be "discussed" by the Conference, was interpreted as a specific offer by the United States to reduce its tariffs.

At this point the President decided to send Moley as his liaison officer to London to convey the need for unity to the demoralized delegation, and "the President's opinions on the significance and implications of his domestic program and its bearing upon the objectives of the Conference," which would explain his desire that the Conference turn away from stabilization and tariff discussions in favor of "long-range objectives." [7] Fantastic rumors circulated while Moley hurried abroad and seemingly superseded his own superior, the Secretary of State. The dollar was falling rapidly, speculators were having a field day, and France and the gold-bloc countries were frantic with fear that they would be forced off the gold standard.

To allay the panic of the gold bloc, Moley drew up a declaration which suggested that steps would be taken to end speculation and that all countries would eventually return to the gold standard. It embodied no specific promise of stabilization, but the President nevertheless rejected it with the statement that the United States must be free to raise domestic prices regardless of what foreign exchange rates might be. It was Moley's turn now to appear repudiated by the President; but the latter was only pushing to an extreme Moley's own faith in economic nationalism.

The President was enjoying a vacation cruise with guests who included Professors George F. Warren and Frank A. Pearson, ardent advocates of the "commodity dollar" theory, and Moley believed they had prevailed upon their host to experiment with their idea that the dollar could be devaluated artificially even below the level it had reached on the international exchange. They believed that purchases of gold by the government at increasing dollar prices would not only reap advantages for the United States in trade, but would also force domestic commodity prices upward proportionately as the gold value of the dollar fell. The President acted

90]

upon the Warren theory later in the year. On July 1 the dollar stood at $4.33 to the pound and was worth only $0.75 in gold—a level lower than that which the President a few days before had suggested as one at which the United States might stabilize. Nevertheless, on July 3 he sent his famous "bombshell" message to the Conference, which in very strong terms rejected stabilization and was interpreted by the powers as a declaration of economic warfare:

I would regard it as a catastrophe amounting to a world tragedy if the great Conference of Nations, called to bring about a more real and permanent financial stability and a greater prosperity to the masses of all Nations, should, in advance of any serious effort to consider these broader problems, allow itself to be diverted by the proposal of a purely artificial and temporary experiment affecting the monetary exchange of a few Nations only. . . .[8]

Warning was then given that the United States would alter the gold value of the dollar in order to control its purchasing and debt-paying power. Later the President commented on the effect of his message:

It is true that my radio message to the London Conference fell upon it like a bombshell. This was because the message was realistic at a time when the gold-bloc Nations were seeking a purely limited objective, and were unwilling to go to the root of national and international problems. The immediate result was a somewhat petulant outcry that I had wrecked the Conference.[9]

A conciliatory statement was made by the American delegation on July 5 to win the support of the sterling bloc, and prevent France from forcing an immediate adjournment and blaming the President for the failure of the Conference. No serious attempt was made to put the Conference on the path desired by the President. Secretary Hull by heroic efforts kept it in session for three more weeks, but its only accomplishments were minor advisory agreements to deal with surpluses of wheat and silver.

It has been said that the London Economic Conference was the world's last chance to check the economic nationalist rivalries which the Axis powers were to intensify with extreme political nationalism to the point of aggression and war. Whatever truth there be in this opinion, the failure of the Conference is attributable to the insistence of the gold bloc that the United States give up further devaluation of the dollar before any other nation made concessions, in equal measure with the refusal of the United States to abandon at the outset a useful adjunct of the domestic recovery program which it had just adopted. The apparent agreement among other nations that, if the United States would not make the first concession and surrender the first favorable conditions in international trade and domestic commodity prices which she had enjoyed since the depression began, they had no further interest in the Conference, argues the one-sided purpose of their participation in it.

Other nations could argue that with the Hawley-Smoot Tariff of 1930 the United States had inaugurated the latest cycle of economic aggressions and that they had hoped the new Democratic administration would also inaugurate a general retreat. But they were doomed to disappointment until the time arrived when the American administration abandoned the primary emphasis of the First New Deal on a rise in domestic commodity prices as the means to recovery. That under the Second New Deal the economic foreign policy of the United States did turn towards international coöperation indicates that the United States did not fail to do its part to establish economic peace before the Axis plunged the world into war.

CHAPTER VI

FALSE RECOVERY

Before the domestic recovery program could be got under-way, its success was anticipated and discounted by a rapid rise in certain factors of prosperity. The index of production rose from 56 in March to 101 in July.[1] Improvement was particularly marked in the steel, automobile, construction, and textile industries. The index of farm prices rose from 55 to 83 during the same period. Retail food prices rose from 59.8 to 71.[2] Wall Street staged a bull market in industrial stocks which rose in price from an average of 63 in March to 109 in July. Monthly stock sales on the New York Exchange which had been less than 20,000,000 in January and February rose to 125,000,000 in June.[3]

These portents of prosperity were widely interpreted as proof that the new administration had already routed the depression. Wiser heads pointed out that no change in fundamentals had as yet been accomplished by the administration, except a slight fall in the value of the dollar. Employment in manufacturing industries rose between March and July from 58.9 to 71.5, and payrolls from 37.1 to 50.8,[4] but purchasing power lagged far behind production and the rise in prices. The boom was compounded of speculation based on cheap credit and expectation of inflation and future profits, expansion of inventories as a hedge against rising prices, and the manufacture at prevailing low wages of surpluses which could be sold at higher prices after NIRA had raised costs, limited production, and stiffened price controls.

Manufacturers, merchants, and investors hurried to change money, which had already begun to fall in value, into goods, which were rising in value. The "recovery" which resulted was false because it was speculative and without sufficient foundation in expanded purchasing power. It left the mass of consumers, who had no surplus funds to exchange for goods, worse off than before, because rising prices reduced the value of their income. The inability of the government to launch its recovery program as soon as the business world perceived the tendencies of the legislation before Congress created a time lag during which businessmen improved their situation and placed the administration policy of a concerted rise of all the factors of recovery under a heavy handicap.

The most speculative elements of the boom were liquidated by the stock market crash of July. A more serious handicap on the administration's recovery program was the decline of production from 101 in July to 71 in November.[5] These were the very months during which the NIRA went into effect. Unlike previous periods of declining stock prices and production, this one witnessed a rise in commodity prices, those of an industry highly affected by NIRA such as textiles rising from 68 to 76.8.[6] Many manufacturers evidently took advantage of the opportunity offered by NIRA to raise prices while they limited production and supplied expanding markets with surpluses built up earlier.

The stock market crash in July and the likelihood that business would evade features of NIRA which were unfavorable to it, particularly the necessary increase in purchasing power through re-employment and higher wages, led the National Recovery Administration late in July to launch a great campaign for immediate compliance with minimum-wage and maximum-hours rules.

In this campaign General Hugh S. Johnson, Administrator of NRA, used to the full his experience during the First World

War as organizer of the draft and of industrial mobilization for war production. He undertook once more the creation of mass support for a concerted national effort to integrate in a vast pyramidal organization all geographic localities and all business enterprises with the government. Before the Act had been passed, Johnson had begun the process of code writing for the ten biggest industries: cotton textiles, bituminous coal, automobile, petroleum, lumber, garment trades, wholesale trade, retail trade, iron and steel, and construction. On July 9, the President signed the Cotton Textile Code, in which a notable clause abolished child labor in the industry. But difficulties multiplied in drawing up the codes for the other industries. The stock market crash of July 21 served as a danger signal that "recovery" to date had been one-sided and would be followed by a general collapse unless purchasing power was swiftly built up.

The campaign was launched on July 24 in a radio address by the President. He asked for immediate and universal compliance with minimum wages of 30 cents per hour, maximum hours for factory workers of 35 per week, and abolition of child labor. These were the terms of the President's Re-employment Agreement, or "Blanket Code." [7] Compliance was to be voluntary, but the right to use the Blue Eagle insignia, encouragement of the public to buy only where it was displayed, and a campaign along wartime lines to create favorable opinion were designed to win acceptance for the Blanket Code without enlisting the coercive powers of NIRA.

The main object of the Blue Eagle campaign to increase purchasing power was clearly favorable to labor, but this was modified by three circumstances. Section 9 of the Blanket Code permitted further price rises if they were "necessary." The NRA machinery was incapable of supervising the interpretation of this Section. Labor was asked to refrain from "aggression," which would mean giving up its chief weapon, the strike, against employers who refused to conform with the spirit or letter of the NIRA, particularly Section 7A. And employers who found the provisions of the Blanket Code too severe were invited to submit codes through their trade associations to cover their particular industries.

The invitation was accepted with alacrity, and the NRA machinery was taxed to the limit in organizing hundreds of codes for particular industries at the same time that it conducted a comprehensive campaign for immediate compliance with the Blanket Code. The Industrial Advisory Board, composed of three cabinet members, the Director of the Budget, the Chairman of the Federal Trade Commission, and General Johnson, supervised the work. Employers, labor, and consumers were represented by three advisory boards which were intended to protect their respective interests. Trade associations submitted codes to the advisory boards, hearings were held to obtain agreement among all interests, and a code authority was appointed to administer each finished agreement. The National Labor Board was established to handle disputes involving Section 7A. The organization was carefully planned to achieve fair distribution of the burdens and benefits of the new law among employers, labor, and the public. Free debate, bargaining, and agreement under the impartial supervision of the government were calculated to ensure achievement of the ideal end of self-government by the interests concerned in planning and execution of a rationalized economic order.

Whether ideal ends which were to be reached through so elaborate a technique could not be approached for sheer lack of time, sound leadership, and correct execution, or whether the conflict of interests between employers and labor was too profound in any case for voluntary coördination, the NRA in practice fell far short of the expectations of even its most ardent supporters. By September 1, over six hundred codes for particular industries, including most of the big ten, were in operation, and a high level of acceptance of the Blanket Code had been reached. Nevertheless, production declined steadily, and the rate of increase of employment and payrolls fell off during September and absolute decline set in by November.[8] Prices, on the other hand, continued to rise, or fell off very slightly.[9]

What had happened? Answers varied, but no one claimed that business had shouldered more than its share of the burdens of the Act, or had failed to win a full measure of benefits. It was pointed out that the trade associations, which had originated the code system, and which were themselves dominated by the largest corporations, had not only formulated the codes but had also dominated the procedure of hearings, amendment, and adoption, while the influence of small businessmen, laborers, and consumers had been very slight. The rules of "fair competition" which had been installed in the codes frequently included more or less avowed price-fixing devices as well as limitations on production which were desired by the largest corporations. The Code Authorities which administered the agreements were largely staffed by representatives of the corporations most interested in controlling enforcement, according to the precedent established by dollar-a-year men in World War days. In an open hearing early in 1934, General Johnson admitted a series of faults of NRA, many of which injured small business or labor or the public, but none of them indicated discrimination against big business.[10]

The National Labor Board was said to be more interested in preventing strikes than in securing enforcement of Section 7A. The Automobile Code and some others contained the "merit clause" which expressly permitted employers to discharge employees on grounds of incompetency. The clause was self-administered by employers, and it was held to encourage nullification of employees' right to join an independent union by discharge of all or leading union members. Employers fought bitterly against collective bargaining, employing labor spies and the whole roster of anti-union tactics. The chief one was the organization of company unions financed and often staffed by the employers or their agents. Such unions were held to misrepresent the interests of labor even when the forms of collective bargaining were observed. A wave of company union organization swept the country when NRA was launched. Under these circumstances it became possible for businessmen to observe the child-labor and hours-and-wages provisions of the codes and at the same time reduce labor costs. Labor-saving machinery was installed, and the stretch-out and speed-up systems were further developed. The charges that cuts in the wages of skilled and semi-skilled labor, and its replacement with unskilled more than offset the gains made by the elimination of child labor and the raising of sweated wages to the minimum levels are supported by statistics of hourly earnings, which show that during the NRA period skilled and semi-skilled categories lost more than unskilled and women workers gained, so that overall hourly earnings declined.[11] Organized labor decided that only by using the strike weapon could labor's share of the benefits of NRA be obtained, and a wave of strikes by A.F. of L. unions occurred during the early fall of 1933. The great majority were called in large-scale industry to oppose company unions and to win rights guaranteed to labor in Section 7A, especially union recognition as bargaining agent. The vexed questions of suitable voting units in large plants and of minority representation in collective bargaining were, for the time being, either evaded by the Labor Board or settled in favor of employers.

While headlines in the newspapers through October featured the more spectacular problems of NRA, such as strikes,

Henry Ford's refusal to sign the Automobile Code, and the waverings of General Johnson between cajolery of violators of codes and threats to "crack down on chiselers," a groundswell of opposition to the whole experiment developed as it became apparent that its promised benefits to the mass of people were not forthcoming. Radicals called the codes a blueprint for fascism, and their administration a sell-out of labor. Labor leaders and liberals complained of the undue influence of business in drawing up and administering the codes, while they admitted the benefits realized, particularly the virtual elimination of child labor and sweatshops. Small businessmen claimed that they could not compete successfully against large corporations because the codes discriminated against them. On the other hand, big business, represented chiefly by the National Association of Manufacturers, launched an attack on the rights granted to labor by Section 7A. The strikes and organizing campaigns conducted by the A. F. of L. led to the fear that in time company unionism would be defeated, and the right of labor to organize and bargain collectively would impose the closed shop on industry. Stricter government supervision and prosecution of violators of codes were also feared because they would limit the degree of hegemony which big business had established for itself under NRA.

By November, 1933, the NRA honeymoon was ended. The first fruits of the recovery program were more disappointing to labor than to any other group. Businessmen had won a fairly favorable position with a rising price level and an expanding market without commensurate increases in costs. And when the results of the farmers' first season of experiment with planned production under the AAA were examined, the rising price of manufactured goods was found to be a direct cause of disappointment for them also.

The Agricultural Adjustment Administration was set up

under George N. Peek as Administrator. Peek had shared much of the experience of General Johnson during and after the First World War, but he lacked Johnson's energy and ability as an administrator. By Peek's account, his General Counsel, Jerome Frank, and Assistant Secretary of Agriculture Tugwell organized a cabal of "collectivists" within the AAA which enjoyed the patronage of the "internationalist" Secretary Wallace, and this cabal plotted to impose acreage control on the farmers, as opposed to Peek's plan of tariff-equalization payments.[12] But "conspiracy" was unnecessary in 1933, because Peek's plan included provision for acreage control when the growing crop gave evidence of creating a super-surplus, over and above the normal surplus for export and too large for tariff-equalization to be achieved. It was the determination of Wallace and Tugwell to institute acreage control for 1934 before the crops were planted, to avoid production of even a normal surplus for export, which led to Peek's resignation in December, 1933. The latter agreed that for the first season "regimentation" of the farmers by acreage control was unavoidable because when the AAA was organized in May crops were already growing which would create a super-surplus. Thus the "plowing-under" program of 1933, which evoked the most severe criticism of any AAA activity, was undertaken willingly by Peek for sound "nationalist" reasons, and not as the program of the "collectivist-internationalist conspirators." The distinction is important in characterizing the First New Deal. That the Wallace-Tugwell plan for acreage control as carried out in 1934 involved an even greater limitation on production than Peek's plan must be understood in the light of its advocates' support of it only until, in Secretary Wallace's words, "radical tariff modifications should suddenly build up foreign purchasing power for our surplus farm products." [13] Tariff reductions were anathema to Peek. However little difference the quarrel made to the actual operation of the AAA in 1933, control of the farm program by Peek is another indication of the initial desire of the administration to conduct its experiments under conservative auspices.

One-fourth of the land on which cotton was growing on July 1 was rented to the Secretary of Agriculture at $6 to $20 per acre in cash and options on cotton owned by the government since the Hoover administration. The cotton plants on the rented acreage were plowed under, but the remaining 30,000,000 acres yielded a slightly larger crop than had 36,-000,000 acres in 1932, because farmers had concentrated on maximizing the yield of their unrented soil. From February to July the price of cotton had risen from 5.5 cents per pound to 10.6 cents. This rise occurred before the AAA had affected the market, and was caused by the campaign of textile manufacturers to process as much cotton as possible before NRA code wages went into effect. In August, after one-fourth of the crop was destroyed, and contrary to the calculations of advocates of the Domestic Allotment Plan, the price of cotton fell to 8.8 cents. To save the program, the AAA organized the Commodity Credit Corporation which used RFC funds to lend farmers 10 cents a pound on their crops. The loans were made only to farmers who signed contracts to take more acreage out of production in 1934, when the full Wallace-Tugwell program was to be installed by renting 15,000,000 acres instead of only 10,000,000. The Commodity Credit Corporation loans successfully sustained the price and helped to raise it to 9.6 cents by November. The net result to cotton farmers in 1933 was an increase in their cash income of more than 50 per cent over 1932 and 1931.[14]

The cotton program was the most successful AAA operation in 1933. Wheat, tobacco, corn, hogs, and sows due to farrow were destroyed. Surplus foods were purchased by the

AAA using FERA funds and distributed to the states for the unemployed, and this work was taken over on October 1 and expanded by the Federal Surplus Relief Corporation. But these efforts were less successful in raising farm prices and income. Total farm income, including government payments and products used at home, increased only 20 per cent over 1932, and was still 14 per cent under 1931. Over one-fourth of the farmers' increase in cash income in 1933 was derived from government payments, which were obtained from processing taxes and added to the cost of manufactured products.[15] The general rise in price of the commodities which farmers bought reduced the real value of their money, so that most of their increase in income was lost.[16]

The course of farm prices during the latter half of the year intensified the difficulties of farmers and matched the decline of industrial employment and payrolls which began in November. Farm prices had risen rapidly from March to July in response to the fall of the dollar and speculative demand. But during those months farmers had little to sell. Beginning in July farm prices fell from an index of 83 to 78 in December,[17] thus reasserting the ancient problem of falling prices during the marketing season.

Dissatisfaction with the AAA became widespread. It was pointed out that the farm products which were benefited were raised chiefly by large landowners, farming corporations, and banks and insurance companies which had become large owners of farm lands through foreclosures; while smaller diversified farmers could rent often only a part of one field to the AAA and they frequently found it not worthwhile. The prices of crops not covered by AAA were even weaker. Farm laborers, who were excluded from the provisions of the NRA, sharecroppers, and tenants usually received no share of AAA checks, or found themselves put off the land as a consequence of the landowners' reduction of acreage.

In the fall, revolt spread once more in the Corn Belt. Quick action by the Farm Credit Administration had relieved the problem of farm foreclosures, but sporadic violence developed into a new strike against low farm prices which Milo Reno and the Farm Holiday Association crudely organized.

Thus the end of the AAA honeymoon coincided with that of the NRA. The decline of farm prices along with industrial employment and payrolls were the chief factors causing danger of a new depression and general dissatisfaction with the administration's recovery program. To save the situation, the President acted swiftly to administer a series of stimulants to the economic system.

CHAPTER VII

THE SHOT IN THE ARM

THE most important action taken by the administration in the fall of 1933 to save the recovery program was in the field of gold policy. The drop in the international exchange value of the dollar when it was divorced from gold in the spring had been accompanied by a sharp rise in domestic prices, stimulation of exports, and restraint of imports. On July 8 it was decided that, in the President's words: "Since the Administration's efforts to raise commodity prices were meeting with success, and other American exporters were finding that their world markets were expanding . . . American gold-mining interests could obtain the benefits of world gold prices" [1] by the government relaxing the restrictions on gold exports. But this action was perhaps premature and influenced the end of the domestic boom later in the month. When it became apparent by the middle of October that NRA and AAA were failing to develop recovery of industrial production, employment and payrolls, and farm prices, it was announced on October 22 that an experiment based on the "commodity-dollar" theory of Professor Warren would be undertaken.

The dollar had ceased its rapid decline in August. The Warren plan called for artificial measures to force the gold value of the dollar to decline still farther, and its sponsors predicted that commodity prices would rise proportionately. Since the prices of manufactured goods were recovering successfully, the administration's first interest was in stimulating farm prices, and it was hoped that these, being more dependent on world prices than the former, would be the greater beneficiaries of the Warren scheme to raise American prices higher than the world level. Furthermore, farm exports were chiefly dependent on price conditions, while exports of manufactures depended more on quality and on patent cartels, so that farm exports could be expected to benefit specially by forced dollar devaluation.

On October 21 it required $29.01 of American currency to buy an ounce of gold on the world market, as compared with $20.67 before March 4. On October 25 the Reconstruction Finance Corporation offered $31.36 per ounce for any newly-mined domestic gold. Sales of foreign gold were also invited beginning October 29. At short intervals the price offered was increased until $34.06 was reached on December 18. The pound was then well above the old par of $4.87, and the dollar could be bought on foreign exchanges for about 60 cents in gold, old value. It was necessary to buy all the gold offered in order to hold the dollar at this "artificial" low level. On December 28 the Federal Reserve Banks were ordered to turn in to the Treasury the gold stocks of the country, which they had been holding since the banking crisis in March, in exchange for notes at the old rate of $20.67, and the "profit" which accrued to the Treasury from the increased dollar value of this gold and of its own stocks held to support the currency, offset the cost of buying new domestic and foreign gold at the new rate.

This forced devaluation of the dollar to about 60 per cent of its former gold content unsettled the markets of the world. Speculators who bought gold for resale to the RFC made killings. Foreign countries believed the United States was guilty of economic aggression on their currencies and trade. France especially complained that the RFC purchases would drain the world of gold and force France off the gold standard.

European manufacturers were convinced that the cheapening of American goods in foreign markets gave American exports an unfair advantage in world trade, and constituted exchange dumping.[2]

These effects of the new devaluation of the dollar were considered by the administration to be justified by the stimulation of American recovery which the action provided. Advantage had undoubtedly been won in foreign trade. But unfortunately for Professor Warren's theory, his prediction that domestic commodity prices would rise automatically with the dollar price of gold was not fulfilled. Commodity prices as a whole fell slightly during November and December. Farm prices, which were most in need of stimulation, fell most, while the prices of manufactures held steady or rose slightly.[3] But it is impossible to say with certainty that the commodity-dollar experiment did not prevent the economic regression of October from developing into a general collapse. Whether or not the experiment should be credited with a partial success, it represented the President's most extreme resort to economic nationalism in the interest of recovery.

In domestic politics the commodity-dollar experiment was opposed not only by the advocates of maintenance of the gold standard at any cost, who were chiefly Republicans, but it also caused the first defections within the ranks of the ruling party. "Sound-money" Democrats, chiefly Easterners with the creditors' point of view, who had not seriously opposed the fall of the dollar to its "natural" level from March to August, were unwilling to support the further devaluation by "artificial" measures which began in October. Secretary Woodin took a leave of absence because of his failing health as the experiment got underway. Henry A. Morgenthau, Jr., whose opinions did not conflict with the policy, became Acting Secretary of the Treasury in November, and

Secretary after his chief's death the next May. Other leading Treasury officials, such as Dean G. Acheson and O. M. W. Sprague, resigned in protest against the new policy. Bernard M. Baruch, James P. Warburg, and other influential supporters of the administration now turned against it. Alfred E. Smith ended the truce with his successful rival and denounced the "baloney dollar" as his first word in a campaign which he was to fight with increasing bitterness.[4]

The second front on which the President attacked the threatened collapse was unemployment relief. The NRA campaign to expand employment and production was failing. The President had been doubtful from the beginning that the PWA would put an appreciable number of the unemployed to work, because of the restriction on it that only the conventional types of public construction and repair projects might be undertaken. Besides this, Secretary Ickes as its Administrator had proceeded in fear of waste and graft with so much caution that very few new projects were opened by fall. Relief rolls began to rise again with the business reaction in October. The prospect of another winter of increasing unemployment determined the President to act.

Harry Hopkins was the most important figure in helping to evolve the administration's relief policy. He had been a social worker in Christadora House, New York City, before his appointment by Governor Roosevelt as chairman of the New York State Temporary Relief Administration. Early in 1933 he became head of the FERA, and after the experience with it and the other extension of Hoover relief policies, PWA, he helped to plan new departures. The most important elements in Hopkins' conception of relief were that the federal government should provide work relief for employables rather than merely funds for direct relief to be administered by the states, that minimum wage rates higher than relief payments should be paid for labor and that the skills of the unemployed should be used and developed. The social effect of giving work at all levels of skill instead of a dole to the unemployed would be profound, and the labor market would be influenced in ways immediately favorable to labor rather than employers by fair wage standards on federal work projects. The centralization of relief administration and the use of federal credit resources would make possible the substitution of nation-wide campaigns to "prime the pump" of recovery by injecting purchasing power into the lowest level of the economic structure, for uncoördinated and financially weak local-relief activities.

A first step towards realization of these objectives was taken on November 8, when the President announced the creation of the Civil Works Administration to put four million unemployed persons to work immediately on federal "made-work" projects. Funds were allocated from FERA and PWA appropriations supplemented by local governments. Wages were paid which represented a great increase in the purchasing power of the unemployed as compared with relief payments. The administrative machinery was entirely federal, with Hopkins at its head.

Confined on one side to work which could be undertaken more quickly and with less expenditure for materials than PWA projects, and on the other by scrupulous avoidance of competition with private enterprise, the CWA made-work projects were frequently no more useful than raking leaves. But the CWA achieved its main purposes. By January over four million persons were at work, suffering which would have been intensified with a fourth winter of increasing unemployment was minimized, and the sudden injection of almost a billion dollars into the hands of buyers helped to sustain the nation's economy. The program was not intended to be permanent, but a solution of immediate problems, and it was ended by April 1. The experiment served as an intermediate stage in the evolution of relief policy from the initial adoption of Hoover policies which appealed chiefly to business interests, to the full-fledged instrumentation in the Works Progress Administration of 1935 of the Hopkins conception, which appealed chiefly to labor interests and became the relief policy of the Second New Deal.

The third action taken to support recovery was the adjustment of NRA regulations to improve the position of small business and labor. On October 22 businessmen in small towns were exempted from observing the Blanket Code, price increases by manufacturers were made subject to investigation, and machinery for handling complaints against business practices was established. On December 16 the National Labor Board's powers were increased as a result of "several flagrant cases of defiance of the Board by large employers of labor." [5] The Board had been established to preserve industrial peace by "passing" on disputes arising under Section 7A. Now its powers were defined to include mediation, conciliation, and arbitration. These alterations of NRA, slight in themselves, nevertheless were the first official recognition of what statistical definitions of the results of the experiment made clear: that NRA was not providing equal benefits for all groups; rather big business was turning it to its own purposes at the expense of small business, labor, and consumers.

A fourth attempt by the President to hold the line of recovery was the creation of the Public Works Emergency Housing Corporation on November 29. Its object was to provide a broad avenue of opportunity for PWA to put its funds to work. Slum clearance and the construction of low-rent housing in congested urban centers were hit upon as the most useful possibilities. However, the Comptroller General ruled that such projects were outside the powers granted by Congress to PWA, and the attempt failed. The desire of the administration to stimulate recovery in new ways was evident, and this method was used during the Second New Deal when legislation was secured.

The stimulants of cwa work relief and dollar devaluation strengthened the recovery program and possibly averted a collapse which had threatened in October and November. No general upturn of all factors of recovery occurred; rather a steadying at levels below those which had been reached in July. Toward the year's end the index of production began a slow rise from 71 in November to 86 in May, 1934.[6] Beginning in January, employment and payrolls also increased.[7] Industrial and farm prices held fairly steady through the first half of the new year.[8]

These results were perhaps considered sufficient to justify a "breathing-spell" during which the main policies of the First New Deal could be further tested. If they failed, the experiments with new policies, especially the cwa and alterations of the nra, already suggested the lines of evolution which would be pursued.

CHAPTER VIII

YEAR OF TRANSITION: 1934

THE year 1934 was one of transition from the First to the Second New Deal. The CWA which was in full swing at the beginning of the year represented a transitional experiment in relief policy. The stabilization of the dollar in January and the Reciprocity Trade Agreements Act of June ended economic nationalism in foreign policy, if the Silver Purchase Act of June be excepted. Acreage control of farm production was fully established. Bitter controversies over NRA featured the slow shift of policy in the field of relations among government, industry, and labor. The year ended with striking approval at the polls of the administration's course, and with momentous decisions which launched major policies of the Second New Deal in 1935.

A corresponding shift in the membership of the Brains Trust accompanied the alteration of the administration's policies. Raymond Moley came home from the London Economic Conference believing that the public misconception that he had been repudiated by the Bombshell Message should be corrected. Failing that, he considered resigning as Assistant Secretary of State, but waited until September to avoid the appearance of a dispute over policy or with Secretary Hull. In reality the Bombshell Message had repudiated the internationalist policies of Secretary Hull and supported the nationalist policies of Moley. After the latter's resignation he continued to assist the President, but on a different footing. He no longer assisted in the formulation of detailed programs, but worked "as a technician at speech construction," as if he were "a plumber and a pipe needed fixing." [1] For a time he still found frequent opportunities, by his account, to "modify or head off" the President's steps, and it was not until the transition to the Second New Deal was completed that he found the President no longer "left the door open to disagreement." [2] Meanwhile the Columbia University professor was increasingly disturbed by the steps which accomplished the transition, by what he considered the doubtful ideas and methods of newer associates of the President, particularly Harry Hopkins, Benjamin V. Cohen, and Thomas Corcoran, and by the distrust which developed between the administration and businessmen, for which he blamed both sides. The degree to which Moley dissociated himself from the administration was a measure of its abandonment of the policies of the First New Deal, of which he had been a leading advocate. By the time of the 1936 election, both processes had been completed.

That the President was ready by the beginning of 1934 to abandon policies of economic nationalism which Moley had supported was suggested by the legislation on gold for which he asked Congress when it convened in January. The commodity-dollar experiment had won a position for the American dollar in relation to foreign currencies which was advantageous. Further devaluation would bring still greater advantage, but the President instead made ready to cooperate with foreign countries for international stabilization of currencies. He asked Congress to set limits of 40 to 50 per cent devaluation of the gold content of the dollar between which he might fix its value from time to time. Congress agreed, and on January 31, the President by proclamation fixed the dollar at 59.06 per cent of its former gold value, which meant that gold would be bought for $35 per ounce and the pound would stand at about $5. This valuation has been maintained ever since. But at the time, as a bargaining device to encourage a stabilization agreement with other nations, the President had power to devaluate still farther. Devaluation of slightly over 40 per cent had already demonstrated its "ability to get rid of a great many of our export surpluses." [3] A compensating feature of the system from the point of view of foreign countries was that unlimited purchases of foreign gold by the United States at $35 per ounce provided a market for new gold as well as old so favorable that marginal deposits, particularly in South Africa, were brought into production. In effect, the United States was subsidizing the import of a foreign commodity at high prices in order to create foreign purchasing power for American goods and thus increase exports. Since American commodity prices had not risen in proportion to devaluation of the dollar, foreigners who sold gold to the Treasury and bought American goods made an excellent bargain.

The Gold Reserve Act of January also provided that two billion dollars of the "profit" which accrued to the Treasury as a result of the new dollar value of its gold and the gold of the country which had been turned in at the old price should be set aside in a stabilization fund, to be used for the purchase and sale of government securities necessary to hold their value steadily at par in relation to the new dollar value. This was another indication that the United States was ready to end the era of unstable financial conditions and speculation.

The new status of the dollar was evidently still too favorable to the United States to make international stabilization of currencies attractive to foreign countries. The gold bloc nations found it impossible entirely to prevent by legal restrictions the drain of gold to the United States, and at the end of the year, Chancellor of the Exchequer Neville Chamberlain told the House of Commons that Britain was not ready for international stabilization because the dollar was being held below its actual value.[4] By 1936, however, Britain and France were ready to make a stabilization agreement with the United States.

After the value of the dollar had been fixed, the President took other steps to break down the economic isolation of the United States. Private banks had become unwilling to make medium or long term loans to finance international trade because the movement of all nations towards managed currencies, foreign exchange controls, and import restrictions had made the collection of such loans problematical. In order to fill the need for such credits, and to give by example an inducement to private banks to return to the field, the President organized under powers granted by Congress to NRA and the RFC two Export-Import Banks. They were operated by public officials, and the government owned their common stock. The first bank was expressly created on February 2 to facilitate trade with the Soviet Union, and the second, established on March 12, was to provide credits for trade with Cuba, but was expanded to include all other countries. In 1936, the two banks became one.

The most decisive step in the turnaway from economic nationalism was the passage of the Reciprocity Trade Agreements Act in June. A year earlier the President had decided not to send a reciprocity bill to Congress, and the Bombshell Message had destroyed Secretary Hull's hopes of reversing at the London Conference the world movement towards higher tariffs. New tariff protection had been written into NIRA and AAA, but it was not used because devaluation of the dollar in effect raised American tariff walls more than enough to compensate for rising domestic prices. At the same time, devaluation and purchases of foreign gold had created purchasing power for American exports, but this effect was expected to be and proved temporary. After the value of the dollar was fixed in January, most of the "free" gold in the world was sold to the Treasury, amounting to $452,000,000 in February and $237,000,000 in March. But most countries took action to protect their stocks, and only surpluses of newly-mined gold were sold to the United States beginning in about April, when the amount sold was $54,000,000, and the average fell to less than $40,000,000 thereafter until the end of the year, with little change in subsequent years.[5]

The President therefore asked Congress on March 2 for reciprocity tariff legislation as an emergency measure. Secretary Wallace told the Senate Committee on Finance that after the United States became a creditor nation during the First World War, its foreign exports had been paid for by American loans to foreign countries. When the loans stopped in 1930, exports declined. Dollar devaluation and gold purchases had created a temporary fund of foreign purchasing power and provided a breathing-spell. But the breathing-spell should be used to lower tariffs in order to increase imports and thereby create new pools of foreign purchasing power. If this were successful, acreage control under the AAA would no longer be necessary, because agricultural surpluses could be sold abroad.[6] Secretary Hull also stressed that the proposal was an emergency measure to meet emergency conditions.[7]

Since the negotiation of trade agreements would necessarily be a lengthy process, the effect the measure would have on the emergency was not clear. Protectionists charged that a general attack on the protective system was intended. To this anticipated objection the President directed the statement in his message to Congress: "No sound and important American interest will be injuriously disturbed." [8] Definition of the qualifiers "sound," "important," and "injuriously" left open a wide area for interpretation, and objection was made to lodging in the Executive the exclusive power to define the terms. Reciprocity agreements negotiated by the Executive would not require ratification by the Senate. Reductions to 50 per cent of existing rates would be within the power of the President. The power to raise rates by a like amount was to be used as a bargaining weapon to break down discriminations against American goods. Administration spokesmen argued effectively that arbitrary controls over foreign trade had been granted to the Executive frequently since 1794, and that the specific power to negotiate reciprocity agreements without referring them to Congress had been granted from time to time beginning with the McKinley Act of 1890.[9] Advocates of the Bill did not stress the facts that reciprocity agreement clauses had previously been placed in essentially protective tariff laws as concessions to low-tariff sentiment and with particular reference to Latin American countries, most of whose products did not compete with American products; or that the Presidents since 1890 had all been protectionists except Wilson, and the reciprocity powers granted them had been virtually unused. It was not expected that Secretary Hull, the country's outstanding advocate of low tariffs for a generation, would allow the opportunity to achieve his lifelong purpose to go to waste.

Opponents of the Bill offered its lack of a guaranty that interested parties would be given a public hearing prior to the conclusion of an agreement as further evidence that the administration intended to break down the protective system. Advocates, on the other hand, were convinced that public hearings would revive the notorious tariff lobbies, bribery, and propaganda campaigns of former periods, and prevent objective decisions. Less attention was paid to a more concrete indication that general tariff reductions might result: most nations had been granted "unconditional most-favored-nation" status in their commercial treaties with the United States, hence the reductions in specific rates in a reciprocity agreement with one country, for which presumably equal concessions would be obtained, would automatically extend to almost all other countries without their making any concessions therefor to the United States. "Global" quotas could be and were written into agreements to prevent unlimited advantage of reductions being taken by nations which had made no concessions. Nevertheless this, and other, aspects of the Bill convinced Raymond Moley that, as he wrote to the President, it was a "'dangerous . . . indirect, roundabout method'" of achieving the "'fixed purpose to lower tariffs on the part of those entrusted with [its] administration.'"[10] Moley expressed the views not only of traditional Republican protectionists, but also of Democrats among whom were important Eastern leaders representing business interests and Westerners whose interest in tariffs on farm produce made them willing to concede protection to manufacturers. The administration, on the other hand, could depend on the support of the Southern wing of the party and of liberal low-tariff sentiment scattered through other sections.

This support and the general prestige of the administration secured the passage of the Bill in spite of sharp opposition in the Senate, and it was signed on June 12. With it, an important foundation of the Second New Deal was laid. The United States, after fourteen years of leadership of the world movement towards higher tariffs, sharply reversed its position and became the leader in an attempt to ameliorate international conditions by reopening the channels of trade. The President declared that "intangible effects which are measured in terms of the spirit of peace and of more friendly relations between Nations"[11] were hoped for, as well as aid to recovery from an expanded foreign market.

Of all the powers, the United States was best equipped to wage a continuing and successful economic war upon the

[117

rest of the world; that it began in 1934 to work for international economic peace and coöperation was of the utmost significance. Perhaps it had begun too late for any effect to be realized of diminution of the economic nationalism and imperialism of the nations which presently organized the Axis. In any case, the United States, by abandoning aggression on foreign economies and leading the way towards international currency and trade coöperation, defined the nature of its influence during the remaining five years of peace. Those who believed that economic peace was a precondition of political and military peace and that an effort should be made to achieve it would not object to the method whereby, without affecting the essential control of Congress over tariffs, the negotiation of trade agreements was removed one step from the influence of domestic pressure groups. That the power was not abused by the Executive is indicated by the renewal of the Reciprocity Trade Agreements Act in 1937, 1940, and even in 1943, when Republicans and conservative Democrats held a majority in both houses of Congress.

The effects of reciprocity on recovery were negligible for a year or more. Agreements with only Cuba and Brazil had been made by the end of 1934. By the end of the first three-year period of the Act's operation, agreements had been made with sixteen countries, including Canada and France, and American exports to these countries were increasing more than 200 per cent faster than exports to other countries.[12] But the hope that export of farm surpluses would make acreage control unnecessary was not to be realized until the Lend-Lease Act was passed in 1941.

In 1934, a great drought and dust storms in the plains country helped the acreage control program to limit production and decrease surpluses. That a natural disaster could be considered a blessing was one of the ironies of scarcity economics. Some farmers called the drought a punishment by God for the sin of destroying nature's bounty. Acreage rental payments were not denied to farmers who abandoned their parched land, and emergency relief payments and credit aids were extended on a large scale to relieve hardship.

The quarrel within the AAA over policy was ended when Peek was shifted to a succession of offices in the foreign-trade field, and Chester A. Davis became Administrator and carried out the acreage control policy without hindrance. It was extended to include sugar beets, sugar cane, and corn, and the total of rental and benefit payments to farmers was more than doubled over 1933.[13] Cattle and other livestock suffering from drought were bought by the AAA and made use of for the unemployed and in other ways which would not disturb market prices. The Frazier-Lemke Farm Bankruptcy Act was passed in June to make it possible for farmers to reacquire on reasonable terms farms lost through bankruptcy, or to suspend bankruptcy proceedings for five years if creditors would not agree to reasonable terms. Interest rates on farm mortgages were decreased by a great expansion of government credit. These measures effectively ended the mortgage crisis in agriculture which the depression had caused.

Farm prices rose through the year, and held fairly firm through the marketing season. The average index for the year was 90 as compared with 70 in 1933, and had not been as high since 1930.[14] Nevertheless, the income of farmers from crops increased over 1933 only $860,000,000 because prices had risen hardly more than enough to compensate for the combined effects of acreage control and the drought. Livestock income increased over $500,000,000, but this represented a considerable decrease of capital in the form of herds sold as a result of the drought. Government payments amounted to more than two-thirds of the total increase of cash farm income, as compared with one-fourth in 1933.[15]

The first full year of AAA operation and the tragedy of the Dust Bowl increased rather than diminished the proportions of the farm problem. Administration experiments were made with resettlement and subsistence farming projects, but they remained minute in scope, and little more was heard of "the over-balance of population in our industrial centers," or of "engaging on a national scale in a redistribution,"[16] as proposed in the President's Inaugural Address. The speeding up of the mechanization and concentration of agriculture in larger units and the displacement of tenants and sharecroppers, which the AAA was furthering, was intensified by the drought and dust storms, and worked to swell the ranks of a new class of migrant farm laborers, whose poverty and helplessness were unmatched by any other group of the population. Their lack of a fixed residence made them practically ineligible for relief and uninteresting to politicians. States, counties, and towns raised "immigration" barriers against them. Their labor, and their children's, was excessively exploited by large farms, which were not subject to NRA codes. Their lack of experience and of fixed employment with a stationary group made the tactics of industrial labor unionism virtually useless to them. The AAA broadly satisfied the large farmers who produced staples which were included in the program. The administration's farm credit system reached farmers whose land produced some sort of income. But the problems of farmers who were dusted out or otherwise lost their land, of tenants, sharecroppers, and migrants were multiplying, and the administration did not for several more years formulate a program which would reach these most depressed groups and constitute a Second New Deal in agriculture.

Meanwhile, a last experiment with the inflation cure for the farmers' ills was forced on the administration by the representatives of the farm and silver states in Congress. They were dissatisfied with the small purchases of silver made under the powers granted by the Thomas Amendment and in accordance with the International Silver Agreement of 1933. A bill introduced by Representative Dies of Texas to permit foreign countries to pay for American farm products with silver valued at one-fourth more than its market price was passed by the House. The Senate amended it to require the Treasury to buy 50,000,000 ounces of silver a month (estimated American production during the whole year 1934 was 25,000,000 ounces), and to issue paper money to the full value of the purchased silver. The President had sought no further legislation on silver. Now he faced the prospect of mandatory and excessive inflation at a time when he was working for stabilization of currencies. He met Congressmen frequently for a month and tried to prevent passage of the Bill. On May 22 he sent a new Bill to Congress which evidently represented a compromise in favor of milder and more elastic silver inflation.

This Silver Purchase Bill declared a policy of increasing the Treasury's silver holdings until they should reach one-third of its gold, and required silver certificates to be placed in circulation in proportion to the silver purchased. The price paid by the Treasury could be raised to $1.29 per ounce (a ratio with gold of about 27 to 1), as compared with the lowest market price of $0.36 in August, 1933. Provisions were made to avoid paying a bonus to silver speculators, one of whom was reported to be Father Coughlin, whose radio sermons were presently to be directed against the administration.

Hearings on the Bill were rushed through, and it was passed and signed on June 19. The processes of nationalization of silver stocks and purchases of domestic and foreign silver at prices which reached $0.78 in April, 1935, were similar to actions previously taken on gold, except that no particular attempt to raise commodity prices was made. The inflationary effect of the silver policy was mild at most, but it paid tribute to the silver mine owners and served to still the ancient "free silver" clamor of farm leaders. If the gold-buying policy endangered the currencies of France and the gold-bloc nations, the silver purchases had similar effects in China, Mexico, Peru, and India. But foreign purchasing power was created, and American exports once more were subsidized.[17]

The chief controversy and the one most fruitful of change in administration policy during the transition from the First to the Second New Deal concerned NRA. Opposition to the experiment mounted steadily. The administration never denied that the rise in industrial prices and profits was outrunning the rise in employment and purchasing power.

The charge that NRA fostered monopoly was vigorously denied by the administration from time to time, but on several occasions in 1934 it also took action designed to break down monopolistic tendencies. Thus on January 20 the President issued an Executive Order:

to provide a practical and rapid way for making effective those provisions of the National Industrial Recovery Act that were designed to prevent persons, under the guise of purported sanctions contained in codes . . . from engaging in monopolistic practices or practices tending to eliminate, oppress or discriminate against small enterprises.[18]

Complainants against monopoly were empowered to appeal their cases from the code authorities to the Federal Trade Commission or the Department of Justice.

To arrive at a definition of monopoly was not easy. The

President pointed out "the conflict inherent in the ambiguities" [19] of the provisions that codes were exempt from the antitrust laws and that the President should not approve a code which permitted monopoly. General Johnson contended that clauses in codes which encouraged price-fixing or price stabilization were not monopolistic if they fixed prices upward and thereby prevented unfair advantage being taken of labor, on the one hand, or prevented large monopolistic groups from slashing prices to ruin small enterprises, on the other. Clauses which limited production and expansion of production equipment he justified as indispensable to the maintenance of prices. However, the evidence, which will presently be examined, showed that not labor but the owners of industry were the chief beneficiaries of high prices.

The President's January Order was perhaps a concession to strong attacks on NRA which were being made especially in Congress. Senators Borah and Nye declared that it was unfair to consumers, labor, and small businessmen, while monopolists gained most advantage. Congressional attacks took a partisan cast insofar as they were led by Republicans, but they were Western progressive Republicans, who supported the larger share of New Deal policies. They were demanding a Senate investigation in January, which the President and General Johnson avoided by agreeing to a review of the experiment by an independent board.

General Johnson has said that in "a moment of total aberration" [20] he suggested the famous radical lawyer, Clarence Darrow, as head of the board. Accordingly, on March 7, the President set up the National Recovery Review Board with Darrow as chairman, to ascertain and report to the President whether any of the codes was "designed to promote monopolies or to eliminate or oppress small enterprises or operate to discriminate against them," [21] and if so, to recommend necessary changes.

Two days before he established the Darrow Board, the President made an important address before the officials of the Code Authorities of six hundred industries in which he vigorously defended NRA, but also told the assembled representatives of industry that the balanced recovery which was the administration's object could only be achieved if industry established low prices and profits, and higher wages and expanded employment. He warned that the antitrust laws "must continue in their major purpose of retaining competition and preventing monopoly; it is only where these laws have prevented the coöperation to eliminate things like child labor and sweat shops, starvation wages and other unfair practices that there is justification in modifying them." [22]

The atmosphere created by the administration in which the Darrow Board went to work was therefore one of mingled defense of NRA against its attackers and warning that businessmen must not give cause for attack. Johnson wanted the Board to report its criticisms to him, but Darrow refused, and obtained from the President a promise of complete independence and of responsibility only to the President himself.[23] Darrow was not interested in surveying the whole of NRA and balancing accomplishments against failures, but only in finding whether certain evils existed. The President described his procedure as more that of a "prosecuting agency to prove a case against big business, than . . . an impartial investigating body." [24] General Johnson wrote that "Bloody old Jeffries at the Assizes never conducted any hearings to equal those [under Darrow] for cavalier disposal of cases. They condemned codes in a half-hour 'hearing' . . . and they refused to allow any explanation. . . . It was a cave of Adullam to which every man who had a grievance, real or fancied, could come to the wailing wall and have his complaint avidly encouraged and promptly underwritten without the slightest inquiry into its merits." [25]

When Darrow sent his first report to the President on May 4, copies were sent by the latter to General Johnson and other officials for comment. The report was not released to the press until May 21, when a vituperative counter-statement was issued at the same time by Johnson. The matter then became clouded in a storm of personalities which provided excitement but little illumination. The three reports of the Board were never printed. Not the least cause of this fiasco was the intemperate tone of the reports themselves, and their casual references to the advantages of socialism. But it is noteworthy that no official of the administration denied the specific evidence in the reports that the Code Authorities were dominated by the trade associations and the latter by the largest corporations, and that price-fixing and production-limitation were sanctioned by many codes and practiced in ways injurious to small business, labor, and the public.[26] The Senate opposition, led by Senator Nye, made full use of the materials in the reports to discredit NRA, and such an administration supporter as Senator Wagner defended the results of NRA only feebly, while declaring himself against the policy of scarcity on which it was founded.[27]

In spite of the administration's refusal to admit the charges of the Darrow Board, several actions were taken which indicated that it believed the charges were not without merit. On May 9, a Policy Board was created to formulate "acceptable, desirable policies as to code provisions." On May 27, an Executive Order suspended efforts to regulate prices and trade practices in the service industries. If 85 per cent of the members of a trade in a given area voted for code provisions, they could be reinstated, but they would not be enforced by NRA beyond the use of the Blue Eagle. Significantly, service industries were not exempted from observance of the labor standards of Section 7A. In June it was announced that henceforth price-fixing would not be permitted in new codes. On July 14, General Johnson set up an Industrial Appeals Board which was empowered to grant relief to small businessmen who suffered from discrimination under the codes or the Code Authorities. And a general reorganization of NRA was discussed for several months before it was undertaken in September.

Rightly or wrongly, opponents of NRA believed that General Johnson had not carried out the intention of the National Industrial Recovery Act, but had unbalanced the codes and their administration in favor of big business. Johnson now took the view that with code-making virtually at an end, and compliance and enforcement emerging as the main problems, he should resign and his functions be subdivided among the members of a board. With this the President agreed. Rumors that Secretary Perkins and Donald Richberg were instrumental in securing his resignation because they found the General too favorable to big business and too high-handed in his methods were, in Johnson's account, not entirely unfounded.[28]

In August, General Johnson returned from a tour of the country and, possibly as a result of his contact with public opinion, exempted many more categories of small business from all code provisions except those guaranteeing collective bargaining and forbidding child labor. On September 24 he resigned from the office of Administrator of NRA. Three days later the President ordered his former office abolished and a National Industrial Recovery Board composed of five officials to take its place. Those who were appointed to these offices were fairly obscure with the exception of the labor leader, Sidney Hillman. The functions formerly performed by Johnson were divided into three parts, each the exclusive province of a branch of the new organization: legislation, or policy making; administration, or code making and revision; judicial, or enforcement, complaints, and disputes.

The general significance of the reorganization of NRA was explained by the President in his fireside chat of September 30:

Let me call your attention to the fact that the National Industrial Recovery Act gave business men the opportunity they had sought for years to improve business conditions through what has been called self-government in industry. If the codes which have been written have been too complicated, if they have gone too far in such matters as price fixing and limitation of production, let it be remembered that so far as possible, consistent with the immediate public interest of this past year and the vital necessity of improving labor conditions, the representatives of trade and industry were permitted to write their ideas into the codes. It is now time to review these actions as a whole to determine . . . whether the methods and policies adopted in the emergency have been best calculated to promote industrial recovery and a permanent improvement of business and labor conditions. There may be a serious question as to the wisdom of many of those devices to control production, or to prevent destructive price cutting which many business organizations have insisted were necessary, or whether their effect may have been to prevent that volume of production which would make possible lower prices and increased employment.[29]

On October 22 the new Board announced that code provisions to limit production would no longer be enforced.

If under NRA the administration had permitted big business to consolidate monopoly with government sanction, and had encouraged substitution of employer-dominated company unions for independent labor unions, the charge of fascism might have acquired some validity. As it was, the monopolistic features of NRA were being whittled away by the end of 1934. The chief reason was the refusal of business to enter into the coöperative spirit on which the experiment

[127

was predicated, to share the benefits of recovery with other groups, or to observe in good faith the provisions of Section 7A in return for its own privileges. Business had won official recognition for its own trade associations and their program, but it had refused to grant similar recognition to independent labor unions and their program. It had enjoyed a virtually free hand in writing and administering the codes, but it had exercised its power chiefly with regard to the immediate advantages which could be won for itself. It did not accept the analysis that the depression had been caused by a failure of purchasing power and that recovery could only be founded on its expansion. The bitterness with which businessmen were beginning to oppose the administration was perhaps partly a recognition that their collectivity had thrown away a chance to remain high in administration councils by failing to pursue a statesmanlike policy during the early days of NRA, and had failed to retrieve its mistake when it had a second chance in the spring of 1934.

A fall of production, employment, and payrolls which occurred in May, coupled with the continued rise of industrial prices, was probably of prime importance in convincing the administration that recovery could not be achieved under the existing NRA system. After dollar devaluation and the CWA had bolstered recovery, the administration had given further trial to NRA, and had defended it against the agitation stirred by the Darrow investigation. But in May production began to fall once more from the index of 86 to 71 in September, so that all the gains since November, 1933, were lost.[30] Nevertheless wholesale prices rose during the same months from 73.7 to 77.6. These were the months of major disillusionment with business policy, ending in reorganization of NRA as the basic expression of the abolition of price-fixing and production limitation. Employment declined during these months from 85.9 to 78, and payrolls from 68.1

to 59.1,[31] and these figures were no doubt influential in determining the corresponding, but slower, change in the administration's labor policies.

In his March 5 address to the NRA Code Authorities, the President had said: "It is the immediate task of industry to re-employ more people at purchasing wages and to do it now." [32] The imminent discharge of 4,000,000 persons by the CWA underlined the urgency of the President's statement. And his growing conviction that employers were using company unions, the speed-up and reductions of pay of skilled and semi-skilled workers to defeat the intentions of Section 7A is suggested by his further remark that the words "free choice" by employees of their representatives in the guaranty of collective bargaining rights meant just what they said. "I ask that the letter and the spirit of free choice be accorded to its workers by every corporation in the United States." [33]

The administration intended that collective bargaining be freely entered into by employers and employees, and it frequently urged that labor refrain from striking while employers were given an opportunity to comply. But the common refusal of employers to meet with representatives of independent unions under any circumstances; their haste to organize company unions which were amenable to their own influence; the host of knotty questions of interpretation of Section 7A which employers precipitated; and the reluctance of the administration to resort to sanctions to enforce labor rights increased the impatience of labor and helped produce another and greater wave of strikes. The number of strikes and of workers involved in the spring and summer of 1934 exceeded all figures since 1922. The militia forces of 19 states were called out, and with police, deputy sheriffs, and company guards killed 46 workers.[34] In 1932, union recognition was the issue in less than 20 per cent of the strikes

[129

called, but in 1934 recognition of a union as bargaining agent under Section 7A was the issue in almost 50 per cent of the strikes.[35]

The American Federation of Labor launched a campaign in 1934 to organize the workers in mass-production industries into craft unions under the guaranties of Section 7A. If employers had permitted the AFL to succeed, they might have been relieved of the necessity of dealing with the more militant Committee for Industrial Organization later. But anti-union tactics, especially widespread use of labor spies and strikebreakers, as well as the timidity of the AFL leadership, the inappropriateness of the craft principle in the great mass-production industries, and the failure of NRA to enforce Section 7A largely defeated the AFL organizing campaign. At the end of the year, AFL membership was still under 3,000,-000. A consequence of this failure was the movement for unionism on industrial principles under stronger leadership, which was led by John L. Lewis of the United Mine Workers and presently split the labor movement into two camps.

This movement was also a response to disappointment with the President's rôle in labor disputes during 1934. On several notable occasions, he intervened in labor disputes to prevent or stop strikes and secure settlements which did not satisfy labor. His method was to appoint a special labor board to investigate and offer arbitration when a threatening situation developed. Thus the Automobile Labor Board in March and the National Steel Labor Relations Board in June averted strikes in those industries, the National Longshoremen's Board induced the leaders of a four-day "revolutionary" general strike on the West Coast in July to submit the issues to arbitration, and the Textile Labor Relations Board served a similar function in the September nation-wide textile strike which involved 500,000 workers. In these and similar situations, labor's use of its most effective weapon was weakened without the administration invoking measures strong enough to compel employers to comply with Section 7A.

The administration furthermore did not support passage of legislation by Congress which would strengthen labor's position under the NRA. By the end of 1933, such corporations as the Weirton Steel Company of West Virginia and the Budd Manufacturing Company of Philadelphia were refusing to obey the decisions of the National Labor Board, and employer-dominated company unions were being used to avoid compliance with the collective bargaining clause of Section 7A. Two Executive Orders in February, 1934, authorized the National Labor Board to hold elections for the determination by employees of their bargaining agents, and to present findings of violations of Section 7A to the Attorney General for possible prosecution, but they left undisturbed the contention of employers that dealing with a company union satisfied the collective bargaining requirements of the law.

Senator Robert F. Wagner of New York, after serving as Chairman of the National Labor Board during its first half-year, concluded that the purposes of Section 7A could be secured only if new legislation were enacted which, as he stated to Congress, would protect the principle of collective bargaining from employer-dominated unions and prevent the latter from destroying or supplanting free labor unions.[36] On March 1, he introduced in the Senate the Labor Disputes Bill to prohibit "unfair labor practices" by employers, among which the following were enumerated: the initiation and financing of company unions, interference with employees' free choice of their representatives, and refusal to recognize or bargain with employee representatives. It also called for the creation of a permanent labor board with power to impose penalties in order to enforce the provisions of the law, mediate disputes, and conduct elections to determine employees' representatives. Extensive public hearings on the Bill were held. Senator Wagner explained to the Committee on Education and Labor that Section 7A had failed because, while it stated the right of employees to bargain collectively, it imposed no obligation upon employers to do so, and their refusal caused 70 per cent of the disputes coming before the Labor Board. The new Bill was based on the successful experience since 1920 of the Railway Labor Board, which had the power to compel employers to recognize representatives chosen by the railroad workers and to make reasonable attempts to arrive at satisfactory agreements with them. A second defect of Section 7A turned upon the employers' interpretation that even when a majority of employees designated an independent union as their bargaining agent, employers were still free to bargain and make agreements only with the minority who designated no representatives or a company union. The third and most important defect was that while Section 7A provided that employees should be free to choose their representatives, it did not prohibit the specific practices of employers which destroyed that freedom. Wagner declared that the success of the recovery program depended upon government support of labor as well as business according to the original intent of the Recovery Act. As things stood, employers trade associations had been greatly strengthened, but labor unions had been resisted at every turn in their efforts to achieve equal rights. The benefits of what recovery had been achieved were consequently distributed unequally in favor of business, and unless a change occurred and purchasing power was built up, a collapse was inevitable.[37]

The conservative press, employers' trade associations, and businessmen in general bitterly opposed the Wagner Labor Disputes Bill. The *New York Herald Tribune* called it the road to fascism.[38] The contrary argument, that independent labor unions were destroyed under fascism, and exactly such employer-dominated organizations as the American company unions substituted by force, was advanced by liberals. The Senate hearing revealed that businessmen heartily approved the NRA as it was then functioning. President Emery of the National Association of Manufacturers defended company unions because they were "modern," and admitted, when pressed by Senator Wagner, that he had opposed Section 7A from the beginning and supported only the parts of the Recovery Act which gave business special privileges.[39] Emery complained that a labor board composed of representatives of both employers and employees could not be impartial because basic interests of the two groups were conflicting.[40] On the other hand, General Counsel Edmonds of the Philadelphia Chamber of Commerce objected to the Bill precisely because it impressed him as having been written by "a man who had been reading Marx on Class War, and thought all employers and employees were standing in opposite corners making faces at each other." [41] President Harriman of the United States Chamber of Commerce feared that the Bill would undo the good which had come from the Recovery Act, and proposed reliance upon General Johnson to work out labor problems with the existing machinery.[42] Johnson failed to appear before the Committee, and it was understood that he disapproved any ban on company unions.[43]

During the months while the Labor Disputes Bill was being considered, a heavy campaign against it in the press and in public speeches was conducted by the National Association of Manufacturers, the Chamber of Commerce, the Iron and Steel Institute, the National Automobile Chamber of Commerce, and other business groups. A frequent proposal was that labor disputes be settled by the Code Authorities.[44]

Since the officials of the Code Authorities were almost exclusively drawn from the trade associations, this plan called for the abandonment of the basic Recovery Act principles of equal rights for business and labor and impartiality in the settlement of their disputes.

The attitude of the administration towards the Labor Disputes Bill was expected to be decisive. It squarely presented to the President the issue whether collective bargaining under NRA should be conducted by company unions or by independent unions. That the President was willing to give businessmen further opportunity to prove their contention that the aims of Section 7A and of the recovery program could be achieved through company unions was indicated during his intervention late in March in the threatened automobile strike. After conferences with leaders of both sides, he arranged a settlement under which the new Automobile Labor Board could recognize company unions as bargaining agents: "The Government makes it clear that it favors no particular union or particular form of employee organization or representation." [45] No restrictions were placed upon employers financing and controlling company unions in the automobile industry. The general opinion of the Senate was that the President had by this agreement registered his disapproval of the Wagner Labor Disputes Bill.[46]

Senator Wagner accordingly permitted his Bill to be amended to remove most of the restrictions on domination by employers of company unions. President Harriman of the Chamber of Commerce thereupon said that the Bill was unnecessary because the President had already sanctioned company unions.[47] Senator Wagner then revised his Bill and secured White House approval of restoration of some restrictions on company unions. The Bill was up for final vote on the same day that the President reached an agreement to settle the strike of steel workers which was to begin that day. This settlement, like that of the automobile strike, made possible the use by employers of company unions. Senator Robinson prevented the Wagner Bill from coming to a vote and secured the substitution of a resolution which merely gave statutory authority to the Executive Orders of February which had provided for elections and prosecutions. Senator Robinson, as Democratic floor leader, was acting on the President's request. Senator Wagner deferred to the President, saying that he was ready to accept the latter's judgment that further trial should be permitted before employer-dominated unions were rejected as bargaining agents.[48] Other progressive Senators were reluctant to support the resolution. Senator Cutting of New Mexico protested that "the new deal is being strangled in the house of its friends." [49] Nevertheless the resolution was pushed through both houses.

On June 29, the President abolished the old National Labor Board and established the new National Labor Relations Board, which permitted the appointment of new members and the resignation of Senator Wagner, whose Bill had no doubt made employers dissatisfied with him.

Thus the administration went very far to avoid coercion of employers and to encourage voluntary compliance with Section 7A. The fall in production, employment, and payrolls in May did not lead the administration to change its labor policy, nor did the new outbreak of strikes which reached epidemic proportions in September. Through the summer months, the President in his public speeches stressed the need for the unity and coöperation of all groups in working for recovery. His mood was not friendly towards the partisans of labor, rather he sought to conciliate businessmen.[50] Possibly he believed that the relaxation of the controls on production and prices in the NRA codes, coupled with a free hand granted to business in the matter of company unions would induce an industrial revival. At any rate, on September 30, when he announced the reorganization of NRA he offered businessmen "a specific trial period of industrial peace" during which they might use their company unions to carry out rather than circumvent the collective bargaining clause of Section 7A. A month later the President in an address to the American Bankers' Association renewed his plea for the coöperation of business on equal terms with other groups:

The time is ripe for an alliance of all forces intent upon the business of recovery. In such an alliance will be found business and banking, agriculture and industry, and labor and capital. What an all-America team that would be! The possibilities of such a team kindle the imagination.[51]

Attempts to conciliate business did not prevent the organization in August of the Liberty League, a combination of čonservative Democrats and industrial leaders, including Jouett Shouse, Al Smith, and members of the Du Pont family, to fight the "radicalism" of the New Deal. The Liberty League was intended to make the rights of property supreme over all other rights, to stiffen the resistance of businessmen to the President's program, to discourage concessions to labor, and to secure the election of an anti-New Deal Congress in the November elections. In the last purpose at least it was unsuccessful. And its extreme attacks on the administration did not strengthen advocates of conciliation on either side.

In spite of his seeming support of company unions, the President retained the confidence of labor. Dissatisfaction with this aspect of the administration program was outweighed by the recognition that other policies worked in labor's favor. A far-reaching program of social security had been initiated. The Railway Retirement Act of June 27 provided pensions for railroad workers after thirty years' service or at an age of sixty-five, the cost to be borne one-third by themselves and two-thirds by the companies. And on June 29, the President had appointed the Committee on Economic Security to prepare plans for a universal program of unemployment and old-age pension insurance, and health and child welfare benefits. New ground was being broken to meet one of the fundamental needs of labor and bring American social legislation abreast of common practice in other industrial nations.

Government regulation of business enterprise was extended to several new fields during 1934. The Securities Exchange Act of June 6 established the Securities and Exchange Commission and charged it with the enforcement of the Securities Act of 1933 and with the prevention of excessive speculation, marginal trading, and manipulation of prices by stock-exchange operators. The Communications Act of June 19 created the Federal Communications Commission to exercise controls over telegraph, cable, and radio corporations similar to those of the Interstate Commerce Commission over transportation. After revelations of fraud in the letting of air mail contracts which occurred under the Hoover administration, and a disastrous attempt to fly the mails by the Army, the Air Mail Act of June 12 was passed to return mail flying to private companies under rigid controls calculated to prevent further fraud. Kidnaping and other crimes were made subject to federal law. These laws were additions to the permanent body of progressive reforms and had long been demanded by liberals. But General Smedley D. Butler created a sensation when he told a House Committee that during the summer of 1934 a group of Wall Street brokers had urged him to lead a fascist march on Washington and overthrow the government in order to protect business interests.

When the President approached the first test of his administration in the November Congressional elections, he had largely lost the support which business had given him during the banking crisis and the first NRA campaign. The concessions which had been made in regard to company unions did not offset the opposition which the many far-reaching reforms produced among businessmen. Nor did the opposition of organized labor to company unions, bitter as it was, prevent the administration from holding the support of labor, which again joined with farmers to elect still larger Democratic majorities to Congress. The President and his aggressive attack on the depression, besides reforms which satisfied the public demand for correction of business abuses which the depression years had revealed, captured the public imagination and won a degree of loyalty among his supporters which no President since Wilson had enjoyed.

The Republican Party had no constructive program to offer as an alternative to the New Deal, and appealed only to fears that "limitless inflation," "domination of an all-powerful central government," and other perils were in the offing.[52] Republican strength fell in the Senate from 35 to 25 and in the House from 113 to 103, and Republican progressives or partial supporters of the administration fared better than those who campaigned on the Party platform.

These results, which violated the usual rule that an administration loses Congressional support in mid-term elections, were described by Charles A. Beard as "thunder on the left."[53] The new Congress was expected to demand an end of concessions to business and a whole-hearted farmer-labor program for recovery and reform. Although the National Association of Manufacturers remained intransigent after the election, the prospect of a more "radical" Congress caused the leaders of the Chamber of Commerce to believe that possibly a mistake was being made in not accepting the President's offers to business of coöperation. Now they made an effort to rally to his support. A series of conferences was held between business leaders and the President. The former made known their support of the more conservative administration leaders, such as Secretaries Hull, Morgenthau, and Roper, Jesse Jones and Professor Moley, and their opposition to the "radicals," including Secretaries Ickes and Perkins, and Hopkins and Tugwell.

Whatever confidences were exchanged and understandings were reached in these conferences, the unbalanced character of recovery could not be gainsaid. In his Message to the new Congress the President found it impossible to say that recovery, after a year and a half, was creating anything besides "substantial benefits to our agricultural population, increased industrial activity, and profits to our merchants." [54] Congress was thereupon asked to legislate a new program which should add labor to the beneficiaries of recovery, and the main program of the Second New Deal, after a long season of reluctance, was launched.

CHAPTER IX

THE GOOD NEIGHBOR

IT WILL be convenient to describe the political foreign policy of the first two years of the Roosevelt administration before taking up the momentous events of 1935 on the domestic front. Political, unlike economic, foreign policy did not undergo a reversal during the early years of the New Deal. Renunciation of imperialism by the United States and coöperation with peaceful nations against violation of treaties and aggression were consistently pursued through the most crisis-ridden period in the world's history.

The foundations of both these aspects of the Good Neighbor Policy had been laid by the Wilson administration, and were built upon by two striking actions of the Hoover administration. In 1904, President Theodore Roosevelt had generalized the imperialist tendencies of his foreign policy by proclaiming as a corollary of the Monroe Doctrine the right of the United States to exercise international police power over Latin America in cases of "wrongdoing" which might lead to intervention by a non-American power. President Wilson reassured Latin Americans that the United States would never again seek an additional foot of territory by conquest, and that it was willing to abandon the Roosevelt Corollary and coöperate with other American republics in multilateral rather than unilateral enforcement of the Monroe Doctrine. But occupations of Central American and Caribbean republics by American troops and supervision of their fiscal affairs by American commissions had continued under Wilson as well as Harding and Coolidge.

The Clark Memorandum of the State Department officially repudiated the Roosevelt Corollary in 1930, and the evacuation of occupied republics was actually begun. In 1932, the Hoover administration also took the first action which revived the Wilsonian policy of international coöperation against aggression. It worked with the League of Nations to condemn Japanese aggression in Manchuria, and announced the Stimson Doctrine under which the United States, in parallel action with the League, refused to recognize the government of Manchukuo which Japan established by force of arms in violation of its treaties.

The Roosevelt administration adopted and sought to expand these two policies. It completed the evacuation of Latin American republics and affirmed the Stimson Doctrine. At the Pan American Conference in Montevideo late in 1933, the United States accepted in a treaty with all the American republics an article which declared that no state has the right to intervene in the internal or external affairs of another. President Roosevelt supplemented this with a promise that "the definite policy of the United States from now on is one opposed to armed intervention." [1]

Such promises became convincing when the administration fulfilled them in a series of treaties with the semi-dependencies of the United States. In August, 1933, it refused to intervene in Cuba when that country presented it with a classical opportunity. The oppressive Machado regime was arousing revolutionary opposition, and the efforts of Ambassador Welles to mediate led to relaxation of dictatorial measures, but finally failed when violence began. Under the Platt Amendment of the Cuban Treaty of 1903, the United States was authorized to intervene when a Cuban government was unable to protect life, liberty, and property. But the President sent warships only to provide relief and escape for American citizens, as might be done when a great power fell victim to civil war, and the naval commanders were given strict orders not to intervene in the internal affairs of Cuba. The new regime of Dr. Grau San Martin was not recognized by the United States on the ground that its ability to control the country was doubtful.

This and the presence of warships led to the charge that the administration's policy was one of coercion. The failure of sugar exports was the basic cause of Cuba's troubles, and the administration took measures to restore her prosperity. American sugar producers were induced to increase the quota of imports which they were willing to allot to Cuba, and a general reciprocity treaty was ratified in 1934. The unexampled step of conferring with other Latin American republics was taken before the decision was made to refuse recognition of the San Martin government, and it was again by agreement that his successor, Carlos Mendieta, was recognized early in 1934. Then a new Treaty of Relations was negotiated which put to rest all doubts as to the policy of non-intervention in Cuba.

The new treaty abrogated the Platt Amendment, under which the United States had the right to supervise Cuban foreign policy and fiscal affairs as well as the right to intervene with armed force. The Senate approved the treaty with only one dissenting vote, and in June, 1934, ratifications were exchanged with Cuba, which staged a three-day celebration of its new freedom. Two months later the reciprocity trade agreement was proclaimed which granted sharp reductions of duties on imports of Cuban sugar, tobacco, rum, fruits, and vegetables, in return for reductions on American exports of foods and manufactures. Under the new agreement Cuban and American exports rapidly increased. The new radical regime of Fulgencia Batista was promptly recognized by the United States, in spite of Batista's program of reforms which would injure American business interests in Cuba, and the new government became stabilized and pacified Cuban political life largely as a result of the restoration of a degree of economic prosperity.

The most important aspect of the reorganization of American relations with Cuba was its demonstration to all Latin America that "Yankee Imperialism" was being voluntarily liquidated, that friendship and coöperation were being substituted for threats and force. If the new policy paid dividends in the form of increased trade, they were not collected exclusively by the United States.

That political anti-imperialism was not merely a new and more suave mask for economic imperialism was strikingly suggested by the manner in which the American protectorate over Haiti was terminated in 1934. After signing an agreement for the ending of United States military occupation, the President of Haiti, Stenio Vincent, appealed to President Roosevelt to end financial control also. The National City Bank of New York owned the National Bank of Haiti which was the Republic's only bank of issue. A loan to the Haitian government had been floated by the New York bank and was being paid out of Haitian revenues, which were collected by officials of the United States government and deposited in the Bank of Haiti. In April, 1934, after conferences with President Vincent, a plan was announced by President Roosevelt which accorded full financial independence to Haiti. It provided for the sale of the Bank of Haiti to the government of Haiti, a promise by Haiti to respect the interests of bondholders, and the transfer to Haiti of supervision over its own revenues. Thus a small but notorious instance of American "finance imperialism" was liquidated. More sensational, if not more significant, tests of the profundity of the administration's opposition to economic imperialism were to come later, particularly in Mexico.

Two further actions in 1934 marked the retreat from imperialism. A treaty with Panama abrogated clauses of the treaty of 1903 by which that Republic was made a semi-protectorate of the United States. And the Philippine Islands were granted self-government during a ten-year transition period at the end of which they were promised independence. As early as 1916, the Jones Act had pledged the United States to give up its control of the Islands as soon as a stable government could be established. The Filipinos made considerable progress in meeting this condition, but it was the depression of 1929 which led to a revival of American interest in their independence. American producers of beet-sugar, dairy products, cordage, and cotton-seed oil believed that imports of Philippine products under the free-trade rule of 1909 injured the sale of their own products in the American market. Manufacturers who exported goods to the Islands under the same free-trade conditions did not strongly oppose agitation for the imposition of tariffs against imports from the Philippines, which could best be achieved by granting them their independence. Labor leaders supported the movement as a means of restricting the immigration of Filipinos whom they considered a menace to the living standards of American workers. Extreme isolationists were anxious that the United States should reduce its commitments in the Far East.

These were the chief motives which led to the passage of the Hawes-Cutting Act over President Hoover's veto shortly before he left office. The Act provided a ten-year period before independence during which a Philippine Commonwealth government would gain experience. Quota restrictions and rising tariff schedules against imports from the Islands would be imposed, and Philippine import taxes against American goods were prohibited. Immigration would be restricted to fifty persons per year. The Act required acceptance by the Philippine Legislature within a year. In October, 1933, that body rejected it as a "death sentence" which would strangle the Philippine economy.

On March 2, 1934, President Roosevelt sent a message to Congress recommending that the Act be extended without other change than provisions to relinquish United States military bases in the Islands and to settle the question of naval bases on mutually satisfactory terms after the transition period. He proposed that a trade conference be called to correct inequalities in the tariff provisions by agreement. The law was thereupon passed as the Tydings-McDuffie Act. The Philippine Legislature accepted the Act as its only opportunity to gain independence, and on the assumption that tariff concessions would be made by the new administration in Washington. But Congress, two days after the law was accepted by the Filipinos, violated its provisions by imposing a special tax against importation of cocoanut oil, and a few days later fixed sugar quotas which further discriminated against the Islands. Efforts of the President to prevent such acts of bad faith were fruitless. Not until 1937 did the Joint Committee on Philippine Affairs meet to consider improvement of trade relations, and its purely advisory work had little success. The economic hardships which separation from the United States entailed and the threat of Japanese aggression made many Filipinos wish for permanent protection by the United States. If the motives and results of the grant of Philippine independence were not all advantageous to the Filipinos, at least their right to choose freely to assume the responsibilities of independence had not been withheld by the United States.

Before the retreat from imperialism had been completed in 1934, the Chaco War between Bolivia and Paraguay gave occasion for the administration to develop the implications of the Stimson Doctrine. Non-recognition of conquests seemed but a feeble weapon against war and aggression. Paraguay was thought to be the aggressor in the Chaco War, and the administration hoped that in coöperation with the League of Nations the United States might determine the aggressor, impose an arms embargo on it while permitting aid to be sent to the victim, and, through mediation if necessary, bring an end to the war. But isolationists in Congress, chiefly from the Western states, believed that discrimination between aggressors and victims would lead to "involvement" by the United States, and possibly to war. In May, 1934, Congress passed a resolution giving the President authority to impose an arms embargo in coöperation with the League on both belligerents, but not on the aggressor alone. Thus it refused to permit any experiment with the policy of collective security, but insisted upon "non-intervention" and "neutrality." Congress refused to change its position in this respect until after the Fall of France in 1940 caused a general awakening. Meanwhile the administration sought what methods were left to it to throw the influence of the United States into the scales against the rise of aggression.

Late in 1934, Bolivia submitted her case to the League Assembly. After Paraguay refused to accept a plan of peace drawn up by the League, the latter recommended that she be embargoed and that Bolivia be assisted to win the war. The administration was unable to add the United States to the powers which embargoed Paraguay without also embargoing Bolivia, but it did work successfully as a mediator with other American republics to bring the war to an end in 1935.

The isolationism of the Senate contributed to the failure of the Geneva Disarmament Conference. When the new administration came to power, the Conference had reached a deadlock in the struggle between France to win guaranties of security and Germany to achieve equality of armaments with the major powers. France and her allies of the Little Entente were unwilling to surrender their military superiority without assurances of military assistance in case of attack. The American delegation had been neutral. In April, 1933, Norman Davis told the Conference that the Roosevelt administration was prepared to abandon its traditional isolationism and to join in efforts for collective security to the extent of entering a consultative pact, provided effective disarmament, especially in offensive weapons, and continuous supervision of armaments were also achieved. A consultative pact would commit the United States to confer on joint defense measures in support of any signatory which became the victim of aggression. This offer was expected to "smoke out" the new Hitler government of Germany, by testing the sincerity of Hitler's argument that Germany's desire to rearm was based solely on the desire for equality. A crisis developed when Hitler called the Reichstag to hear a statement of policy, for it was feared that he would withdraw from the Conference rather than consent to equality through disarmament.

On May 16, the day before the Reichstag was to convene, the President sent his "Appeal to the Nations" to all governments, urging that no government assume responsibility for blocking peace efforts, and endorsing the Davis proposals. Hitler's address the next day was conciliatory. Five days later Davis told the Conference that if the nations agreed on disarmament measures the United States would not take any action to defeat efforts for collective security against an aggressor nation. This meant that it would not sell arms to an aggressor, or refuse to sell arms to a victim of aggression or to nations which supported the victim.

By this time isolationists in the Senate had taken alarm.

A resolution granting the President authority to declare an arms embargo against any nation had been endorsed by the previous administration and had passed the House without attracting attention on April 17. Now, on May 27, it was reported by the Senate Foreign Relations Committee as amended to provide that the President might lay an embargo only against all the parties to a dispute. He was forbidden to single out an aggressor nation, or to permit arms shipments to powers which enforced sanctions against an aggressor. This amendment served warning that the Democratic Senators from Western states who had come to power with the new administration, and who were largely progressive on domestic issues, were isolationist in foreign policy.

The administration did not challenge the Senate. Its economic nationalist policies for domestic recovery no doubt weakened its attempts to pursue an internationalist foreign policy on political questions. The powers at the Conference lost interest in the Davis proposals after the Senate Committee in effect repudiated them. In October, Hitler took advantage of the obvious disunity of the powers. A proposal which Norman Davis endorsed, that, after a preliminary period, the heavily-armed powers should disarm until Germany should find itself on a basis of equality, was opposed by Hitler even before France could register its fears for its security. Germany announced its withdrawal from the Conference and from the League of Nations. The Conference dragged on, but without hope of success.

Congress took further action in 1934 which served notice to aggressors that the United States would not subordinate extreme interpretations of national interest to considerations of collective security. In 1933, payments of war debts to the United States were made in full only by Finland, while Britain and four other countries made small "token" payments and France and four more countries defaulted completely.

The administration made only mild representations to the defaulting nations, and assured those which made token payments that they were not considered to be in default. Defaults and token payments stirred up the desire for reprisals among many Congressmen. Senator Hiram Johnson of California had long been a severe critic of the American bankers who had sold bonds of the Allied governments to American investors prior to the entrance of the United States in the First World War. He and many others attributed the nation's declaration of war on Germany to the influence of such bankers and bondholders. He had led a Senate investigation which aimed to prove this contention, and in 1933 he introduced legislation to forbid the continued purchase or sale of securities of governments in default on their war debts to the United States government. The law would have ended the negotiability of existing as well as future bond issues in this country of the governments concerned. On the objection of the State Department it was dropped. But the continued failure of nations to pay their war debts angered Congress sufficiently to revive the Bill in 1934 and to pass it with an amendment which made it apply only to future bond issues of governments in default.

The President was away from Washington when the Bill was passed, and it was said that this prevented him from using his influence against it: but he signed it without objection when he returned. The Attorney General ruled that the Johnson Act required a debtor nation to pay the next installment in full to avoid default and the penalties of the Act. Only Finland enjoyed a favorable trade balance with the United States, and only Finland continued to pay. Those nations like Great Britain which had previously made token payments pleaded the Johnson Act as abolishing the advantage of not being technically in default which token payments had given them. If the purpose of the Johnson Act was to encourage payment of the war debts, it failed dismally, and caused a net loss of the token payments. But the Act was widely supported as an isolationist measure which would reduce the motives for the United States entering a future war.

Pacifist sentiment grew strong in the United States during these years. The main focus of political action was the armaments industry, against which sensational attacks were being published. *Merchants of Death* by H. C. Engelbrecht and F. C. Hanighen [2] described the instigation of war scares between nations by salesmen of the armament industry to create markets for their products. "Arms and the Men," in *Fortune* for March, 1934, provided convincing details of the international connections, the political and propaganda methods, and the profits of the industry. These and other accounts were influential in causing the Senate to adopt Senator Nye's resolution for a full-scale investigation of the munitions industry by a special committee.

The President sent a special message to the Senate on May 18 in which he recommended generous support for the investigation. He described attempts of the United States to secure international supervision and control of armaments, and added:

The peoples of many countries are being taxed to the point of poverty and starvation in order to enable Governments to engage in a mad race in armament which, if permitted to continue, may well result in war. This grave menace to the peace of the world is due in no small measure to the uncontrolled activities of the manufacturers and merchants of engines of destruction, and it must be met by the concerted action of the peoples of all Nations. [3]

Efforts to secure international control of armaments failed, partly because of the isolationist sentiment of Congress. To the President such efforts complemented the policy of collective security: both were intended to keep the United States out of war by keeping war out of the world. But to isolationists efforts to keep war out of the world involved the risk of the United States engaging in war against aggressors who did not directly attack the United States. They believed that the United States could best remain at peace by refusing to take sides against aggressor nations. To them the revelations of the Nye Munitions Investigation gave arguments for purely national supervision of the armaments industry as the complement of their refusal to allow the administration to discriminate between aggressor nations and their victims. The majority of the Republican Congressmen were isolationists, and with like-minded Democrats they were able to impose their policy on the administration. In the Neutrality Act of 1935 their program was made into law.

In lesser matters than issues of collective security the administration was nevertheless able to show its opposition to the aggressor nations. It made some attempt to pursue a strong policy towards Japan. The League of Nations was notified that the United States would continue the Stimson policy of non-recognition of conquests in violation of treaties. The Hoover administration had failed to build up the strength of the Navy to levels authorized by the Treaty of Washington of 1922 and the Treaty of London of 1930, while Japan had fully built up to her ratio of 7 in the formula 7-10-10 for Japan, Britain, and the United States. By 1930, Japan had begun to ask for equality. It was granted increases over the strength allowed in 1922, but Britain and the United States maintained that equality would give Japan general offensive naval superiority, because defense of her more localized possessions did not require the same armaments as defense of the scattered possessions of Britain, and of the two vast coastlines and distant insular possessions of the United States.

A Naval Conference was scheduled for 1935 prior to the expiration of the treaties. In March, 1934, the President signed the Vinson Act which authorized building up the United States Navy to full treaty strength. In 1933, some building had been begun with funds allocated by the PWA, but no new appropriations were made, and the plan of the Vinson Act remained in abeyance until 1938. In December, 1934, Japan, after once more demanding equality on grounds of prestige, gave the required two years' notice that after 1936 it would no longer observe any naval limitations. On the same day the United States Navy announced plans for fleet maneuvers in Far Eastern waters.

The disruptive and aggressive attitudes of the new Hitler government in Germany caused minor but indicative reactions by the Roosevelt administration. Discriminations against American citizens as compared with others in the payment of German debts led Secretary Hull to make strong representations. When Germany claimed that its trade situation made transfers difficult, the Secretary answered that the policies of the Nazi government were responsible for the popular boycotts of German goods which were being pursued in many countries. After the passage of the Reciprocity Trade Agreements Act, Germany was placed on a "blacklist" of powers who should receive no concessions under the agreements because they practiced discriminations against American goods.

In sharp contrast with the administration's policies towards Germany and Japan was its effort to establish better relations with Russia. The conviction of many Americans that official recognition of the Soviet regime would compromise the moral, economic, and political rectitude of the United States made this country the last important power to withhold recognition, and there was a certain historical justice in the situation, for Tsarist Russia had been the last important power to recognize the revolutionary government of the United States. Fear that the Roosevelt administration would not be orthodox on the question led to a mass protest against recognition of Russia in April, 1933, by over one thousand organizations, including groups which identified themselves with fascism, and the American Legion, the Catholic Daughters of America, the American Federation of Labor, and the Daughters of the American Revolution.[4] But the desire of American businessmen to secure protection of their increasing trade with Russia, the menace to both countries of Japanese aggression, and the conviction of many that Russia would throw its weight on the side of international coöperation for collective security and peace created strong sentiment in favor of recognition. Such a veteran isolationist as Senator Borah of Idaho declared that world peace and disarmament would be furthered by the establishment of diplomatic relations with Russia.[5]

At the London Economic Conference the American delegates were observed in frequent consultation with Soviet delegates. Immediately thereafter, in July, 1933, the administration approved an RFC loan of four million dollars to American exporters to finance the sale of surplus cotton to the Soviet Union. This served to demonstrate the possibilities of Soviet trade.

In October, the President with great simplicity cut through the tangle of grievances which separated the two countries by inviting the Soviet government to send a representative for discussions with him in Washington. Maxim Litvinov, Peoples' Commissar for Foreign Affairs, arrived in November. His conversations with the President resulted in mutual recognition of the two governments, provision for the exchange of diplomatic representatives, and an exchange of letters in which Litvinov for Russia guaranteed to prevent activity in Russia which aimed to overthrow the United

States government, and pointed out the Soviet laws and practices which would protect American nationals in the exercise of religious freedom and other rights in Russia. The Soviet government waived its claims for damages arising from the American military expedition to Siberia in 1918. Other vexed questions of claims of the United States for loans made to preceding Russian governments and for expropriations of American property during the Russian Revolution, and of Russian claims for damage done by the American military expedition to Archangel in 1918, were postponed, and they troubled relations between the two countries during the succeeding years.

American exports to Russia increased after recognition was granted, but not as fabulously as some had expected. The continued existence of the Communist Party in the United States and the attendance of its leaders at meetings of the Communist International in Moscow were objected to as contrary to the engagement of Litvinov. But the Communist International and its affiliates had ceased to advocate revolution, and had turned to collaboration with socialist and democratic parties in a united front against fascism and aggression, so that the issue assumed less importance. It was not seriously proposed that the United States again break off relations with Russia, and a minimum of coöperation in the interests of trade, world stability, and peace was maintained.

Political foreign policy was the only field in which the Roosevelt administration illustrated no important evolution: from the beginning, anti-imperialism and collective security were its constant objectives. Congress supported the former objective, and it was rapidly and successfully instrumented. But collective security was unacceptable to the majority in Congress, and the administration was thwarted in its efforts to achieve that one alone among all of its major domestic and foreign policies. It is also true that the administration was chiefly interested in domestic policy until 1938, and did not press a foreign objective on Congress when powerful opposition arose. Popular opinion seemed to support Congress overwhelmingly in its opposition to collective security. The President never vetoed an act which imposed isolationism on the administration, nor did he appeal to the people for support of collective security until 1937.

CHAPTER X

LAUNCHING THE SECOND NEW DEAL: 1935

THE President's Annual Message to Congress on January 4, 1935, launched the Second New Deal. It announced a fresh start almost as if a new administration were being inaugurated. Achievements of the previous two years were dismissed perfunctorily: credit was taken for recovery only in the fields of agriculture, industrial production, and profits. Social justice was the new goal. Reform was declared to be inseparable from recovery. The ultimate human objectives of reform the President sought to rescue from the confusion of piecemeal efforts:

We find our population suffering from old inequalities, little changed by past sporadic remedies. In spite of our efforts and in spite of our talk, we have not weeded out the overprivileged and we have not effectively lifted up the underprivileged.

This did not mean that the "profit motive" would be destroyed; but its definition was fairly unorthodox:

By the profit motive we mean the right by work to earn a decent livelihood for ourselves and for our families.

The attitude towards more conventional definitions of the profit motive was made clear:

We have . . . a clear mandate from the people, that Americans must forswear that conception of the acquisition of wealth which, through excessive profits, creates undue private power over private affairs and, to our misfortune, over public affairs as well. In building toward this end we do not destroy ambition, nor do we seek to divide our wealth into equal shares on stated occasions. We continue to recognize the greater ability of some to earn more than others. But we do assert that the ambition of the individual to obtain for him and his a proper security, a reasonable leisure, and a decent living throughout life is an ambition to be preferred to the appetite for great wealth and great power.

Security of the men, women, and children of the nation was named as the central objective. A program was submitted to Congress designed to establish three types of security —"a program which because of many lost years will take many future years to fulfill." Stranded populations in the city and country should be rescued by better use of natural resources and intelligent distribution of means of livelihood. Unemployment and old-age insurance, benefits for destitute children, mothers, sick and physically handicapped persons should provide security against the major hazards of life. Housing was the third part of the program. Each of these problems of security had already been the subject of experimentation and comprehensive studies. But the President now gave up expectation that unemployment would be solved immediately by private enterprise and the NRA, and asked that it be dealt with in ways which would carry out the program for security. Recovery would be stimulated by the federal government pouring purchasing power into the hands of the least privileged groups, rather than by encouraging price rises which would increase profits and "seep down" in the form of higher wages to groups which would use their increased purchasing power to stimulate recovery. The shift from the latter program to the former, which was the shift from the First to the Second New Deal, was neither absolute nor sudden. The most practical justification for the change was the failure of the First New Deal, particularly NRA, to produce sound economic recovery, and the security program of 1935 was launched only after thorough experiment with the more conservative methods of achieving recovery.

The justification which the President offered for the new approach to unemployment was the "stark fact" that in spite of employment gains under NRA and the PWA program, approximately five million unemployed were still on the relief rolls. To continue to dole out relief to them would produce "spiritual and moral disintegration fundamentally destructive to the national fibre." The millions who were being attracted by the Townsend Movement, Father Coughlin's Social Justice, Huey Long's Share-Our-Wealth, and many other panaceas were perhaps in the President's mind when he spoke of saving "not only the bodies of the unemployed from destitution but also their self-respect, their self-reliance and courage and determination."

An estimated one and a half million who were on the relief rolls were unemployable. These the President wanted turned back to local agencies which would be assisted by federal social-security funds. The remaining group were employable, and Congress should establish a greatly enlarged and unified plan to provide employment for them by the federal government on projects such as slum clearance, rural electrification, and soil reclamation which would at the same time serve other purposes of the security program. The new work relief program would supersede FERA and all but a few normal public building operations of the PWA. Payment of the workers should be at a security wage level, higher than the existing dole but not so high as to discourage acceptance of private employment.

Besides the security program, the President suggested legislation to clarify and renew the National Industrial Recovery Act, strengthen anti-crime measures, reform public-utilities holding-company practices, and improve the forms and methods of taxation. Abnormal world conditions required continuation of acreage control in agriculture.[1]

The broad political significance of the launching of the security program of 1935 was that it ended the period during which the administration had supported economic policies of businessmen and established new ties of mutual support between the administration and all other groups of the population. The Message contained no invitation to businessmen to coöperate with the new program. By its nature they could have no immediate effect upon its success or failure. Rather a warning was issued that speculative profits should not be sought or any action taken which would slow the program.

Many developments influenced the formulation of the new program. Dominant groups of businessmen had shown their determination to resist all compromise or coöperation with the administration when its policies had been drawn up partially by business leaders and were designed to benefit all groups equally. This resistance was climaxed by the organization and activities of the Liberty League which drew class lines across party divisions. Thus it could be said that issues of class interest and antagonism had been introduced not by the administration but by its opponents. The defeat of the Liberty League in the 1934 elections resulted in a new Congress which was eager to carry out an anti-business program as an inevitable consequence of the efforts of the League to override party divisions and elect Congressmen on grounds of class interest. If conservative Democrats abandoned their party in favor of a program which exclusively benefited property interests, the obvious strategy of the leaders of the Democratic Party was to design a program which should appeal more exclusively to farmers and laborers, and compensate for the loss of conservative support by winning over the minority of farmers and laborers who had remained loyal to the Republican Party.

The rise of the Committee for Industrial Organization, which brought employees of the great mass production industries into the labor movement and added a new militancy to it, also influenced the new orientation of the administration. The CIO and its aggressive leader, John L. Lewis, were determined to take advantage of the promises which had been made to labor during the early days of the NRA. They had fought the conservative unionism of the American Federation of Labor which was easily defeated by labor spying and company unionism in the mass-production industries. The refusal of businessmen to deal with organized labor had quickly disillusioned the CIO with the promises of businessmen and the administration, and it strove to end the tolerance by the administration all through 1934 of the refusal of businessmen to coöperate with the recovery program in ways favorable to labor. More broadly, the rise of a militant labor movement in the United States was contemporaneous with the suppression of the labor movement and the rise of reaction and fascism abroad, which led many Americans to welcome the growth of a powerful labor movement as a guaranty against the spread of fascism to the United States. Many leading American writers who had abandoned hope for the cultural and political health of their country during the period of reaction after the First World War were appalled by the ferocious forms which reaction assumed abroad. They began to rediscover the values of American democracy, and to work in sympathy with the labor movement to renovate and strengthen the institutions of democracy as protection against American reaction. Innumerable novels, dramas, and historical, economic, social, and political studies were published which expressed resurgent faith in American institutions and exposed the meaning and danger of reaction. The Second New Deal was synchronized with the new currents of American thought, and the growing ranks of liberals, who had been largely skeptical of, and even opposed to, the First New Deal, gave ardent support to the administration.

That the administration was lagging behind rather than leading the labor movement and resurgent liberalism was suggested by the limited scope of the security program as compared with the subsequent enactments of Congress. Several of the most important laws of the Second New Deal, including the Wagner Labor Relations Act and the Fair Labor Standards Act, were still opposed by the administration. The security program itself was eagerly and completely enacted by Congress. On January 17, the Social Security Bill was introduced and strongly recommended in a special message. The Bill looked to the states to assume responsibility for the relief of unemployables, but federal aid was offered to the states for this purpose and for health service agencies in proportion to the states' own appropriations. A federal tax on employers' payrolls, beginning at 1 and reaching 3 per cent in 1939 would build up funds for unemployment insurance. States which established approved insurance systems suited to local needs could receive and administer up to 90 per cent of the payments which employers within their borders had made. The remaining 10 per cent would be used to aid the states in meeting administrative expenses. The only feature of the Bill which would be exclusively federal was a plan for old-age pension insurance under which a tax of 1 per cent on both the wages of employees and the payrolls of employers would reach 3 per cent in 1949, and provide funds for pensions of from $10 to $85 per month for life for qualified employees who retired at 65.

Extensive hearings were held on the Bill. Most of the criticism came from those who considered it too limited in scope. The organized ranks of Dr. Townsend's Old Age Revolving Pension movement made a determined effort to substitute their scheme, which called for payments of $200 per month to the aged, to be derived from a universal 2 per cent tax on commercial transactions. The cost was estimated to be $20,000,000,000 per year, but since recipients would be required to spend their checks each month, it was expected that the depression would be incidentally cured. Townsend was put on the stand at the hearings on the administration Bill, not to provide a platform for him, but to discredit his movement by revealing the unsoundness of its theory, and by airing the squabbles among its leaders, the unsavory character of some of them as well as the private gains which they made from the contributions of their members. The motive was to turn the sincere followers of the Townsend movement against it and to attract them to the moderate program of the administration.

Spokesmen of the American Federation of Labor opposed the taxes on wages and payrolls, and proposed new taxes on incomes as the source of insurance funds. Many objections were made to the cutting down of purchasing power by taxes on wages. This argument was adopted by some conservative opponents of the Bill. President Emery of the National Association of Manufacturers declared that industry did not want to pay taxes for the social security of its employees. At the other extreme of opinion, Earl Browder, the head of the Communist Party, opposed the Bill on the ground that it was the responsibility of the wealthy alone to provide all funds needed for the relief of the unemployed, the aged, and other disadvantaged groups.[2]

Supporters of the Bill found themselves in the position of moderates who refused to intensify radicalism by rejecting all proposals but made concessions which would minimize agitation for extreme measures. The only important difficulty over passage developed in a struggle between the Senate and the House for incompatible amendments. After a deadlock all amendments were abandoned except one to eliminate the administration's proposal that workers be allowed voluntarily to buy larger annuities than the compulsory pensions would provide. This amendment was a concession to private insurance companies which would have found the government competing with them for business.

The Social Security Act was passed in August and signed by the President with the statement that it did not provide complete protection against the "hazards and vicissitudes of life," but would give "some measure of protection to the average citizen," and by flattening out the peaks of inflation and the valleys of deflation would lessen the force of possible future depressions and provide "an economic structure of vastly greater soundness." [3]

In his Annual Budget Message of January 3, the President requested that $4,000,000,000 be appropriated for giving work to employables on the relief rolls. This amount would be added to the national debt, all other expenses of the government being met by income. On January 24, he submitted the Reports of the National Resources Board and the Mississippi Valley Committee of the PWA, in order to demonstrate how relief work would be integrated with planned development of natural resources, especially land and water. In April, Congress appropriated funds, and on May 6, the Works Progress Administration was established.

Harry Hopkins was made Administrator of the WPA, and as head also of the FERA he had direct charge of transferring unemployables to local relief agencies and employables to the WPA projects. A Division of Applications and Information received suggestions for projects from any public or private source, and the Advisory Committee on Allotments transmitted plans to the President for approval and assignment of funds. The WPA utilized some forty existing administrative agencies of the federal government to organize projects which fell in their fields. Three important new agencies were organized: the Agricultural Resettlement, Rural Electrification, and National Youth Administrations. For smaller projects such groups were organized as the Federal Theatre Project, the Historical Records Survey, and many others. Some estimate of the variety and scope of WPA projects may be obtained from a random selection of a small fraction of its accomplishments during its first two years: 1,634 new school buildings, 105 airport landing fields, 3,000 tennis courts, 3,300 storage dams, 103 golf courses, 5,800 traveling libraries established, 1,654 medical and dental clinics established, 36,000 miles of new rural roads, 128,000,000 school lunches served, 2,000,000 home visits by nurses, 1,500 theatrical productions, 134 fish hatcheries, 1,100,000 Braille pages transcribed, and 17,000 literacy classes conducted per month.[4]

The great majority of WPA workers were unskilled laborers, but projects were organized whenever possible to use skilled and professional workers in activities for which they had been trained. Wages during the first year were paid on the "security" basis at a level higher than relief payments but lower than prevailing wages, and ranged from $15 per month for unskilled farm labor in the South to $90 per month for professional services in New York City. The objection that security wages encouraged private employers to lower their wage scales, especially after the invalidation of NIRA, led the administration in 1936 to raise the hourly rates on WPA projects to the prevailing level, but to reduce the number of hours worked per month so that the monthly totals remained at the security level.

The WPA was attacked through its stormy career from opposite viewpoints. Workers especially in the largest cities organized themselves into unions, of which the Workers' Alliance became the most militant. Even traditionally individualistic artists organized a union. These groups demanded the rights usually advocated by labor unions, especially representation on the administrative level, and on a few occasions conducted strikes against the WPA. The administration ruled that workers could not strike against relief of their economic distress, but efforts were made to receive and consider workers' proposals. These chiefly concerned details of administration and opposition to systems of discharging workers periodically. Failure to give work to all the eligible unemployed and frequent dismissals were also criticized. On the other hand, the WPA became a chief target of opponents of the administration. Charges of waste, coddling, and vote-getting motives became common. The WPA worker leaning on his shovel between rare dabblings in the dirt became a standard cartoon figure and the butt of innumerable jokes. Where labor efficiency could be measured, as on building projects, it was demonstrated that WPA labor was less productive than labor privately employed. To this the administration could answer that private employers had naturally dismissed their least efficient workers, and that the difference in cost between direct relief and the WPA program was more than repaid by the vast quantities of useful projects which were completed. And the use of work relief as a means of restoring purchasing power and achieving recovery seemed to be justified by the general prosperity which set in late in the summer of 1935 and suffered no relapses as had all previous upswings, for two years, after which the "recession" of 1937 followed the dismissal of the majority of WPA workers.

The Resettlement Administration was the response of the administration to the growing recognition that the AAA program did not aid, and in some respects injured, smaller diversified farmers, tenants, sharecroppers, and migrants. The main interest of the RA was in the farmers whose land was not productive enough to repay cultivation. The presence of

over one million farm families on relief rolls had caused the
FERA to undertake demonstration projects whereby sub-
marginal land was purchased and devoted to forest, wild
life, park, grazing, and other uses which were calculated to
end erosion, restore productivity, and make the land socially
useful. These projects were turned over to the RA and WPA
labor was used on them. RA credits aided farmers from sub-
marginal lands to resettle on productive land where their
labor might become profitable. From the Department of the
Interior, the Subsistence Homesteads Division was also taken
over by the RA with its projects which were continued on a
modified basis. Individual acreage was enlarged to provide a
higher living standard, and the amortization period of loans
was extended.

The RA also attacked the problem of farm tenancy, which
had been growing at an alarming rate until over 40 per cent
of all farmers had become tenants. Farms were bought by
the RA and sold on easy terms to tenants selected for their
character and ability. Various types of rehabilitation work
were carried out, such as the granting of small emergency
loans, assistance to groups of small farmers in buying heavy
farm machinery on a coöperative basis, instruction in better
farming methods, and assistance to young people to establish
themselves as farmers. The most controversial activity of the
RA was the creation of the Greenbelt Towns, which were experiments in planned suburban communities for low-income
city workers. Each community was built by WPA labor and
designed for about seven hundred families as a village sur-
rounded by a belt of farm and wood lands on which the
residents could supplement their wages. A corporation of
which all the villagers were members governed the town,
paid taxes, and collected rents out of which it repaid to the
government its investment. Only three communities were
established in the vicinity of Washington, Cincinnati, and

Milwaukee. These and the subsistence homestead communities, of which about thirty were organized, were storm centers of controversy. They were cited as proof that the administration harbored socialist or collectivist plans and wished to undermine individualism by regimentation and assertion of government responsibility. Those who sympathized with the experments pointed to the free and self-governing institutions of the communities, the incentives to ambition for better living which they provided, and their value as experiments for the possible solution of pressing economic and social problems.

An important criticism of the RA was that it encouraged the increase of agricultural production at a time when the AAA was seeking to reduce it in the interest of higher prices. In answer to this the President wrote:

> The task of resettling is to take farm families off . . . inferior land and move them to land where they can raise a fair proportion of the total national crop of any particular product. That total national crop, in turn, is so controlled by a crop-reduction program that a decent price may be obtained for all the farmers who have together produced that total. It is not that each resettled farmer is necessarily going to raise more crops on his new land than he did on his old. The important point is that when he does raise his share of the total crop, he is not compelled to lose money because of the difficulty and expense of making his bad land produce his farm products.[5]

The scope of the work of the RA was not sufficient to make it more than an experimental demonstration. After two years only 5,000,000 acres had been purchased, and 4,441 families had been resettled.[6] Cultivation of sub-marginal land and farm tenancy were only slightly affected, and sharecropping not at all. The Southern Tenant Farmers Union was organizing sharecroppers with some success, and it protested that the administration's major agricultural program, the AAA, was injuring all farm groups except the larger owners. The growing class of migrant farm laborers was the most distressed of all farm groups. The RA was only an intermediate step towards the general solution of the problems of poorer farm groups, which was not undertaken until the Farm Security Administration was established in 1937.

The Rural Electrification Administration was established in May, 1935, to provide loans at low interest and WPA labor for the extension of power lines to farm homes where private utilities found too little opportunity for profit to undertake the investment. The sales of electrical appliances were expected to be stimulated by the REA program. Priority was given to projects which would distribute the power of publicly owned plants. In some areas conflicts developed between private companies whose owners feared the regulation of their rates which public ownership of power lines would make possible, and the REA projects. The threatened development of REA lines frequently stimulated the extension of power lines into rural districts by private companies and the lowering of their rates.

The National Youth Administration which was established in June, 1935, was intended to give to unemployed young people "their chance in school, their turn as apprentices and their opportunity for jobs—a chance to work and earn for themselves." [7] The problems of youth were particularly acute by 1935. Besides the obvious results of the depression, the NRA had caused industries to discharge about 1,500,000 workers of under 16 years, and minimum wage scales caused employers to give work to experienced laborers rather than to train apprentices. The Civilian Conservation Corps was expanded and placed under the WPA, but it gave work to only a half million boys at most, and none to girls. Early in 1935, a survey showed that 3,000,000 people between 16 and 25 years of age were on relief, or one in every seven. Tens of thousands had left dispiriting homes and taken to roaming as tramps. Many turned to crime as a means of livelihood.

As an emergency measure the WPA established shelters to care for transient youths. The main object of the NYA was to return young people to schools and colleges and otherwise prepare them for socially constructive careers. In all cases work experience rather than direct relief payments was used to inculcate self-reliant habits. Schools and colleges were provided with funds and given control over their expenditure for part-time employment of students in clerical, library, laboratory, and other positions in the institutions. Vocational training, guidance, placement service, and apprentice agreements with private employers were organized by the NYA. Special WPA projects which would provide valuable work experience were developed for the employment and training of young people. By 1936, almost 600,000 were being reached at a given time by the various NYA activities. A striking feature was the participation of the young people themselves in the administration of the NYA, which was encouraged as training in citizenship.

During this period political organizations of youth, some of which were radical, attracted growing memberships, and a large number of them federated into the National Youth Congress. The latter organization attracted wide attention by its militant demonstrations against war and fascism and in favor of more thorough-going relief and reform policies by the government. Such activities sometimes caused more worry than did the problems which the depression had brought to youth, and led to the accusation that the administration was coddling young people and nourishing class antagonisms. Supporters of the NYA argued that it gave to youth a practical demonstration of the creative and corrective powers of democracy and of the social value of work and self-help, which would compensate for the economic

[169

ills which made radical political solutions popular. If social-ism attracted youthful supporters during these years, it was a remarkable fact that in the United States alone of all indus-trial nations, fascism won practically no adherents among young people.

The third part of the security program, "decent homes," was not made the subject of new legislation until 1937. In the meantime the activities of the Federal Housing Adminis-tration, first established in August, 1934, were expanded. Notes and mortgages for the repair and modernization of old and the construction of new homes and small business structures were insured by the FHA, so that a field which pri-vate bankers had not found profitable was entered by them on a large scale. The Housing Division of the PWA was re-tarded by the extreme caution which affected all PWA activi-ties. A program of loans to limited-dividend corporations which would construct low-cost housing in slum districts was frustrated by the high cost of land, promotional schemes by private enterprises, and other factors, so that only 7 out of 533 contemplated projects were carried out. Direct federal construction of slum-clearing housing was largely prevented by the refusal of a Circuit Court in July, 1935, to admit the power of the government to exercise the right of eminent do-main in acquiring slum properties. Early in 1936, the Comp-troller General ruled that no subsidies but full economic rent must govern the rents charged tenants in the few projects which were being constructed. The George-Healey Act was passed to authorize partial subsidies. Organization of local bodies which should construct slum-clearance projects with limited federal aid was encouraged and slowly realized. The difficulties which beset the housing program prevented any great progress until experience, growing public demand, and the Housing Act of 1937 finally made possible the provision of low-rent housing for appreciable numbers of slum dwellers in cities.

Besides the three proposals of the security program, improvement in the forms and methods of taxation had been asked for by the President in January, 1935. In June, he sent to Congress the famous special message on tax revision which was variously called a "soak-the-rich" scheme, an act of revenge on wealthy opponents of the administration, an attempt to reassert the administration's prestige after the first series of decisions of the Supreme Court invalidating New Deal laws, and a concession intended to draw to the administration the support of the members of Senator Huey Long's "Share Our Wealth" movement. The latter analysis of the significance of the message is possibly supported by internal evidence: "Social unrest and a deepening sense of unfairness are dangers to our national life which we must minimize by rigorous methods" [8] of ending favoritism to great wealth in taxation.

Senator Long had supported the administration only briefly after it came to power. He had opposed returning the banks to the control of their owners and other measures of the First New Deal, especially NIRA, which he considered a sellout to Wall Street. His political machine in Louisiana began to suppress all opposition by methods which ranged from placing the election machinery in the exclusive control of Long appointees to the use of secret police. Complaints that liberty was being destroyed in Louisiana came to the White House, and the federal administration refused to turn Louisiana patronage over to the Long machine. In June, 1933, an interview with the President began with the Senator's refusal to take off his straw hat and proceeded through various types of offensive behavior and attempts to dominate the President. After it was over Long said to Postmaster General

Farley: "What the hell is the use of coming down to see this fellow? I can't win any decision over him." [9]

The "Kingfish" thereupon went into total opposition to the administration, and used tactics of debate and filibuster to disrupt the administration's program in the Senate. He also organized the Share Our Wealth Society to win a personal following beyond the boundaries of his state. Local clubs were set up over a wide area, and the Senator engaged in an intensive campaign of appeals to less literate elements of the population, especially rural Southerners, with whom he had considerable success. Observers believed that his claim of March, 1934, was not unduly exaggerated: "Two hundred and fifty-four thousand earnest men and women are now dedicated to an unrelenting fight to divide up the wealth of this Land of Plenty so that children will not starve and their parents beg for crusts." [10] He demanded that the federal government guarantee an income of $5,000 per year to every family, thus making "Every Man a King." This pill was sweetened for conservatives by "limitations" of private fortunes to $50,000,000, of legacies to $5,000,000, and of incomes to $1,000,000 per year. In this propaganda vicious attacks were made on Wall Street as the source of capitalist iniquities, and the administration was pictured as being its tool:

> Black Sheep, Wall Street, have you any gold?
> Yes, sir; yes, sir; all I can hold.
> Thanks to the New Deal I've made a billion more
> And I've stuck it all away in my little chain store. [11]

The significance of Long's anti-capitalism was indicated by the outcome of a conflict with oil companies in Louisana. After raising threats to ruin the companies by taxation, the campaign was suddenly dropped after an alleged private deal between politicians and companies. Improvements of state roads, free textbooks in schools, free hospitals, and expansion of the University of Louisiana were pointed to as proof of the Senator's sincerity as a reform leader. But the graft with which later trials and investigations revealed state activities to be riddled suggested that his reforms were burdens to the people rather than improvements of their condition. The Long combination of captivating oratory and propaganda, impossible promises, unlimited corruption, and ruthless destruction of civil liberties in the interest of building a one-man political machine and wiping out all opposition made observers declare that it was the most dangerous of the native fascist movements of the period. Unlike the leaders of smaller groups, Long did not avow fascist doctrine: he was said to remark that in the United States fascism would arrive in the guise of anti-fascism.

Long's feud with the administration became relentless. Department of Justice officials brought suit against members of the Long machine after finding evidence that they had failed to pay taxes on income from corrupt sources. Long worked to obtain personal control of federal-unemployment and work-relief funds allocated to Louisiana. Among other devices, the state legislature under his dictation enacted laws which would give the Governor and the Tax Board control over PWA loans. The motive was said to be not merely the desire for graft but unwillingness that any political, business, or unemployed opponents of the Long machine should benefit by federal funds. The national administration under these circumstances refused to make allotments for Louisiana, on the grounds that state control was not permissible under the federal laws governing the administration of funds, and that their distribution on the basis of need would be compromised. In the Senate, Long's fantastic tirades and filibusters against the administration made him notorious throughout the nation. His Share Our Wealth clubs grew to ominous dimensions by 1935. It was commonly expected that he would challenge the President for the Democratic nomination for the Presidency in 1936.

In the summer of 1935, Long established martial law in Louisiana and took complete control of the state as dictator in all but name. Secret police terrorized opponents and abolished judicial guaranties. Municipal government was reduced to subservience. Courts were subjected to limitations in procedure which made them ineffective. Taxes and appropriations and expenditures were no longer subject to audit. In September, Long was assassinated by the son of an opponent, and the machine and dictatorship he had built up were gradually liquidated while the state made its peace with the federal government. Many of Long's henchmen were brought to trial. Others, like the Reverend Gerald L. K. Smith, cast about for new opportunities.

The Long movement had become of national importance within and outside the Democratic Party when the President issued his special message on taxation. At first Long praised the program in a letter to the President. He conceded that the wind had been taken out of his movement and that the Share Our Wealth clubs would support the President.[12] Later he thought better of his praise, and turned to strenuous opposition of the program on the ground that its terms were too moderate.[13]

The Presidential message asserted that "our revenue laws have operated in many ways to the unfair advantage of the few, and they have done little to prevent an unjust concentration of wealth and economic power." [14] The sources of modern wealth were declared to be not only personal thrift and industry but also speculation, the labor and coöperation of the masses of the population, and the advantages and protection which government confers upon corporations. The dominant purpose of tax revision should be the redistribution of tax burdens according to ability to pay. Higher taxes on inheritances and gifts were justified on the ground that taxation of "static wealth" would not disturb the mechanisms of production. Higher taxes on large individual incomes would reduce the "disturbing effects upon our national life" of great wealth and carry out the "very sound public policy of encouraging a wider distribution of wealth." [15] The existing laws taxed an income of $5,000,000 at the same rate as one of $1,000,000, while a person with an income of $6,000 paid double the rate of one with $4,000.

Besides eliminating such inequities in individual income taxes, the principle of ability to pay should be extended to corporation tax rates. In place of the existing uniform corporation income tax of 13¾ per cent, the rate for smaller corporations might be reduced to 10¾ per cent, and the rates graduated to a level of 16¾ per cent on the highest corporation incomes. Such a system would be particularly fair because small corporations were more subject to state taxes and regulations than large corporations which were engaged in interstate commerce. To prevent evasion of the tax by the device of numerous subsidiaries and affiliates, a tax should be levied on dividends received by corporations. For later consideration the President suggested the elimination of unnecessary holding companies in all types of business, discouragement of unduly large corporate surpluses, a constitutional amendment to permit federal taxation of the income from subsequent issues of state and local government securities, and similar state powers over the income from federal issues.

A Wealth Tax Bill was written to carry out the President's recommendations, and it was debated in Congress largely in terms of the Long Share Our Wealth program. Long's opposition to the Bill because it was too moderate materially assisted in its passage, for his intransigence and unwillingness even to begin with cautious measures were regarded as further proof of dangerous demagoguery. Conservative opposition to the Bill was stronger after it passed than before it became clear that a more extreme measure would not be substituted under the influence of Long. Congress installed minor changes in the Bill. Inheritance taxes were eliminated and estate taxes increased. Income tax rates for small corporations were only lowered to 12½ per cent and only increased to 15 per cent on all corporation incomes in excess of $50,-000, but additional taxes were levied of 6 per cent on profits in excess of 10 per cent, and were graduated to 12 per cent on profits in excess of 15 per cent. Taxes on individual incomes above $1,000,000 were graduated steeply to 75 per cent on income in excess of $5,000,000. Holding companies which were used for the management of private fortunes were heavily taxed. The Wealth Tax Act was passed and signed on August 30.

Considerable public opposition to the Act developed on the ground that it was punitive. Roy W. Howard, owner of a chain of newspapers which had generally supported the administration, wrote to the President that businessmen who had once supported the New Deal were becoming increasingly hostile because they believed that the President had refused to broaden the tax base and had recommended the Wealth Tax measure in order to gain revenge on business rather than revenue. Business, he wrote, needed to have its fears allayed and a "breathing spell" from further experimentation. The President replied:

The tax program of which you speak is based upon a broad and just social and economic purpose. Such a purpose, it goes without saying, is not to destroy wealth, but to create broader range of opportunity, to restrain the growth of unwholesome and sterile accumulations and to lay the burdens of Government where they can best be carried. This law affects only those individual people who have incomes over $50,000 a year, and individual estates of decedents who leave over $40,000.

. . . Taxes on 95 percent of our corporations are actually reduced by the new tax law. . . .

Congress declined to broaden the tax base because it was recognized that the tax base had already been broadened to a very considerable extent during the past five years. . . .

. . . What is known as consumers' taxes, namely, the invisible taxes paid by people in every walk of life, fall relatively much more heavily upon the poor man than on the rich man. In 1929, consumers' taxes represented only 30 percent of the national revenue. Today they are 60 percent, and even with the passage of the recent tax bill the proportion of these consumers' taxes will drop only 5 percent.[16]

Then the President declared that the basic program to which the administration was pledged when it came to power "has now reached substantial completion and the 'breathing spell' of which you speak is here—very decidedly so." [17]

Less sympathetic businessmen than Roy Howard were appalled at the legislation passed during the 1935 session, and treated the "breathing spell" as a bad joke, for besides the security program and the Wealth Tax Act a series of laws to regulate business and to strengthen labor had been passed which were of major importance in the construction of the Second New Deal.

In March, the President strongly urged Congress to pass the Public Utility Holding Company Bill which had been written on the basis of special reports by the Federal Trade Commission and the National Power Policy Committee. The use of the holding company device during the twenties in order to exploit investors and to operate electric power and gas companies had become one of the major scandals of the period when public investigations and such incidents as the collapse of the Insull system revealed the methods which had been used. The abuses which the pyramiding of holding

[177

companies made possible were many. The purchase of a small amount of stock in an operating company by a holding company gave the directors of the holding company voting control over the operating company, and by assembling such control over great numbers of operating companies a holding company found that buyers would readily purchase its stock issues on the assumption dividends would rise with the economies which large scale organization would make possible. By raising tier upon tier of holding companies, which were related to other holding companies as well as to operating companies, an intricate web could be created which only the promoters, if anyone, understood, and high pressure methods could be used to unload endless series of stock issues on the public. Dividends were often falsified, being actually paid out of capital, and market prices rigged by pools. Commissions, legal fees, and other promotional profits could be saddled on the system with impunity. The high rates charged for electricity and gas to the public, and losses by investors ultimately paid for the exploits of the promoters. In 1925, holding companies controlled about 65 per cent of the electric power industry. By 1932, only the thirteen largest holding companies controlled 75 per cent of the industry. Natural-gas trunk pipe systems had been similarly centralized.[18] The resulting system of control of a vast industry by promoters who had made only slight investments, if any, the President in his message to Congress called "private socialism," and he declared that its destruction was essential if governmental socialism was to be avoided. The Bill recommended to Congress did not require the abolition of holding companies which performed demonstrably useful functions in terms of economies and efficiency of management; but a "death sentence" clause set a term of five years at the end of which any holding company which could not demonstrate its useful character would be forced to dissolve. The President declared that "except where it is absolutely necessary to the continued functioning of a geographically integrated operating utility system, the utility holding company with its present powers must go." [19] He drew particular attention to the vigorous campaign which the companies were waging against the Bill:

I have watched the use of investors' money to make the investor believe that the efforts of Government to protect him are designed to defraud him. I have seen much of the propaganda prepared against such legislation—even down to mimeographed sheets of instructions for propaganda to exploit the most farfetched and fallacious fears. . . .

Such a measure will not destroy legitimate business or wholesome and productive investment. It will not destroy a penny of actual value of those operating properties which holding companies now control and which holding company securities represent in so far as they have any value.[20]

The "death sentence" caused a bitter fight which lasted through the session of Congress. The House deleted it when it first passed the Bill, but the Senate retained it. Both houses held investigations of charges that the utility companies and the administration were using extreme methods to bring pressure to bear on Congressmen. Administration leaders were accused of threatening Congressmen with the withdrawal of patronage. Tom Corcoran, an official of the RFC and intimate of the President, denied Representative Brewster's charge that the administration through Corcoran had threatened that it would stop the Passamaquoddy Dam Project in Brewster's state of Maine unless the Representative voted for the "death sentence." A former manager of a telegraph office testified that telegrams of protest against the Bill had been sent from his office over names taken by utility lobbyists from the telephone directory. The Senate found a record of $700,000 spent to oppose the Bill by one of the largest holding companies, the Associated Gas and Electric Company. Philip H. Gadsden, chairman of the main lobby organization, the Committee of Public Utility Executives, whose papers had been seized by the Senate committee, admitted that he had spent about $150,000 in creating sentiment against the Bill, and that in addition he had disbursed $150,000 in "lawyers' fees." [21]

The House was led to accept a Senate offer of compromise on the "death sentence" only after the President announced his willingness to accept the compromise also. The Act as it was signed on August 28 permitted two levels of holding companies above operating companies, but otherwise maintained the "death sentence." The Securities and Exchange Commission was given power to regulate the financial practices of utility companies, and the Federal Power Commission received authority over the organizational provisions of the Act. After the new law was passed, utility companies largely disregarded it and depended upon the federal courts to come to their rescue by declaring the law unconstitutional. Over fifty suits were immediately instituted, and some lower federal courts upheld the companies. The Supreme Court ultimately upheld the constitutionality of the law.

The Motor Carrier Act and the Air Mail Act, which were signed in August, recognized the growth of competition with the railroads of bus, truck, and air transportation, and gave to the Interstate Commerce Commission powers to regulate rates, finances, and labor in the new fields which largely matched the powers it had long exercised over the railroads. The Banking Act of 1935, the Tennessee Valley Authority Amending Act, and the Gold Clause Act all clarified previous enactments. In May, Congress passed the Patman Bonus Bill, which called for inflation of the currency by issuance of greenbacks to the amount of $2,200,000,000 in order to pay war veterans immediately the full value of their adjusted service certificates which had been intended to mature in 1945. The President took the unprecedented step of delivering in person to a joint session of Congress a powerfully reasoned veto message. The veterans' lobby was not convinced, and the House overrode the veto, but the Senate sustained it by a narrow margin. The President's action was widely praised as evidence that he drew a sharp line against unsound inflationary devices for increasing purchasing power even though this one gave him an opportunity to win the support of a powerful special interest group.

The Wagner-Connery Labor Relations Act, which was passed in 1935, was as important in the structure of the Second New Deal as the Social Security Act, but it was not in the strictest sense an administration measure. The refusal of the administration to accept it in 1934, and the change to a favorable attitude towards it after it was passed by Congress in July, 1935, was a significant aspect of the evolution of administration policy from the First to the Second New Deal, and was closely related to the decision to abandon the keystone of the First New Deal, the NIRA.

On February 20, 1935, the President recommended to Congress the extension of the NIRA for two years beyond its expiration in June, 1935. His request emphasized that the rights of labor under the law should be strengthened, and that the abuses of business should be curtailed:

We must make certain that the privilege of coöperating to prevent unfair competition will not be transformed into a license to strangle fair competition under the apparent sanction of the law. Small enterprises especially should be given added protection against discrimination and oppression.[22]

The message also cited the gains of labor under NRA, particularly the re-employment of about 4,000,000 people, the elimination of "the age-long curse of child labor," the outlawing of the sweatshop, and the release of millions of workers from starvation wages and excessive hours of labor. Business had gained from the Act by being freed in part from dishonorable competition and destructive business practices and by safeguards for small enterprises. Consumers had gained by "less gouging in retail sales and prices than in any similar period of increasing demand and rising markets." [23]

But the President's favorable analysis of the effects of NIRA was poorly supported by the "Report on the Operation of the National Industrial Recovery Act," which was also made public in February by the Research and Planning Division of NRA. This report pointed out, for example, that payrolls in December, 1934, were only about 60 per cent of their level in 1926, while dividends and interest were 150 per cent of their total in 1926. The income of those who received interest and dividends was 50 per cent higher than in 1926, even though the national income was nearly 40 per cent lower and production had declined 33 per cent as compared with the earlier years.[24] Obviously, NIRA was not the only cause of the situation; but it had been intended to correct it. The President's new work relief program was also eloquent of the failure of NRA to accomplish what had been expected at its launching. By emphasizing the constructive achievements of the system and·asking for modifications of the law which would expand them, the President indicated that he had not yet given up the original conception that the great majority of businessmen could be induced to coöperate with a planned recovery program with social objectives.

A Congressional investigation of NRA was already underway when the President sent his message. Most of the investigators were hostile to the experiment from the liberal standpoint, and they concentrated on complaints against it rather than on the achievements which the President had summarized. Officials of the administration who appeared as witnesses admitted weaknesses of NRA, but asked for further opportunity to iron them out. Donald Richberg declared that "it is true that under some codes these [small] enterprises have suffered, but it is not true that the major effects of the codes have been injurious to small private enterprise." [25] William Green asked that the law be extended for two years even though labor had not obtained the benefits it expected, because the alternative was loss of the legal rights which organized labor had acquired. Defenders of the law pointed out that many of the recommendations of the Darrow Review Board had been put into effect and that the monopolistic tendencies of the first series of codes had been to some extent eliminated. Polls of the leading employers' organizations showed that members of the Chamber of Commerce favored continuation of NRA by almost three to one, while members of the National Association of Manufacturers opposed it by three to one.[26] General Hugh Johnson supported extension. He now admitted objections to the law, particularly that it promoted monopoly, which he had formerly denied and was inclined to agree they had been valid then; but that since his own "bad administration" had been ended, errors which he had made were in process of correction. He declared that the largest industries' leaders were divided between two views regarding the codes: some opposed them as restrictions on their freedom, while others believed that the system was inevitable and aimed to win control over it for themselves. Section 7A had substantially failed in its original purpose because of conflicting interpretations; clarification was the main need, and he was inclined to favor special legislation for that purpose. The General recommended: "Clean up NRA—don't destroy it. Let us scrub our infant offspring vigorously but let us not throw the baby down the drain pipe with the dirty water." [27]

In opposition to the proposal to extend NIRA, the advice of Kirton Varley on how to bring fascism to the United States was quoted from his book, *Gospel of Fascism:*

Study Italian practice in organizing the corporations and profit by the experience gained there. Organize the industrial organizations under the NRA administration into guilds with the same end in view.[28]

Considerable objection to NRA was made because it was based on the theory of economic scarcity. The chief tactic of the opponents of the law was to delay action by Congress until the Supreme Court should have handed down its decision on the constitutionality of the original Act. The administration, on the other hand, preferred to postpone tests until corrections in the law had been made.

The proposal to extend NIRA was also intended to prevent passage of the Wagner Labor Relations Bill and the Black Thirty Hour Bill, both of which were being pressed in Congress once more and by groups largely identical with the liberal and progressive opponents of NIRA. The Black Bill was being considered for the third time. Each time it had become broader in scope, and now it covered virtually all industries and classes of wage earners. Senator Black offered it as a means of increasing purchasing power and of returning the unemployed to work in private industry. Representative Connery introduced it in the House. Through January and February, hearings were held which showed once more the division of opinion between businessmen who opposed such a drastic measure and labor leaders who approved it.[29] The Bill was successfully sidetracked. In spite of support by such progressive leaders as Senators Borah, LaFollette, and Norris, motion to consider the Bill in the Senate was defeated on April 8, largely by the votes of those who wished to wait until the question of NIRA renewal was settled.

The Wagner Labor Relations Bill was not so easily set aside. The Bill embodied the main provisions of the author's Labor Disputes Bill, which had been dropped at the President's request in 1934. The heart of the measure was the outlawing of employer-dominated company unions and the enforcement of the right of collective bargaining through representatives chosen by employees. Representative Connery introduced a similar bill of the same name in the House. Through the spring, the administration gave no support to the Wagner-Connery Bill, but labor made its strongest fight of the session for it. Extensive hearings in both houses were largely repetitious of hearings on the same proposal which had been held in 1934, but both sides presented their views with greater force. Again the National Association of Manufacturers and the industries which had organized company unions under NRA were the most aggressive opponents of the measure. The Liberty League took active part in the campaign. The chief argument of the opposition was that the Bill presupposed an unalterable antagonism between employers and employees, while company unions were founded on the principle of coöperation between the two groups, and on the actual mutuality of their interests. This argument was answered by pointing out that the Bill, on the contrary, presupposed that the "class struggle" was not so inevitable that it could not be resolved by collective bargaining on the basis of mutual interests. Company unions which were financed and dominated by employers did not express the mutual interests of both classes, but the exclusive interests of the power that held the purse. Company unions which were not financed by employers would not be outlawed under the Bill. Employers already had their own organization in their management bodies: equality and mutuality could only be achieved by granting to labor the right to its organization, which must then have an opportunity to coöperate with the employer through collective bargaining. The argument that the leadership of labor unions was sometimes corrupt was answered by pointing out that some corporation managements had also been shown to be corrupt, particularly, as was revealed by the Senate investigation of civil liberties by the LaFollette Committee, in their anti-union activities; that such instances were not reasonable grounds for the refusal of labor unions to deal with management or management to deal with labor unions: checks on such practices were available to union members as to stockholders of corporations, short of infringements of public law which were subject to regular court proceedings.

The Bill declared that representatives chosen by the majority of workers in a particular factory unit should be the exclusive bargaining agents of all the workers in the unit. This clause aroused the particular support of labor leaders who recalled that the President had established the same principle in an Executive Order of February 1, 1934, and that on February 4, Johnson and Richberg for NRA had laid down the contrary rule, that representatives of a majority in a given unit could speak only for that group, while representatives of a minority could bargain with equal authority for its group, and that individuals could bargain for themselves, even to the point of making contracts containing different wage and other provisions. The opportunity which this rule gave to employers to break any union organization by granting better terms of employment to company union or non-union members, and, after union members had lost interest in their organization, changing to less favorable terms or refusing entirely to bargain, was described as an effective technique which was commonly used to evade the intent of the guaranty of collective bargaining which labor had received in NIRA. William Green said of the Johnson-Richberg rule:

This interpretation, I say to you, took the heart and teeth and soul out of Section 7(a); and we have never been able to overcome that interpretation because the administration itself never protested the interpretation.[30]

Senator Wagner stated a recent conference of the National Association of Manufacturers at White Sulphur Springs had adopted a rule that when a majority of the members of a trade association agreed on a certain trade practice it would also bind the minority. This, he declared, was an example of the imposition of majority rule on business, while the same rule was denied to labor.

The growth of labor unrest and strikes was cited as proof that the spread of company unions and the emasculation of Section 7A did not solve the problems of labor relations. Most strikes grew out of the refusal of employers to recognize and bargain with an independent union even when it had a majority among the employees. While the hearings were going on, strike situations were developing in the automobile, rubber, and building service industries, each of which could be solved by recognition of an independent union. The lesson was made explicit by William Green:

I do not mind telling you that the spirit of the workers in America has been aroused. They are going to find a way to bargain collectively. The day of individualism is past, and they are tired of it, because they have been exploited. If they are denied the right to bargain collectively in an orderly way and through orderly processes, they are going to use their economic strength, and the American Federation of Labor will encourage them to use it, support them in using it. . . . The establishment of labor in our whole economic and political system in a place where it belongs must be recognized. Labor must have its place in the sun.[31]

To the Senate, Green made it plain that the AFL leadership was feeling the pressure of the growing militancy of the rank and file of labor: "We cannot and will not continue to urge workers to have patience, unless the Wagner bill is made law, and unless it is enforced, once it becomes law." [32] Francis Biddle, the chairman of the existing National Labor Relations Board, supported the new Bill as the solution of the problems which faced his Board. He also showed its connection with the general recovery program:

I think it is obvious that where labor is a party to and can bargain collectively, and with power behind the bargaining, that there is a greater chance for high wages; otherwise there would be no attempt to resist the burden by the employers. The real reason the employer resists this bill is because the employer knows it will increase purchasing power. [33]

The arguments of the opponents of the Bill were defensive, but the record of labor relations during the previous two years did not reflect favorably on the existing system. It became clear that the Bill was acquiring considerable support in Congress and among the public. Supporters of the Bill discussed at length the provision of the Connery measure in the House for a labor board within the Department of Labor as compared with the Wagner provision for an independent board whose members could not be removed except for cause. Secretary Perkins feared that an independent board would usurp the mediatory activities of the Department of Labor. Senator Wagner answered that he would not oppose the Secretary's plan if she were going to be Secretary of Labor forever, but since it would be necessary to provide for the future, independence of judgment for personnel who exercised quasi-judicial functions could be permanently secured only by making the board free of Executive control. Wagner's view prevailed, and the House altered its Bill to suit the Senate version.

When the Bill reached the floor of the Senate, a last effort was made by Senator Tydings of Maryland to prevent it from favoring independent unionism. He offered an amendment which forbade coercion of employees by labor unions. This provision was presented as one which was required by fairness in order to match the ban on coercion by employers of their employees. It would have prevented organizational drives by independent unions to the same extent that employers were forbidden to urge their employees to join company unions. It would have changed the law from one which favored organized labor to one which would limit labor organizations to such as a group of employees in a particular factory could set up for themselves. A successful labor movement had not developed in any country under such conditions. It was the equivalent of forbidding organizational activities by employers' trade associations, or such "coercive" measures as the majority rule principle of the National Association of Manufacturers. The Tydings amendment was defeated on these grounds by a vote of 50 to 21 on May 16.

On May 14, the Senate had voted to extend NIRA for ten months. Senator Wagner was asked whether his Bill did not overlap the NIRA. The Senator was unwilling to oppose the administration's request for extension of NIRA, and he answered that his Bill defined the rights of labor more clearly than Section 7A and implemented them with provisions for enforcement: it would stand independently of NIRA. At the same time the silence of the President was interpreted to mean that he was not yet ready to accept the Wagner-Connery Bill. On May 16, the liberals and progressives of the Senate, most of them Democrats, passed the Bill by an ample majority of 63 to 12.

Eleven days later the NIRA was declared unconstitutional by the Supreme Court in the famous "sick chicken" decision. This placed a new significance on the Wagner-Connery Bill. The administration indicated that it would ask for re-enactment of NIRA after changing its terms to meet the constitutional objections of the Court. But it never pressed for re-enactment aggressively, and ultimately it dropped the proposal entirely. In the meantime supporters of the Wagner-Connery Bill passed it through the House by a large majority.

Faced with the alternative of vetoing a bill which was strongly advocated by his own supporters within and outside of Congress, the President signed the Wagner-Connery National Labor Relations Act on July 5. It was the only important law of the whole New Deal period which the President had not initiated or at least advocated before its passage. But he supported the law strongly once it was passed, and by 1936 he was taking the lead in advocating re-enactment of the remainder of Section 7A, so that a wages and hours bill was passed in 1938 as the Fair Labor Standards Act.

The re-enactment in stronger form of the section of NIRA which was favorable to labor, coupled with the failure to re-enact the sections which were favorable to business, displays the evolution of policy away from the First New Deal and the major significance of the Second New Deal.

The passage of the Social Security Act, the WPA program, the Wealth Tax Act, laws subjecting public utility holding companies and new forms of transportation to federal regulation, and the National Labor Relations Act made the 1935 session of Congress perhaps the most important one in the field of domestic liberal-progressive reform in the nation's history. Labor supplanted farmers and business as the chief beneficiary of legislation for the first time.

But before the session had closed, the Supreme Court had shown that the whole structure of the New Deal, including the laws most recently enacted, was in danger of destruction at the hands of the conservative majority of the justices, and the greatest crisis of the administration was precipitated.

CHAPTER XI

THE SUPREME COURT OBJECTS

At LEAST once in every generation the Supreme Court has been an issue in partisan politics. Jefferson, Jackson, and Lincoln had been among the eminent critics of the Court who attacked it as dangerous to the success of popular government. Decisions that duly enacted federal laws were unconstitutional and need not be obeyed, such as had been made only twice before but with increasing frequency after the Civil War, were the most important cause of friction between the Supreme Court and the other two branches of the government, the states, and the people. Students of the Court's history are inclined to believe that it has been beneficially influenced by its encounters with adverse public opinion. Certainly it has not been uninfluenced by factors other than judicial considerations. Judicial "statesmanship" is the laudatory way of describing the decisions of the Court which showed a willingness to make an unchanging Constitution respond to political, social, and economic changes. "The Supreme Court follows the election returns" is the more coarse way of describing the same phenomena. The most intense of all conflicts involving the Supreme Court was precipitated by its decisions of 1935 and 1936 which invalidated a large part of the New Deal.

The justices of the Supreme Court since the Civil War had been on the whole conservative in the double sense of insistence upon restriction of the powers of government to the letter of the Constitution narrowly interpreted, and lack of sympathy with liberal or progressive reforms. Many of the justices had specialized in the practice of private corporation law before taking seats on the great tribunal, and the rarity of a Democratic administration during the period had given Republican presidents more opportunities to appoint justices. When the Roosevelt administration came to power, three Justices, Brandeis, Stone, and Cardozo, were classed as liberals, four, Van Devanter, Sutherland, McReynolds, and Butler, were conservatives and two, Roberts and Chief Justice Hughes, were "roving" conservatives who occasionally agreed with the liberals. The preponderance of the conservatives was slight, but not all of them were the oldest members of the Court, and in any case the new President had no chance to appoint a new justice during his entire first term in office. Meanwhile it required the vote of only one of the two roving conservatives to invalidate a law which left room for conflicting interpretations concerning its constitutionality.

The great unresolved problem which faced the Court was whether the states and the federal government had constitutional authority to legislate the social and economic reforms which were being enacted in the United States in common with every other democratic industrial nation. Before January, 1935, the Supreme Court gave no sign that it would interpret the Constitution narrowly in order to invalidate the experiments of the New Deal. In fact, two decisions of 1934 which upheld a Minnesota mortgage moratorium law and a New York law to regulate the price of milk suggested that the Court was willing to interpret the Constitution broadly in order to permit emergency and reform legislation to be enacted. But decisions of lower federal courts were being based on strict interpretations, and by 1935 the highest court was called upon to render the final verdicts.

On January 7, the Supreme Court decided the "Hot Oil" case adversely to the administration. Section 9C of NIRA gave the President authority to prohibit the interstate transportation of oil in excess of the amount permitted by state laws in order to encourage restriction of production in conformity with the general purposes of NIRA. The Court held Section 9C to be an unconstitutional delegation to the Executive of legislative authority which belonged to Congress, because the law did not provide sufficient guidance for the President or adequate limitations or controls of his authority.[1] The decision called into doubt the constitutionality of the whole of NIRA, since other sections of the Act gave the President equal or greater "legislative" authority. In a vigorous dissenting opinion, Justice Cardozo declared that Section 9C and the general intent of NIRA gave the President discretion as to the occasion but none whatever as to the purpose and means of administering the prohibition of "hot oil" in interstate commerce, and that the Section was therefore not an unconstitutional delegation of legislative authority. This comment, and suggestions which appeared in the majority decision, indicated the possibility of saving the NIRA as a whole by redrawing it to specify more exactly the rules and limitations for the President's guidance. But opponents of NIRA in Congress prevented its revision before the Supreme Court rendered a decision on the whole Act in May.

In the meantime, the administration won an ambiguous victory in a series of decisions on the validity of the abrogation of gold payments for public and private debts. The Court held that the federal government had authority under the money power to override the gold clauses in private debts and those of state and local governments. Holders of federal gold certificates were told that, while the federal government had no power to violate its pledge of payment in gold, the holders' right to receive gold was meaningless because Congress did have the power to forbid the possession of gold. The Court refused to decide the further question whether holders of federal gold certificates had the right to receive currency payment according to the old dollar value of gold or according to the new higher value of gold, because holders had not shown that they had suffered any actual loss as a result of the government's payment according to the old value. This left open the possibility that the Court might uphold suits against the government to recover loss of purchasing power suffered by holders of gold certificates, who were paid in the old value in currency, as a result of the rise in commodity prices and the devaluation of the gold content of the dollar. But the federal government can be sued in any case only when it deigns to give its consent. The President in June asked Congress to withdraw the government's consent to be sued in the Court of Claims on its gold obligations, and the Gold Clause Act was accordingly passed and signed on August 28. This ended the possibility that the Court could require that owners of gold certificates be given compensation for devaluation which holders of other forms of money could not receive.

On May 6, the Court invalidated the Railroad Retirement Act of June, 1934, on the grounds that particular provisions of the law violated the due process clause of the Fifth Amendment, and that imposition upon employers and employees of a pension system for employees was an unwarranted extension of the government's power to regulate interstate commerce. The former objection was chiefly based on the pooling of pension payments made by employers and employees into one fund from which pensions would be paid when employees became eligible without regard for the contributions made by particular companies. Thus companies whose employees were on the whole younger than others' would find their property taken away without "due process of law." In the second objection, the Court found no relation between pensions and the efficiency and safety of interstate commerce. Pensions, like medical attention, education, housing, and other matters were "really and essentially related solely to the social welfare of the worker, and therefore remote from any regulation of commerce as such." [2]

Chief Justice Hughes entered a dissent in which Justices Cardozo, Stone, and Brandeis joined. He pointed out that while particular provisions of the Act might require revision, the general assertion that pensions had no relation to the efficiency and safety of interstate commerce was answered by the practice of the railroads themselves, most of which had pension plans, and by previous decisions of the Court which upheld such regulations as employee accident compensation laws. The Chief Justice declared that it was not the duty of the Court to pass on the wisdom of particular regulations of commerce by Congress. This dissent, with its far-reaching implications for social reform legislation, lacked one vote of becoming the governing decision. As things stood, the Court prevented the administration from providing social security for workers in the railroad field, which had always been the first to come under new types of federal regulation, and thereby threw serious doubt upon the constitutionality of the much more extensive Social Security Bill which was before Congress.

The Social Security Bill was nevertheless passed as an application of the power to tax for the general welfare. And the special needs of railroad employees were met by the Wagner-Crosser Railroad Retirement Act which was signed on August 29. The President had been advised that division of the contents of the invalidated law into two laws would meet the conditions of constitutionality. The Wagner-Crosser Act provided for the payment of pensions to railroad employees out of the general funds of the Treasury in promotion of the general welfare. A second law, signed the same day, laid a special tax on railroads and their employees. The two laws were later tested in court, but before a decision was rendered, the railroads agreed to install a universal pension plan voluntarily. In 1937, legislation which was of undoubted constitutionality was accordingly enacted, and it superseded the two laws of 1935.

The Court's invalidation of the original Railroad Retirement Act proved to be no insurmountable barrier to the achievement of the purposes of the law. A decision of May 27, which told the President that he had overstepped his power when, on October 7, 1933, he had removed William E. Humphrey from the Federal Trade Commission, established a rule of permanent importance. The Federal Trade Commission had been established during the Wilson administration to investigate violations of the antitrust laws and check abuses of business without requiring court action for minor infractions. During the subsequent Republican administrations, appointments which were made as the seven-year terms of incumbents ran out staffed the Commission with men who seemed to be less interested in obtaining obedience to the antitrust laws than in encouraging businessmen to accept the codes of trade practices which were advocated by the largest corporations. Commissioners who were not sympathetic to the original purposes of the body transformed it from one devoted to correcting the abuses of big business to one which coöperated with big business.

The Securities Act of 1933 placed upon the FTC the responsibility of administering a further reform of business practices, and the provision of appeals from code authorities to the FTC made it important also to the success of NRA. One of the requirements of the law which established the FTC was that not more than three of the five Commissioners should be members of the same political party. Humphrey was a Republican of notoriously conservative views, who had been reappointed to the Commission by President

Hoover in 1931. In order to obtain a Commission which should be not unfavorably disposed towards the laws it would administer, President Roosevelt twice asked Humphrey to resign on the ground that his opinions would make it impossible for him to carry out the policies of the administration. The Commissioner refused to resign, and the President removed him from office. But Humphrey refused to admit that his opinions would make him guilty of the charge of inefficiency, which was named in the law as a cause for removal. He insisted that he was still a member of the Commission, and when he died the executor of his estate sued for unpaid salary.

The attorney for the government cited a previous case in which the Supreme Court had decided that the President might remove an administrative officer for other causes than those named in the law which created the office, even if the officer served, as did Humphrey, in a quasi-judicial capacity. But the Supreme Court now decided unanimously that such quasi-judicial and quasi-legislative bodies as the Federal Trade Commission and the Interstate Commerce Commission were agents of Congress rather than of the President, and that the President therefore had no power to remove their officers except for causes designated by Congress. "For it is quite evident that one who holds his office only during the pleasure of another, cannot be depended upon to maintain an attitude of independence against the latter's will." [3]

The far-reaching importance of this decision, increasing as it did the independence of all quasi-judicial and quasi-legislative bodies, would no doubt be appreciated by liberals when conservatives next won control of the Executive. In 1935, however, the decision seemed to many to be a reversal of the previous rule in order to prevent the installation of an effective reform administration.

Another decision handed down on May 27 found the

Frazier-Lemke Farm Bankruptcy Act of June, 1934, unconstitutional. A Kentucky farmer who had mortgaged his property to a bank had defaulted, and the bank had foreclosed. He refused the bank's offer to take the farm in satisfaction of the mortgage, but took advantage of the Frazier-Lemke Act to secure a reappraisal which fixed the value of the farm at about one-half of the mortgage. The bank refused to accept this price, and the farmer, under further provisions of the Act, obtained a stay of proceedings for five years during which he retained possession of the farm subject to a small rental fixed by a court. The Supreme Court held that the Act as thus applied had taken property rights from the bank and was void:

For the Fifth Amendment commands that, however great the nation's need, private property shall not be thus taken even for a wholly public use without just compensation. If the public interest requires, and permits, the taking of property of individual mortgagees in order to relieve the necessities of individual mortgagors, resort must be had to proceedings by eminent domain; so that, through taxation, the burden of the relief afforded in the public interest may be borne by the public.[4]

This decision refused to take into account the special powers which an emergency might temporarily justify, which had been the basis of the Court's approval of the Minnesota mortgage moratorium law in 1934. But the sponsors of the federal law rewrote it to meet by changing details the objections of the Court, and this new Frazier-Lemke Farm Mortgage Act was passed and signed on August 29.

The third decision on May 27 invalidated the NIRA. A test case which attacked an especially vulnerable position of NRA arose because the Schechter Poultry Corporation of Brooklyn, New York, refused to obey the Live Poultry Code of Fair Competition. Chickens which had been brought to New

York from other states were bought from commission merchants by the Schechter Corporation, transported to Brooklyn, killed, and sold to retail merchants for local sale and consumption. The Corporation claimed that the chickens had ceased to be "in" interstate commerce when it bought them, and that regulation of its operations under the interstate commerce power of the federal government was unconstitutional. The attorney for the government claimed that the depression in the market for chickens had "affected" interstate commerce insofar as it reduced the number of chickens imported into New York from other states, and that regulations of the Corporation's business which were calculated to remove burdens and increase the flow of interstate commerce were therefore within the power of the federal government. The Corporation had paid wages which were below the code minimum and thereby reduced purchasing power in a way that restricted the flow of interstate commerce, and it had sold "unfit chickens" which did not meet the standards of fair trade practice laid down in the code, thereby further reducing the market for chickens and the flow of interestate commerce by creating distrust of that commodity among consumers.

The Supreme Court decided in favor of the Corporation, on the ground that its operations had only an "indirect" effect upon interstate commerce. If the federal government had power to regulate everything which had an indirect effect upon interstate commerce, "there would be virtually no limit to the federal power and for all practical purposes we should have a completely centralized government," [5] which was manifestly not the purpose of the Constitution. If the decision had gone no farther, the NRA would have lost its power to regulate such businesses as had only an indirect effect upon interstate commerce, while retaining its power to regulate those which were clearly interstate in scope.

But the Schechter Corporation also claimed that Congress had by passing the NIRA attempted an unconstitutional delegation of its legislative functions to the Executive. The codes of fair competition were laws made by the President, and only Congress has the power to make laws. The government argued that Congress had not delegated its law-making power, because in NIRA it had laid down policies and standards, such as the elimination of unfair methods of competition in wages and hours of labor, and the methods, such as the procedure of hearings, which governed the President. The Court decided this question also in favor of the Corporation, because "the discretion of the President in approving or prescribing codes, and thus enacting laws for the government of trade and industry throughout the country, is virtually unfettered." [6] Such quasi-legislative and quasi-judicial agencies as the Federal Trade Commission and the Interstate Commerce Commission were constitutional because Congress had itself determined the codes of laws which the commissions enforced, and had given those bodies merely the power to make subordinate rules and interpretations in order to apply the codes to particular cases. NIRA gave the President power to approve the codes themselves, as well as the power to establish the agencies which carried them out, and it was therefore an unconstitutional delegation of legislative power.

Justice Cardozo in a concurrent opinion in which Justice Stone joined, explained that the limitations on the President's discretion which he had pointed out in Section 9C when the Hot Oil case was decided were not present in the remainder of NIRA, and that it therefore gave the President in effect "a roving commission to inquire into evils and upon discovery correct them." [7] Cardozo and Stone furthermore agreed that the Schechter Corporation's business was intrastate, which precluded its regulation by the federal government under the interstate commerce power. Thus the hope that a "liberal" majority might be won for NIRA was dashed, for the decision was unanimous that it was unconstitutional. Commentators rang the changes on the theme that the Schechter Corporation and the Supreme Court had changed the famous Blue Eagle into an "unfit chicken."

During the week after May 27, the President held three press conferences in which he discussed the situation precipitated by the decisions of the Supreme Court, especially the invalidation of NIRA. He suggested the confusion which the latter decision caused, and the frantic desire of many people to retain the benefits of NIRA, by showing correspondents the letters and telegrams which were flooding the White House. He declared that competitive lowering of wages and increasing of hours were the inevitable response of not only inveterate exploiters, but also of businessmen who could not otherwise meet the low prices which such competitors charged for their products. Such devices as loss leaders would again give large department stores and chain stores advantages over small businessmen.

The President hit upon the Court's narrow interpretation of interstate commerce as the most significant aspect of its decisions. Similar application of the commerce clause could result in the invalidation of the AAA, the SEC, and many other parts of the New Deal. He remarked that when employers had sought injunctions against striking miners the Court had often interpreted the commerce clause very broadly and granted injunctions; the Schechter decision "seems to be a direct reversal in saying that where you try to improve the wages and hours of miners, the coal suddenly becomes a purely local intrastate matter, and you can't do anything about it. Of course, here the shoe is on the other foot." [8] The President said that turning back to forty-eight states control over the multifarious complexities of modern industry and agriculture in an economy which had become national would create "a perfectly ridiculous and impossible situation." [9]

You see the implications of the decision. That is why I say it is one of the most important decisions ever rendered in this country. And the issue is not going to be a partisan issue for a minute. The issue is going to be whether we go one way or the other. Don't call it right or left; that is just first-year high school language, just about. It is not right or left—it is a question for national decision on a very important problem of Government. We are the only Nation in the world that has not solved that problem. We thought we were solving it, and now it has been thrown right straight in our faces. We have been relegated to the horse-and-buggy definition of interstate commerce.[10]

Correspondents were allowed to use the "horse-and-buggy" phrase as a direct quotation, and it became famous overnight. The President refused to tell correspondents whether he had a plan for "the way out," but they were made to understand that he did not intend to abandon the New Deal without a struggle. Correspondents spoke of the Dred Scott Decision, civil war, and constitutional amendments, suggesting an analogy with the most famous previous conflict over the Supreme Court, but they were only told that suggestions for "the way out" which were received at the White House were being sent to the Department of Justice.

It has been shown that the very practical "way out" of rewriting legislation to meet constitutional objections was used to recover the Railroad Retirement Act and the Frazier-Lemke Farm Mortgage Act. For a time the same method seemed destined to be used in order to re-establish the NRA. The Petroleum Act of February 22 had met the objections to Section 9C by Congressional enactment of more specific rules to govern the President in prohibiting the interstate transportation of "hot oil." In the Alcohol Control Act of August 29 Congress enacted the provisions of the NRA Liquor

Code and established the Federal Alcohol Administration under the Treasury Department to administer the rules.

The Guffey-Snyder Bituminous Coal Stabilization Act of August 30 was aptly called the "little NRA," and fully demonstrated the way in which all of the codes and all the objectives of NIRA might have been restored. The Bituminous Coal Bill had first been sponsored by John L. Lewis of the United Mine Workers Union to strengthen the NRA in the soft coal fields. In May, before the NIRA decision, the President had refused to support it. A strike was threatened by the mine workers. After the invalidation of NIRA the President made the Bill an administration measure. It virtually duplicated the provisions of the Bituminous Coal Code. The work of the former Code Authority was delegated to a new National Bituminous Coal Commission, which was required to draw up and administer a code embodying the mandatory provisions of the law. These included price-fixing, production limitation, and labor guaranties, the latter to be administered by a new Bituminous Coal Labor Board. The possibility that coal mining would be defined as intrastate commerce was met by avoiding any provision for judicial action against violators of the code and by making observance nominally voluntary. A tax of 15 per cent on the market value of coal which they mined was imposed on producers, and nine-tenths of the tax was remitted in the case of producers who complied with the code. Wages and hours provisions required the agreement of two-thirds of the producers and one-half of the miners in a given area.

This law was strongly urged upon Congress by the President, who feared that the end of NIRA would revive in the soft coal fields the over-production, cut-throat competition, and low labor standards of previous periods. In a letter of July 6 to the chairman of the House committee which was considering the Guffey-Snyder Bill, the President said that

the soft coal situation was so urgent and the benefits of the
Bill so obvious that doubts should be resolved in its favor,

leaving to the courts, in an orderly fashion, the ultimate question
of constitutionality. A decision by the Supreme Court relative to
this measure would be helpful as indicating, with increasing clar-
ity, the constitutional limits within which this Government must
operate. The proposed bill has been carefully drafted by employers and employees working coöperatively. An opportunity should
be given to the industry to attempt to work out some of its major
problems. I hope your committee will not permit doubts as to
constitutionality, however reasonable, to block the suggested
legislation.[11]

The last sentence of this letter was frequently quoted out of
its context to "prove" that the President wished to defy the
Supreme Court. But the Guffey-Snyder Act was passed by
Congress and signed on August 30.

The Wagner-Connery National Labor Relations Act of
July 5 re-enacted the guaranty to labor of collective bargaining in Section 7A of NIRA. When the 1935 session of Congress ended, therefore, the wages and hours and child labor
provisions of Section 7A and the codes which had covered
some six hundred industries, excepting petroleum, liquor,
and soft coal, were the parts of NIRA which had not been re-
enacted. The other two laws which the Supreme Court had
invalidated had been entirely re-established. The "way out"
had evidently been found. In 1936, the administration for
the first time supported the re-enactment of wages and hours
and child labor provisions, and the law was passed as the
Fair Labor Standards Act in 1938. Since the Wagner Act
and the Fair Labor Standards Act together imposed on employers labor provisions which were at least as strict as the
labor provisions in most NRA codes, the ultimate residuum of
lost legislation after the 1935 decisions of the Supreme Court

amounted to only the fair trade practice provisions of all but three of the NRA codes.

These fair trade practice provisions had originally been advocated by business. In many codes they had amounted to the imposition on an industry of price and production conditions which were more favorable to the largest corporations than to small competitors, and had fostered monopoly. The administration had made an effort to prevent monopolistic clauses from being written into codes, but not until after the first series of codes had been written, and its efforts were only slightly successful. It had also worked to increase the importance in codes of such clauses as the prohibition of loss leaders in order to establish trade practices which would be favorable to small competitors, and these efforts met somewhat greater success. It was a debatable question whether the codes as they stood in April, 1935, were helpful or harmful to small business. When the President had asked for the renewal of NIRA, he had expressed the hope that revision of the law would result in the strengthening chiefly of its labor provisions. But this objective was achieved through the two separate labor laws. It is impossible to say without evidence which is not now available when and why the President gave up interest in the revival of the fair trade practices of the great body of NRA codes. Prior to 1938, he spoke several times in general terms of the desirability of re-establishing NRA in modified form, and for a time after the Schechter decision he encouraged voluntary action by businessmen. But he never made a specific recommendation to Congress. Three things are clear: the codes could all have been re-enacted in constitutional form; even before the invalidation of NIRA the President was concerned to eradicate the monopolistic tendencies of the codes, and he was determined not to revive their monopolistic features after that decision; and the evolution of administration policy away

[205

from the codes and towards an active anti-monopoly program was in both cases completed in 1938 when the codes were no longer mentioned and a campaign of antitrust prosecutions was begun. It seems to be a just implication that the fair trade provisions of the NRA codes, alone of all the New Deal casualties in the Supreme Court, were not revived because the administration considered them to be more favorable to monopoly than to competition, to big business than to small. In such a decision the great majority of liberal-progressive Congressmen and other leaders would concur.

In any case, 1933 and 1938 represent the extreme limits between which the business policy of the New Deal evolved into its opposite: from support of big business to opposition. The slow pace at which this change of front was accomplished, carried out as it was in a vast complex of developments which involved many fields besides the NIRA problem, suggests that the invalidation of NIRA was an incident of minor importance and that the basic cause of the change remained the refusal of business to coöperate with the First New Deal which was intended to distribute fairly among all groups the burdens and benefits of recovery and reform.

An intriguing question is whether the major recovery which began promptly after NIRA was invalidated helped to convince the administration that the fair practice provisions of the codes had been harmful rather than beneficial. The harmful effects of the termination of the codes upon hours and wages of labor which the President had predicted were not apparent in statistical summaries. Payrolls in manufacturing industries rose from an index of 69.1 in July, 1935, to 110.1 in May, 1937. Employment increased from 89.2 in June, 1935 to 112.3 in July, 1937, a level which surpassed that of 1929.[12] The index of industrial production also rose steadily from 85 in May, 1935, to 118 in May, 1937.[13] Wholesale prices, after an almost continuous rise from 59.8 in February, 1933, to 80.1 in April, 1935, then held steadily within a few tenths of 80 until August, 1936, having fallen more than they rose during that period, and subsequently rose to 88 by April, 1937. Farm prices had passed the index of 100, which was the average of the "prosperity" years of 1909 to 1914, in September, 1934, and they rose to 130 in April, 1937.[14]

In short, sound and balanced recovery, which had never been achieved under the First New Deal, in either quantity or quality, was inaugurated with the summer of 1935. For the first time the rise in prices did not absorb the increase of workers' and farmers' income. From April, 1935, to July, 1936, while employment, payrolls, and production all increased rapidly, industrial prices did not rise at all. At the same time, farmers' prices did gain. The combination of these developments created the type of recovery which had been the objective of the administration. A revival of competition with low unit profits compensated for by expanding production, which in turn was supported by increased purchasing power, argued that the invalidation of NIRA was an important cause of the recovery.

Another important factor was the creation of purchasing power by the WPA. The latter and local and national direct relief programs were supporting about ten million persons, including the dependents of the unemployed, during the summer months. The transfer of many more of the unemployed to WPA projects and the resultant increase of their incomes occurred during the fall months and coincided with the strong upswing of recovery. The expansion of private employment was never sufficient before the Second World War to permit general reduction of the WPA program without risking the recovery gains which had been made. The pump seemed to be in permanent need of priming. Other factors besides the revival of competition and the WPA program, such as the accumulation of demand during the depression years for producers' goods, were undoubtedly influential in creating the recovery of 1935 to 1937. But all of the policies of the Second New Deal were intended to create recovery primarily by increasing the purchasing power of the mass of the population, and it was a recovery which corresponded with the objectives of the Second New Deal which actually occurred. The policies of the First New Deal had been intended to create recovery primarily by raising prices, with the expectation that corresponding recovery of employment, production, and purchasing power would occur: the primary purpose had been achieved, but not the other objectives which would have justified the price rise. The success of the Second New Deal as compared with the First was the most important political fact of 1936. It led inevitably to the conviction that the newer policies should be strengthened and extended.

This conviction dominated the administration, Congress, and the public during 1936, and the latter emphatically registered the fact in the November elections. But meanwhile the Supreme Court handed down several more decisions which were unfavorable to the administration, and these, unlike the decisions of 1935, threatened to break down the structure of the Second New Deal.

Amendments of the Agricultural Adjustment Act had been signed on August 24, 1935, in an effort by the administration to make it conform with constitutional doctrines recently laid down by the Supreme Court. Congress withdrew previous apparent delegations of legislative power to the Executive, actions of the administrators of the law were ratified, and control over agriculture was limited to products which clearly entered interstate commerce. Initial experiments with the parity-price and ever-normal-granary system, which might be substituted for acreage control, were provided for, but the new system was not developed on a large scale until

1938. In the meantime it was hoped that acreage control would be found constitutional.

An action under the original AAA to collect processing taxes from a cotton textile factory gave rise to the case in which the law was tested before the Supreme Court. The mill had gone bankrupt, and the receivers claimed that the processing tax was unconstitutional because its purpose was not to raise revenue but to obtain funds from a particular group of citizens, processors of agricultural products, and to use them to "purchase" compliance by another group of citizens, farmers, with the regulation of agriculture by the system of acreage control, a regulation which was outside the power of the federal government and invaded the rights of the states. Eloquent oral arguments were made on both sides, and many special briefs were filed by farmers' organizations and by processors as *amici curiae*.

The decision of a majority of six members of the Court was that the Agricultural Adjustment Act was unconstitutional. In the majority opinion, which was written by Justice Roberts, sharp remarks were made in answer to the wave of criticism which had greeted the decisions of the previous year:

It is sometimes said that the court assumes a power to overrule or control the action of the people's representatives. This is a misconception. . . . When an act of Congress is appropriately challenged in the courts . . . the judicial branch of the Government has only one duty,—to lay the article of the Constitution which is invoked beside the statute which is challenged and to decide whether the latter squares with the former. All the court does, or can do, is to announce its considered judgment upon the question. The only power it has, if such it may be called, is the power of judgment. This court neither approves nor condemns any legislative policy. . . .

The question is not what power the Federal Government ought to have but what powers in fact have been given by the people.[15]

The last sentence had obvious bearing on the statements to the press which the President had made, and hinted that a constitutional amendment was the proper recourse of those who desired an end to "horse-and-buggy" decisions. The stress on "judgment" implied that human fallibility in handling judicial abstractions, rather than differences in political philosophy, was the cause of split decisions. However, the fact that when the Court divided, the same justices were almost invariably on the side of liberal interpretation of the Constitution, while others were equally consistent on the side of conservative interpretation, suggested to many observers that the decisions of the Court were not the product of "accidental" differences in judicial interpretation, but rather were the result of sympathy with particular political and economic philosophies and interests.

The decision held that the AAA processing tax was not a true tax but an expropriation of money from one group for the benefit of another. Such an exaction might nevertheless be validly used for regulatory purposes which were within the powers of Congress. In its argument the government had not claimed the interstate commerce power but the power to tax and appropriate for the general welfare as the constitutional authority for the Act. It pointed out that Congressional power to appropriate in aid of agriculture under the general welfare clause had long been unquestioned, even though power to regulate agriculture was not expressly committed to the federal government by the Constitution. The Court replied that since no specific taxes had been laid to provide funds for previous agricultural appropriations, the question of constitutionality had never come up because no redress was possible even if the grants were unconstitutional. And the AAA benefit payments to farmers were not grants in aid, but were made in pursuance of acreage control contracts, which, even if voluntary, were still regulatory in purpose. The Constitution had not specifically granted the power to regulate agriculture to Congress, therefore "Congress has no power to enforce its commands on the farmer to the ends sought by the Agricultural Adjustment Act. It must follow that it may not indirectly accomplish those ends by taxing and spending to purchase compliance." [16] The Court gave many illustrations to show how the principle of the AAA could be used to purchase compliance with federal regulations in every sphere which was reserved by the Constitution to the states. The general-welfare clause of the Constitution could not be intended to permit the federal government to destroy all the powers of the states, which the Constitution itself guaranteed, and to become an unlimited central government.

Justices Brandeis, Cardozo, and Stone dissented. The latter affirmed that the Court was concerned only with the power of Congress to enact statutes, not with their wisdom, but he implied that the AAA was being invalidated because the majority of the justices thought it unwise. He asked for self-restraint by the Court, because, unlike the legislative and executive branches, there was no other check on the Court's exercise of power. The power of Congress to lay an excise tax on the processing of agricultural products had not been denied, nor did the decision of the majority declare that the expenditure of public money to aid farmers was outside the power of Congress to provide for the general welfare. The majority had attempted to show that the tax and the expenditure were invalid because they "purchased" compliance with a regulation of agriculture which invaded the powers of the states by pointing out how all state powers might similarly be invaded. Justice Stone declared that the same rigid application of the majority decision would lead to even more absurd consequences:

The government may give money to the unemployed, but may not ask that those who get it shall give labor in return, or even use it to support their families. It may give money to sufferers from earthquake, fire, tornado, pestilence or flood, but may not impose conditions—health precautions designed to prevent the spread of disease, or induce the movement of population to safer or more sanitary areas. All that, because it is purchased regulation infringing state powers, must be left for the states, who are unable or unwilling to supply the necessary relief. The government . . . . may appropriate moneys to be expended by the Reconstruction Finance Corporation "to aid in financing agriculture, commerce and industry," and to facilitate "the exportation of agricultural and other products." Do all its activities collapse because, in order to effect the permissible purpose, in myriad ways the money is paid out upon terms and conditions which influence action of the recipients within the states, which Congress cannot command? The answer would seem plain. . . . If appropriation in aid of a program of curtailment of agricultural production is constitutional, and it is not denied that it is, payment to farmers on condition that they reduce their crop acreage is constitutional.[17]

Justice Stone called the decision of the majority "a tortured construction of the Constitution" based on suppositions "addressed to the mind accustomed to believe that it is the business of courts to sit in judgment on the wisdom of legislative action," and pleaded that "language, even of a constitution, may mean what it says: that the power to tax and spend includes the power to relieve a nationwide economic maladjustment by conditional gifts of money." [18]

The argument in favor of the constitutionality of the AAA seemed as convincing as its opposite, and many concluded that only the "accident" which placed a majority of justices who held conservative economic and political views on the bench at the moment decided the issue.

The invalidation of the AAA on January 6, 1936, faced the administration with a chaotic situation. Payments to farmers under contract were stopped, until Congress made special appropriations to complete payments to farmers who had complied with their contracts. On January 13, the Supreme Court ordered that $200,000,000 of taxes which had been collected from processors be returned to them. Secretary Wallace called this a "legalized steal" because processors had already passed on the taxes to purchasers of their products. The status of loans on cotton and corn crops which had been made by the RFC on the assumption that the borrowers would comply with acreage control was in doubt. More broadly, the end of acreage control threatened to revive surpluses and ruin farm prices.

The President quickly reassured farmers that equality for agriculture remained a dominant policy of the administration. Secretary Wallace called a conference of farm leaders from all over the country, and they expressed a revived interest in various schemes to subsidize exports of surpluses. At a press conference on January 10, the President had objected to such schemes because they would encourage the expansion of farming operations on marginal land, particularly in the Dust Bowl, when soil conservation, the turning back to pasture and forest and soil-building crops of depleted and eroding land was the basic need of agriculture. He did not say whether unwillingness to dump American produce on foreign markets and consequent intensification of the world movement towards economic nationalism also made him object to export subsidies, but he declared that the quota system which many countries were already using to restrict their imports of American farm products would make a subsidy program impracticable.

A week later the President told the press that the Soil Conservation Act of 1935, which had seemed of minor importance when it was passed, might be broadened by amendment to make possible the limitation of agricultural production by payments to farmers in return for soil conservation activities of many kinds. The prevention of erosion required interstate control, and had long been accepted as within the power of the federal government. If the Soil Conservation Act was amended to include the power to stop depletion of soil by failure to rotate crops as a contributory factor in erosion, the results sought for by the AAA might be achieved. Not contracts to limit production, but leases to the government of land which the farmer thereupon could not use for soil-depleting crops, would be the chief technique of the new system. Under the AAA, soil conservation had been a secondary object while prevention of surpluses in order to raise farm prices had been the primary object: now their positions would be reversed.

This program was approved by farm leaders. Unexpected support came from ex-President Hoover, who advocated the scheme with the proviso that it be administered by the land-grant colleges of the states in order to prevent the growth of bureaucracy. The Bill which took shape in Congress provided for initial administration by the Soil Conservation Service of the Department of Agriculture, and transfer of administration to the states by a gradual process which was to be complete by January 1, 1938. Recognition of the one-sided benefits of AAA appeared in provisions that tenants and sharecroppers should receive a proportion of the new payments to landowners.

The Soil Conservation and Domestic Allotment Act passed Congress by large majorities and was signed on March 1, 1936. By rapid organization in every county of farmers who elected administrative leaders and decided on the soil conserving measures which should be undertaken in their neighborhood, the program was put into effect in time to bring the 1936 crops under control. The individual farmer who agreed to coöperate with the program undertook to practice various methods of plowing and cultivation which would check erosion, to substitute grasses and legumes for soil-depleting crops such as cotton, tobacco, corn, and wheat, and to practice soil-building with chemical fertilizers and in other ways. In return he received compensation out of the general funds of the Treasury for labor to check erosion which aided the national program or for the lease of land to the government. The increasing public awareness of the problems of farmers of the Dust Bowl, and, just as the law was being passed, a series of great floods in the New England states, Pennsylvania, New York, and the Ohio valley, enlarged public support for the new Act. It was still subject to the criticism that it represented a policy of economic scarcity, but in 1938 this criticism was largely met by the second Agricultural Adjustment Act. The invalidation of the first AAA, like that of the NIRA, had little influence on the long-range evolution of the administration's policies. The "legalized steal" of the processing taxes was compensated for by a new tax on processors. The net result of the AAA decision was not the abolition of acreage control but the new soil-conserving efforts which the government obtained in return for the benefits paid to farmers. The aims of raising the prices of farm products and the purchasing power of farmers were expressly stated in the Soil Conservation and Domestic Allotment Act. The Court's decision might be said to have caused an expansion rather than an abandonment of the administration's agricultural program.

The administration won a limited victory on February 17, 1936, when the Supreme Court found constitutional the power granted to the TVA to sell electric power to local distributors in competition with private utility companies. Only Justice McReynolds dissented. The majority found that production of electricity was an incident of the defense and navigation functions of the TVA dams, and denied that the government could be restricted in its right to dispose of its property. Justice McReynolds dissented, arguing that sale of electricity and competition with private companies were primary aims of the TVA, and that its purchase of transmission lines was therefore illegal. Further issues were not touched upon in the case.[19] The administration could call the decision a victory, but opponents of TVA were not deterred from undertaking tests of its constitutionality on other grounds.

A severe blow to the administration came with the Court's voiding of the Guffey-Snyder Bituminous Coal Stabilization Act on May 18. In different parts of the decision the Court divided six to three and five to four, because Chief Justice Hughes joined the liberal minority on some points. The majority declared that the tax which was almost wholly refunded to producers who complied with the Bituminous Coal Code was not a tax but a penalty to coerce submission to regulations of wages, hours, working conditions, and the guaranty of collective bargaining. These regulations could not be justified under the general welfare power, because the latter was limited by the Constitution to the power to tax to promote the general welfare, and this tax was not a true tax. Nor could the regulations be justified under the federal power to regulate interstate commerce, since the effect on interstate commerce of working conditions in the mines was only indirect. The authority given to majorities of the miners and owners in particular districts to fix conditions of labor and trade for their entire districts was an unwarranted delegation of legislative authority, and furthermore violated the due process clause. The doctrines of narrow interpretation which had appeared in earlier decisions, especially the invalidation of NIRA, were repeated in stronger terms.

But the NIRA decision had been unanimous, and now a strong minority of the justices declared, in effect, that the Guffey Act had fairly eliminated the unconstitutional features of NIRA. Standards fixed by Congress in the new law were found to be at least as rigid as those found in other laws which had been upheld, so that the charge of undue delegation of legislative power was denied. Interstate commerce was directly affected by the price and labor conditions under which coal was mined. Due process of law had been observed, inasmuch as "an evil existing, and also the power to correct it, the lawmakers were at liberty to use their own discretion in the selection of the means." [20] The tax was termed a penalty which was justified by the necessity to secure submission to a constitutional statute.

The Guffey Act was not re-enacted until 1937 after the shift of Justice Roberts had transformed the liberal minority of justices into a majority. In the meantime, the invalidation of the Act increased doubts as to the constitutionality of the Wagner Labor Relations Act. A committee of lawyers of the Liberty League assured employers that the Act was invalid and might be disobeyed without fear of the penalties which were attached to it. A federal wages and hours law seemed impossible under the new decision of the Court. The immediate consequences in the soft coal fields were drastic. The conditions were restored which had led the administration to advocate price-fixing even after it had turned against that policy for industry as a whole. The widespread practice of illegal mining by "poachers" made it virtually impossible for mine owners to pay wages above the starvation level.

The Guffey Act decision seemed to leave open the possibility that at least the states had the power to regulate the wages of labor. But this assumption was proven to be groundless on June 1 by the last of the great series of decisions unfavorable to the administration. New York State had passed a minimum wage law for women and children in 1933, which required that a commissioner and board fix minimum rates to meet the minimum cost of living necessary for health and that the rates be not less than the reasonable value of services rendered. In 1923, the Supreme Court had declared unconstitutional under the due process clause of the Fourteenth Amendment a District of Columbia law which had provided that women's wages be fixed to meet the minimum cost of living without consideration for the factors of health or the value of services rendered. In the New York law, the latter clause was intended to protect employers from violation of due process, and the health clause was intended to bring the law into a sphere which was indubitably within the power of the states.

The owner of a laundry refused to pay the minimum wage which the board fixed for women in his industry. He won his case before the highest New York court, but the federal Supreme Court accepted an appeal by the state government. Many other states which had similar laws aided in the argument and filed briefs in support of the New York law, while employers' associations filed briefs against it. The Supreme Court voted five to four against the constitutionality of the New York law. Justice Butler for the majority found that the law was not distinguishable from the District of Columbia statute. Fixing the minimum wages of women deprived them of their freedom to make contracts which had been guaranteed to them by the Fourteenth Amendment in its declaration that a state may not deprive a person of life, liberty, or property without due process of law. The "state is without power by any form of legislation to prohibit, change, or nullify contracts between employers and adult women workers as to the amount of wages to be paid." [21]

Justice Stone for himself and Justices Brandeis and Cardozo, and Chief Justice Hughes both wrote dissenting opinions. The latter pointed out the elaborate and fair procedural methods required by the law in order to guarantee that no employer should be at a competitive disadvantage in paying minimum wages, and he found the necessities of due process thereby fulfilled. He declared that many women, and children as a class, were not on a level of equality in bargaining with their employers. Freedom of contract in their relations with employers was illusory. Wages insufficient to support life caused many women employees to be placed on public relief rolls as a burden to all taxpayers while they were working for a private employer and should be supported by just payment for their labor. "We have repeatedly said that liberty of contract is a qualified and not an absolute right." [22] The Court had upheld many restrictions on the freedom of contract. The power of the state specially to protect women was one of the outstanding traditions of legal history. Nothing unreasonable appeared in the New York law. The Chief Justice cited the famous criterion of his great predecessor, John Marshall: "The end is legitimate and the means appropriate. I think that the act should be upheld." [23]

Justice Stone stated that he agreed with all that the Chief Justice had said, but that he was unwilling to support even the invalidation of the District of Columbia law:

There is grim irony in speaking of the freedom of contract of those who, because of their economic necessities, give their services for less than is needful to keep body and soul together. But if this is freedom of contract no one has ever denied that it is freedom which may be restrained, notwithstanding the Fourteenth Amendment, by a statute passed in the public interest.[24]

He emphasized that low wages of women had been demonstrated to produce ill health, immorality, and deterioration of the race. Congress, seventeen states, and twenty-one foreign countries including Great Britain and four commonwealths had enacted minimum-wage regulations, and this precluded for him any assumption that it was a remedy beyond the bounds of reason. Then Justice Stone gave the authority of three justices to the charge which had become common in public debate on the Supreme Court:

It is difficult to imagine any grounds, other than *our own personal economic predilections*, for saying that the contract of employment is any the less an appropriate subject of legislation than are scores of others, in dealing with which this Court has held that legislatures may curtail individual freedom in the public interest.[25]

And a remarkable justification of the New Deal was offered:

In the years which have intervened since the [District of Columbia minimum-wage] case we have had opportunity to learn that a wage is not always the resultant of free bargaining between employers and employees; that it may be one forced upon employees by their economic necessities and upon employers by the most ruthless of their competitors. We have had opportunity to perceive more clearly that a wage insufficient to support the worker does not visit its consequences upon him alone; that it may affect profoundly the entire economic structure of society and, in any case, that it casts on every taxpayer, and on government itself, the burden of solving the problems of poverty, subsistence, health, and morals of large numbers in the community. Because of their nature and extent these are public problems. A generation ago they were for the individual to solve; today they are the burden of the nation.[26]

Such an opinion as Justice Stone's gave laymen to believe that they might understand the meaning of Supreme Court decisions without being versed in the metaphysics of the law. Those who believed in the aims of the New Deal, and others who could be objective, seemed to be relieved of any obligation to accept the opinion of the majority of the Court that the invalidated law was necessarily unconstitutional, or that the program of the administration was likely to undermine American institutions. And if evidence were desired that somehow justice had gone astray, common sense could supply it: the Fourteenth Amendment had been passed ostensibly to protect the newly-emancipated Negroes of the South from oppressive state laws; the due-process clause had originated as a protection of citizens against arbitrary judicial process; to use this Amendment and this clause to "protect" exploited women against an "oppressive" law which would raise their wages and abolish sweatshop competition among employers was indeed ironic, for it turned weapons which had been forged against oppression into the instruments of oppression. If the Court could no longer rely upon the accustomed respect of citizens for the judicial quality and justice of its decisions, common sense and the authority of dissenting justices seemed to be responsible.

The President in a press conference on June 2 carefully confined himself to the request that everyone should read "all three" opinions of the Court, and a factual description of the situation:

The President: It seems to be fairly clear, as a result of this decision and former decisions, using this question of minimum wage as an example, that the "no-man's-land" where no Government—State or Federal—can function is being more clearly defined. A State cannot do it, and the Federal Government cannot do it. I think, from the layman's point of view, that is the easiest way of putting it and about all we can say on it.
Q. How can you meet that situation?
The President: I think that is about all there is to say on it. . . .
Q. I think there are dangers in the existence of that "no-man's-land."
The President: I think that is all there is to say about it. . . .[27]

The invalidations by the Supreme Court of the Guffey-Snyder Bituminous Coal Stabilization Act and New York Minimum Wage Act precipitated the greatest crisis of the Roosevelt administration. Selective re-enactment of the other laws which the Court had voided made those decisions possibly an aid and certainly no hindrance to the construction of the Second New Deal. But no similar "way out" presented itself in the terms under which federal and state labor regulations had been declared unconstitutional. And the central measures of the Second New Deal, the Wagner Labor Relations Act and the Social Security Act, seemed equally vulnerable and incapable of substitution.

Before the President had more "to say" on the dangers of the constitutional "no-man's-land," he would ask the people for a ratification of the Second New Deal.

CHAPTER XII

THE GREAT LANDSLIDE: 1936

As the administration entered the election year of 1936, its greatest asset was that it could claim it was achieving the degree and kind of prosperity which had been its chief aims. Employment by private industry was increasing, and the full scope of the problem of a permanent surplus of labor had not yet been revealed: in 1936, the solution of unemployment by continued expansion of private industry seemed to be a reasonable expectation. "We are on our way," and "we planned it that way," were apt slogans for the campaign.

The President had promised that his method would be experimental. The first body of policies had met with significant failures as well as some success. With a flexibility which was perhaps the most outstanding characteristic of the administration, it substituted for the first policies another group which was producing the great desideratum: a widely distributed prosperity. The banking system had been first saved and then reformed. After the devaluation of the dollar and the rebuff to the London Economic Conference, the value of the dollar had been stabilized, and in September, 1936, international stabilization of currencies was achieved. Expansion of credit by loans of federal funds, especially to farm and home owners, and by other methods had halted deflation and saved the creditor class; but the low-interest rate on federal loans and its effect of lowering the interest rates charged by private lenders, besides rising prices and wages and other inflationary developments, greatly benefited the debtor class. Relief and public works programs had at first been continued with the FERA and PWA on the basis of the Hoover policies. After the intermediate experiment with the CWA, an entirely new policy of security for the unemployed and priming the pump of industry by increasing purchasing power had been established by means of the WPA and the Social Security Act. Tariffs were being lowered by a series of reciprocity agreements after plans to raise them still higher had been abandoned. The program of economy in government had been carried out until Congress overruled the administration, and deficits incurred for the relief of unemployment were at first smaller than the Hoover deficits but mounted rapidly with the expansion of work relief. The growth of administrative agencies absorbed the increased revenues which came with recovery, but the Wealth Tax Act and undistributed profits tax of 1936 shifted more of the burden of taxation to wealthier groups. Acreage control and soil conservation were used to raise farm prices. When injuries to small farmers, tenants, sharecroppers, and migrants became apparent, the first steps were taken towards special aid and protection for these groups. Labor, whose ambition to achieve the full promise of NIRA had for a time been discouraged by the administration in favor of appeasement of business, began with the passage of the Wagner Labor Relations Act and the Social Security Act to receive the whole-hearted support of the administration in acquiring long-deferred rights and privileges. Business had at first been granted immunity from the antitrust laws and government support in establishing the codes of fair-trade practices originated by the trade associations. It had lost the confidence of the administration by pursuing monopolistic objectives, and refusing to carry out the labor provisions of Section 7A in ways which would produce sound economic recovery based on widely distributed prosperity. Then it lost the codes themselves at the hands of the Supreme Court, and the administration did not restore more than three of them out of six hundred. At the same time, reforms of specific business practices, such as the SEC and the Public Utility Holding Company Act, which had been begun during the period of the First New Deal, were multiplied during the later period.

By 1936, the administration had virtually abandoned its initial program of carrying out plans which were formulated by all three of the major interest groups in the nation, business, farmers, and labor, and of making each of these groups the direct beneficiary of government action to help it improve its status. Business had in effect been dropped from the coalition. It was expected henceforth to benefit from government action only indirectly as a result of a vast expansion of government action directly beneficial to labor and farmers. The government's direct relations with business were now almost wholly regulative and were intended to restrict the untrammeled pursuit of profits insofar as it conflicted with the general welfare.

The stage was set for an electoral campaign which would be fought largely on class lines and with the bitterness that such conflict engendered.

The President's Annual Message of January 3, 1936, announced the theme of his campaign for re-election. The more harmonious relations among the republics of the Western hemisphere, which were being developed under the Good Neighbor policy, were contrasted with the growth of autocracy and aggression in the rest of the world. Amelioration was being offered to the world by the United States:

In the field of commerce we have undertaken to encourage a more reasonable interchange of the world's goods. In the field of international finance we have, so far as we are concerned, put an end to dollar diplomacy, to money grabbing, to speculation for the benefit of the powerful and the rich, at the expense of the small and the poor.

The struggle for peace in foreign affairs was identified with the struggle for the New Deal at home:

> Peace is jeopardized by the few and not by the many. Peace is threatened by those who seek selfish power. . . .
> The evidence before us clearly proves that autocracy in world affairs endangers peace and that such threats do not spring from those Nations devoted to the democratic ideal. If this be true in world affairs, it should have the greatest weight in the determination of domestic policies.
> Within democratic Nations the chief concern of the people is to prevent the continuance or the rise of autocratic institutions that beget slavery at home and aggression abroad. Within our borders, as in the world at large, popular opinion is at war with a power-seeking minority.

The forces which produced fascism abroad were identified with the big-business opponents of the New Deal. A small but powerful minority of financial and industrial groups had dominated the government under the Republican administrations, and had abdicated in 1933, "but now with the passing of danger they forget their damaging admissions and withdraw their abdication. . . . They steal the livery of great national constitutional ideals to serve discredited special interests"; they carry the property interests entrusted to them into partisan politics; they control business associations; "they engage in vast propaganda to spread fear and discord among the people—they would 'gang up' against the people's liberties."

The principle of government of this group is shown by its members' principles in their own affairs: "autocracy toward labor, toward stockholders, toward consumers, toward public sentiment." If they believe that the New Deal has hindered recovery, let them propose the repeal of specific laws which have been passed, "let them no longer hide their dissent in a cowardly cloak of generality." They threaten something more menacing than a return to the past. "Our resplendent economic autocracy does not want to return to that individualism of which they prate," but to gain control of the new instruments of public power which are wholesome and proper only in the hands of "a people's Government":

In the hands of political puppets of an economic autocracy such power would provide shackles for the liberties of the people. Give them their way and they will take the course of every autocracy of the past—power for themselves, enslavement for the public.[1]

The message proposed no new legislation. It promised that no further tax increases would be necessary and that relief appropriations would be reduced for the next fiscal year. The election campaign was to be conducted as a defense of laws already enacted, and an appeal for approval of their general principles and philosophy, with a promise that during a second term in office the administration would further instrument those principles.

Much of the legislative product of 1936 was not planned for by the administration. The Soil Conservation and Domestic Allotment Act was substituted for the AAA. A law for immediate payment of the soldiers' bonus, the Adjusted Payment Compensation Act, was passed once more, and repassed over the President's veto on January 24. The law was less inflationary than that of the previous year, since it required payment not in unsecured greenbacks, but in negotiable, nine-year, interest-bearing bonds. The President's veto had reminded Congress of the terms of his personal appeal in

1935, but to no avail. After the law passed, he made an effort to convince veterans that they should hold their bonds, or use them only for constructive purposes.

The invalidation of the processing taxes of the AAA, the costs of the new Soil Conservation and Domestic Allotment Act, and of the soldiers' bonus made new revenue necessary in spite of the promise of no new taxes in 1936. The President decided to ask Congress on March 3 to prevent the regular budget (exclusive of relief expenditures) from becoming unbalanced by the unforeseen expenses. He proposed that temporary and recurrent taxes totaling slightly over one billion dollars be levied, and that not merely revenue but tax reform be the object of the legislation. The failure of many larger corporations to distribute their profits as dividends was providing wealthy stockholders with a means of avoiding the payment of surtaxes on their private incomes. A steeply graduated tax on undistributed profits, and repeal of the existing income tax on corporations would benefit small businesses and those whose ownership was widely distributed, because such companies ordinarily distributed their profits anyway, and would make tax avoidance by large, close-held corporations and their owners more difficult. A special "windfall tax" was also proposed, to compel those companies which had shifted the AAA processing taxes to consumers and then recovered them from the government under the Supreme Court's ruling, to give them up as "unjust enrichment." [2]

On June 22 an act was signed which substantially followed the President's suggestions. The undistributed profits tax was graduated from nothing for a business which distributed all its earnings to 42.5 per cent on corporations which failed to distribute 57.5 per cent of its profits. The new law was an extension of the principles of the Wealth Tax Act of 1935 inasmuch as it gave further relief to small enterprises, and

228]

increased the rates on large corporations unless they distributed their profits, in which case they were taxed according to the still more steeply graduated personal-income rates of the earlier law. The new law aroused the anger of businessmen, who regarded it as a punitive measure which penalized the building up of corporation surpluses for purposes of expansion or protection against hard times. On the other hand, bank credit at low interest and investment capital were becoming plentiful, and it was pointed out that these conditions were extremely favorable to business expansion. Nevertheless, the failure of business to take sufficient advantage of these conditions was attributed by businessmen to the reduction of personal incentive to take risks as a result of high personal-income taxes and the new restrictions and regulations which had been imposed on business. Many authorities believed that expansion of investment was the most important problem which the administration failed to solve.

Another indication of the administration's desire to strengthen small business was the Price Discrimination Act of June 20. This law was designed to reduce the advantages in price which chain stores often received from producers by large-quantity purchases. These advantages made it difficult for owners of one or a few stores to meet the competition of the chains and remain in business. The rapid growth of a few great retail-chain corporations and the elimination of many small businessmen had caused a wave of punitive state tax laws against the former. Under the new federal law, price discrimination which was found by the Federal Trade Commission to support monopoly, reduce competition, and involve interstate commerce was to be abolished by the Commission directing that the quantity on which the lower price was charged be reduced, so as to give the small retailer equal competitive opportunity.

Other problems of monopoly were made difficult by the

administration's desire that competition should not be at the expense of labor or discourage increased production. In March, the President announced to businessmen that the antitrust laws, which were directed only at combinations in restraint of trade, did not prevent coöperation within industries to increase production and employment.[3] But price-fixing and production-limitation, which had been tolerated for a time under NIRA, were vigorously attacked by the President during the election campaign. Progressive Republicans also attacked monopoly, and charged that the administration's policies were favorable to it. A small beginning was made towards an anti-monopoly campaign when, in June, the President ordered the first antitrust prosecution of his administration. A suit was directed against the steel industry, in which price-fixing among nominal competitors was traditional. A general campaign against monopolies was not begun until 1938.

The spring floods of 1936 led Congress to pass several acts to improve control of rivers, but little new work was done for lack of appropriations. The President supported the Wagner Housing Act for slum clearance. It passed only the House during this session. Several minor laws in favor of labor were passed the significance of which was the diligence of the administration in finding methods to support labor which had been left open by the decisions of the Supreme Court. The Walsh-Healy Government Contracts Act established minimum wages, maximum hours, favorable working conditions, and prohibited child labor in industries which were working on contracts for the government. The effect of the law was to revive the labor provisions of NRA codes for a limited group of companies. The Strike-breaker Act prohibited the interstate transportation of persons to interfere with labor stoppages. The recruiting of thugs in large cities by professional agencies which shipped them to employers for purposes of breaking picket lines and otherwise intensifying industrial strife had become "big business," and the law was intended to reduce its scale if not abolish it. The Merchant Marine Act prevented the use of foreign labor to maintain low labor standards for seamen. It required that at least three-fourths of all ships' crews be American citizens, and prescribed hours and conditions of work. The administration did not support the general wages and hours bill which was once more introduced in Congress, whether because it was still unwilling to support so "extreme" a measure, or because the Supreme Court had blocked the way. But during the campaign the President approved the principle of such a law.

The paucity of important new legislation in 1936 was the more striking when it was compared with the projects which were maintained in the stage of preliminary investigation and presented to Congress only in 1937. The "emergency" character of the administration's program disappeared in 1936 with the achievement of recovery. In the activities of the election campaign as well as in Congress, the opportunity was used for stock-taking, formulation of principles, and planning of future action.

In this mood the President made three addresses prior to the Democratic Convention on themes which defined his candidacy for renomination: "New Approaches to Old Problems," "The Period of Social Pioneering Is Only at Its Beginning," and "Nationwide Thinking, Nationwide Planning, and Nationwide Action Are the Three Great Essentials to Prevent Nationwide Crises." These addresses did not sustain the note of defiance of "economic autocracy" which had been sounded in the Annual Message. A series of addresses made on a tour in June to the Texas Centennial Exposition renewed the attack on big business.

No important rival aspirants for the Democratic nomination appeared. The President and Vice President Garner were renominated on June 27 at the Convention in Philadelphia by acclamation. Conservative Democrats, among whom Alfred E. Smith was conspicuous, sent a letter to the Convention urging repudiation of the President and the New Deal, but it was not read to the delegates. Practical unanimity on nominees such as had not occurred at a Democratic convention for generations made possible the substitution of a simple majority for the two-thirds rule. The significance of the change was that the solid South lost its determining voice in the making of Party nominations. The growing conservatism of Southern Democratic leaders was being evidenced by the formation of the Southern Committee to Uphold the Constitution, with a program like that of the Liberty League, and led by Governor Talmadge of Georgia and a group of dissidents of the deep South; but the abolition of the two-thirds rule made the South less important in future struggles among the sections over the naming of national candidates and the formulation of the national platform. A concession to the Southern wing of the Party was made by a promise that the size of state delegations in conventions would be reapportioned on the basis of Democratic votes cast in future elections. But the main seat of the South's power was in future to be in Congress, where the growing willingness of Southern Democratic conservatives to vote with Republicans against the administration gave the South decisive influence.

The platform adopted by the Philadelphia Convention chiefly pointed with pride at the record of the administration. The "self-evident truths" were laid down that the test of representative government was its promotion of the safety and happiness of the people, that Republican rule had impaired them, and that the administration had put the nation back on the road to health and prosperity by humanizing the policies of the government. It would continue to rid the land of kidnapers, bandits, and malefactors of great wealth who defrauded and exploited the people. The policies of the Second New Deal, rather than the First, were emphasized as those which had been successful and would be further developed. Monopolies and economic power concentrated in the hands of the few were still the masters of the producer and the enemies of the consumer. They, and drought, hours and wages, child labor, and many problems could not be handled by forty-eight separate actions by the states, and if they "cannot be effectively solved by legislation within the Constitution, we shall seek such clarifying amendment as will assure to the legislatures of the several States and the Congress of the United States, each within its proper jurisdiction, the power to enact those laws. . . ." [4] An obvious strategy would have been to make a constitutional amendment the main issue of the campaign, as the adverse decisions of the Supreme Court were the main obstacle to the completion of the administration's program. But it was subject to many objections: it raised abstract and difficult questions of constitutional law, not easy to bring to life for the electorate; it would concentrate attention on mechanical means rather than concrete ends; the general disagreement as to what the contents of such an amendment should be, and even whether an amendment was necessary or the best means of breaking the "judicial blockade," would turn debate into fruitless channels; and, most important of all, the President and his administration and policies, not the Supreme Court or the Constitution, were on the ballot for the voters' decision. The plan of the Judiciary Reorganization Bill which the President sent to Congress in 1937 had not been formulated before the November election. In the meantime, the Court issue was kept in abeyance with generalized assurances that it would somehow be resolved.

In his address accepting renomination the President made his famous attack on "economic royalists":

The royalists of the economic order have conceded that political freedom was the business of the Government, but they have maintained that economic slavery was nobody's business. They granted that the Government could protect the citizen in his right to vote, but they denied that the Government could do anything to protect the citizen in his right to work and his right to live. . . .

These economic royalists complain that we seek to overthrow the institutions of America. What they really complain of is that we seek to take away their power. . . . In their blindness they forget what the Flag and the Constitution stand for. Now, as always, they stand for democracy, not tyranny; for freedom, not subjection; and against a dictatorship by mob rule and the overprivileged alike. . . .

Governments can err, Presidents do make mistakes, but the immortal Dante tells us that divine justice weighs the sins of the cold-blooded and the sins of the warm-hearted in different scales. . . .

There is a mysterious cycle in human events. . . . This generation of Americans has a rendezvous with destiny.

In this world of ours, in other lands, there are some people, who, in times past, have lived and fought for freedom, and seem to have grown too weary to carry on the fight. . . .

I believe in my heart that only our success can stir their ancient hope. They begin to know that here in America we are waging . . . a war for the survival of democracy. . . .

I accept the commission you have tendered me. I join with you. I am enlisted for the duration of the war.[5]

Several possible strategies were open to the Republican Party in 1936. The support of big business and conservatives was assured. In the latter group might be included a substantial proportion of small business and middle-class groups and smaller percentages of farmers and laborers. Since 1932, the Republicans had probably lost strength among farmers and laborers which was not compensated in numbers of votes by the greater unity of wealthier groups. If a worse defeat than that of 1932 were to be avoided, it would be necessary to win Western farmers and Eastern laborers away from the administration. Progressive Republicans, chiefly from the farm states, worked to impose such a strategy on the Party. They intended to offer to farmers and workers a program which should recognize and meet their needs, and include strong planks in opposition to industrial and financial monopoly. Their candidate for the Presidential nomination was Senator Borah of Idaho. During the months before the Convention, he made a number of addresses which attacked monopoly, accused the New Deal of furthering the concentration of economic power in the hands of the few, and advocated reforms which differed from those of the administration only in greater emphasis upon the needs of farmers rather than laborers. His candidacy had many characteristics in common with that of Theodore Roosevelt in 1904 and 1912, but, unlike Roosevelt in 1904, Borah failed to win the support of conservative Eastern Republicans.

A second strategy called for opposition to the New Deal looking toward repeal of all its more original measures, and defense of the policies of previous Republican administrations with a view to their revival. Ex-President Hoover and Senator Vandenburg of Michigan were the leading candidates in advocacy of such a program. It was thoroughly supported by the attitudes of businessmen to the experiments of the New Deal and their desire for a return to the friendly coöperation between business and government which prevailed during the twenties. The weakness of this strategy was its abdication of leadership of progressive voters, especially farmers and workers, practically none of whose responsible leaders raised a voice in praise of "the good old days." Western Progressive Republicans would undoubtedly repeat their support of the Democratic candidate rather than submit to the exclusive control of the Republican Party by conservatives. In 1932, the distinctions between the Hoover policies and those of the Democratic candidate were less apparent than in 1936. The evolution of the New Deal away from the partial continuation of Hoover policies during the first period, and towards policies thoroughly opposed by big business, reduced the problematical aspects of another race between the same, or similar, candidates and ensured an even more severe defeat for a conservative Republican candidate in 1936 than in 1932. The ex-President's desire for the nomination could be respected as the natural wish of a sincere, able, and unfortunate leader to justify and retrieve his failures, but the inexorable fact that an awakened and critical electorate would not accept policies which fulfilled the demands of only one major sectional-class interest group caused the practical politicians of the Republican Party to deny Hoover or Vandenburg the nomination and businessmen their hopes for the immediate destruction of the New Deal.

The third strategy was that of compromise. It called for a candidate and a program which should be, in the terminology of earlier Republican inner-party struggles, neither "mugwump" nor "stalwart," but "half-breed." Promises of policies favorable to farmers and workers and restrictive of abuses of big business, and certainly no threat to repeal outright the New Deal, coupled with an aggressive attack upon the mistakes, inefficiencies, improvidence, and dangerous constitutional tendencies of the administration which would justify alterations of its policies, could win the support of wider groups of the population than those attached to a narrowly pro-business program without sacrificing the support of conservatives and businessmen themselves. Such a program could hold Progressive Republicans in line and win farm states, and at the same time split the labor vote to bring over its more conservative groups and join them to middle-class and business groups in order to win majorities in Eastern states. Conservative Democrats led by Alfred E. Smith would be brought still closer to the Republican Party without unduly antagonizing the followers of Borah. Strong emphasis on states' rights, the natural constitutional doctrine of opposition to the New Deal, might even win the support of dissident "Jeffersonian" Democrats and break the solid South.

A candidate who was closely identified with neither the conservative nor the progressive wing of the Party—a "half-breed"—would be the obvious choice for a leader to carry out this strategy. William Randolph Hearst had abandoned his support of the administration in 1934 when most men of great wealth began to find that its reforms outweighed its initial support of the business program for recovery. He was said to be particularly opposed to the prospect that his newspaper employees would become strongly organized for collective bargaining, and the administration's policy of collective security in foreign affairs seemed to him a betrayal of its promise not to advocate joining the League of Nations. Early in the 1936 political season, Hearst made a visit of inspection to Governor Alfred Mossman Landon of Kansas, and presently his chain of newspapers began aggressively to support the Governor for the Republican nomination. Landon's program of economy in governmental expenditure, and successful balancing of the state budget were presented as the most specific proof of his qualification for the Presidency. His duplication of the principles and virtues of President Coolidge were dwelt upon to suggest that the halcyon days prior to the crash of 1929 could be revived by appropriate federal policies.

This was the first notice given to the country as a whole of the availability of Governor Landon. From the point of view of Republican strategists, Landon was a businessman associated with the oil industry who was at the same time identified with a great farm state, so that he might be made attractive to farmers without risking the "irresponsibility" towards business of a Borah. He had supported the Bull Moose campaign of Theodore Roosevelt in 1912, which would appeal to liberals. He was not identified with the adamant opposition to the New Deal, but, on the other hand, he had shown little interest in the progressive legislation which Western governors usually advocated. It would hardly be expected that he would refuse the guidance of the leaders of his Party if they gave him the nomination. The colorless personality of the Governor and his vagueness on issues other than economy were for a time admired as proof of his simple common sense and homespun American virtues.

The Landon "boom" which had been inaugurated by the Hearst press made headway steadily until he was nominated with little opposition early in June at the Cleveland Convention of the Republican Party. Frank Knox, the owner and editor of the Chicago *Daily News*, and a former Progressive who had become a strong opponent of the New Deal, was nominated for Vice President. Throughout the campaign the aggressive personalities of Knox and of John Hamilton, Chairman of the Republican National Committee, tended to overshadow the Republican Presidential nominee.

The Republican Platform listed grievances against the administration after the model of the Declaration of Independence. "America is in peril" were the first words. For three years, the traditions of the nation and the Constitution had been ignored, a dictatorial bureaucracy had been established, and waste, extravagance, and appeals to class prejudice had ruled the administration. A more limited sphere of government activity was advocated. But the indictments of almost no New Deal policies went so far as to advocate repeal of laws which had been passed. In fact, government regulation of business enterprise, including the new fields of public utilities and securities, was supported, and only a limitation of the powers of regulative agencies was advocated. The agricultural program of the New Deal was approved with the statement that it was made up of Republican policies, which, however, the administration "misuses . . . to serve partisan ends." [6] Reciprocity tariff policy was condemned, but a promise to adjust import duties prevented accusation of unmitigated high protectionism.

Most extraordinary was the pledge to "protect the rights of labor to organize and to bargain collectively through representatives of its own choosing without interference from any source." [7] This was a concession to labor, inasmuch as it endorsed the clauses of the Wagner Labor Relations Act which outlawed employer-dominated company unions, and at the same time an assurance to businessmen that if they could not control labor unions, neither could independent unions continue the current campaign to organize the workers in the mass-production industries in the manner of the CIO. Further concessions to labor were advocacy of state laws and interstate compacts to abolish sweatshops and child labor, and to establish hours-and-wages rules for women and children. How the latter could be carried out in the face of the Supreme Court's invalidation of the New York Minimum Wage Act was not made clear. The return of unemployment relief activities to the states suggested that the WPA should be abolished, but a public works program for emergency employment was advocated, and the attitude on WPA remained ambiguous. The purposes of the Social Security Act were approved, while it was hinted that to defray its cost a sales tax should be substituted for taxes on both employers and employees. A balanced budget was advocated by the Republican no less than the Democratic Platform, and neither one could very well point with pride at its record in this respect. The Republican suggestion that tax revision should end the principles of the Wealth Tax Act of 1935 and the Undistributed Profits Tax Act of 1936 was the most important specific promise to repeal New Deal legislation and the most unequivocal plank in support of private wealth and big business. A statement on the gold content of the dollar might or might not mean that a Republican administration would revaluate the dollar or re-establish the full functions of the gold standard. In the field of foreign affairs the Republican Platform was slightly more isolationist in tone and more opposed to collective security than the Democratic Platform.

Greatest stress throughout the Republican document was placed upon extravagance and expansion of federal authority as requiring correction by a change of administration. But the promises of economy and devolution of federal power were not supported by substantial explanations of what expenditures and federal agencies would be abolished. On the other hand, many general and ambiguous statements could be interpreted to mean in their totality the abolition of the New Deal. It was in the latter sense that the Platform was increasingly interpreted by Republican leaders as the campaign progressed. In his address of acceptance, Governor Landon made two provisos: he would advocate a constitutional amendment if necessary to validate state wages-and-hours laws, and he would not favor revaluation of the gold content of the dollar so as to penalize domestic recovery. These qualifications were taken as a sign that the Governor would independently assert a more favorable attitude toward the New Deal than the Party leaders desired. In the course of the campaign, the Governor's "independence" was not again asserted, and he followed the trend towards refusal of compromise with the New Deal. It remained true that no responsible Republican leader proposed in specific terms the repeal of all or even a significant number of New Deal laws.

The possibility of an insurgent third party rising to challenge the administration did not die with Huey Long. The latter's Share Our Wealth movement was inherited by the Reverend Gerald L. K. Smith, a minister from Shreveport, Louisiana. Smith had been Long's chief organizer of local clubs, and when the remains of the Long machine made peace with the administration, the minister attempted to establish himself as the national leader of the Share Our Wealth movement. His chief assets were its mailing lists and a skill in demagogic oratory somewhat inferior to Huey Long's. He formed an alliance with Doctor Townsend, and led him to submerge his plan for old-age pensions, which had lost some of its point with the passage of the Social Security Act, in an amalgam with the Share Our Wealth program. The new plan was to impose a universal transactions tax to obtain revenue for compulsory spending by the unemployed. Presently a minimum income of $5,000 per year would be achieved for everyone. At the same time, the privileges of private-property owners would be increased, and extended to embrace even such services as police protection. Smith's propaganda and frenzied speeches appealed chiefly to hatred for the New Deal, minority-racial groups, professional competence, and radicalism. His fanatical harangues and cynical methods changed the tone of the Townsend movement, which had had a certain dignity and pathos.

Smith next formed a combination with Father Charles E. Coughlin, the "Radio Priest" of Royal Oak, Michigan. Coughlin had gradually built up a national radio audience by transforming religious talks into orations on public issues, and in the process became a master of radio technique. He found his guiding principles in Papal Encyclicals. The reconstruction of society on moral foundations was his general argument, and inflation of the currency his chief specific nostrum. He was particularly interested in raising the price of silver, as was his leading backer and adviser, Frank Keelon, who was an operator in foreign exchange. Coughlin was said to participate in the councils of the administration during its first year in office. But he demanded more extreme inflationary action than the administration would undertake, and became a violent opponent of the Second New Deal. He singled out the President for bitter personal attacks, and grouped him with his other hatreds, whom he pictured as controlling the policies of the administration: "godless capitalists," labor unions, Jews, international bankers, and communists.

In 1934, Coughlin organized the National Union for Social Justice and launched a newspaper, both of which became effective agencies for the dissemination of his propaganda. Smith and Coughlin had much in common besides their hatreds. Both were self-appointed leaders of movements which appealed to rancours and ignorance among lower middle-class, "poor white," and socially mal-adjusted groups. They coupled crude versions of orthodox patriotism and religion with dire threats of the imminence of direct action, and they seemed fairly deliberate in their attempt to create an American reproduction of the forms and formulas which in other countries were subverting democracy and establishing various national brands of fascism and nazism. Their weaknesses were an inability to unite behind one leader; the refusal of any responsible leaders of important groups or sections to join with them; and, most of all, the successful sponsorship of progressive reforms by the New Deal administration, which maintained the faith in democratic institutions and methods of the great majority of the groups, especially the lower middle class, poorer farmers, and unemployed, upon whom the depression bore hardest. In 1936, however, it was not yet clear whether the Smith-Townsend-Coughlin coalition would remain on the "lunatic fringe" of American politics or move to the center of the field.

The decision to launch a third-party movement was made public in June, when Smith, Townsend, and Coughlin announced their support of Representative William Lemke of North Dakota for the Presidency. It was said that the nominating convention had been held in a telephone booth, and certainly the "Union Party" presented no examples of the self-governing techniques of a traditional American political party. Lemke had been closely identified with the farm program of the administration, but he had failed in a recent attempt to force on it an extreme inflationary measure. He did not concentrate his fire on the President as did his three supporters. During the campaign he advocated the farm legislation, including inflation of the currency and mortgage relief, which was traditional in the farm states. His friends found his sudden conversion to the Smith-Townsend-Coughlin doctrines inexplicable. It was expected that he would bring the votes of the independent Farmer-Labor Party groups in Minnesota and the Dakotas and other Western groups into the Union Party. Father Coughlin sought to popularize his candidate with such devices as the name "Liberty Bell Bill," but Lemke was ineffectual as a candidate, an opinion which was summed up in the remark that the Liberty Bell was cracked.[8]

Father Coughlin promised to give up his radio speeches if Lemke polled less than ten million votes. The size of the membership of the Union Party's constituent organizations seemed to make this a fair gamble. Some observers saw the possibility that the Union Party would take away enough votes from the Democratic candidates to ensure a Republican victory. But in November only 890,000 votes were cast for Lemke, and these were thinly scattered from Massachusetts to North Dakota. For a short time the priest was off the air.

The parties of the left also hoped to win an influential

minority vote in the 1936 election. Norman Thomas was nominated for President by the Socialist Party. He had run for office annually for many years, and the regard in which he was held by the public seemed to increase in proportion to his futility as a vote-getter. In 1936, he and his Party refused all connection with the Communist Party and its united-front policy. The New Deal was described as proven to be a failure by the persistence of unemployment, and the Democratic Party as a coalition of liberal dreamers, Southern reactionaries, and corrupt Northern city machines. Thomas advocated immediate abolition of capitalism and establishment of socialism. He polled 190,000 votes.

Earl Browder was the candidate of the Communist Party, which in 1936 concentrated on defeat of the Republican Party as the "chief enemy" of the American people, along with its "reactionary allies," Hearst, the Liberty League, and Wall Street. Browder called Lemke "a stooge for Landon," and the Union Party "the product of a Hearst-Liberty League intrigue." Browder did not advocate socialism as against capitalism, but rather proposed that progress and democracy be defended against reaction and fascism.[9] Since a "united front" with neither the Socialist nor Democratic Party was possible, the strategy of the Communist Party evidently was to instruct its members to vote for the Communist candidate, while those who were sympathetic with the current policies of the Communist Party without being members were asked to vote for the Democratic candidate. The vote which Browder polled was under 80,000, and corresponded closely with the actual membership of his Party.

The minor parties of extremism were unable in 1936 to increase their strength or threaten the supremacy of the traditional parties of moderate liberalism and conservatism. At a time when parties of the extreme right and left in most countries were rapidly growing at the expense of moderate parties, the American people cast the largest total vote in history but gave a total of only 2.9 per cent of their votes for extremist candidates. The latter polled even fewer votes than in 1932, when they won 3.1 per cent of the total. This does not mean that Americans were not caught up in the currents of unrest which were sweeping the world, but rather that their traditional parties, in different degree, were able to accommodate and respond to the need for new policies and programs to meet new conditions and problems.

The chief effect of new currents on American party alignments was to be found not in the course of the minor parties but in the shifts in allegiance by voters from one to the other of the old parties. A few craft unions of the American Federation of Labor were the only labor groups to refuse to support the administration. Labor's Non-Partisan League was organized by leaders of both the AFL and the CIO to support the administration and progressive candidates of any party in Congressional and local contests. The American Labor Party in New York pursued this policy with remarkable success. Some leaders of the Grange supported Landon, but practically all other farm groups advocated the re-election of the President. A fairly ineffective group known as "Businessmen for Roosevelt" attempted to develop support among businessmen for liberalism and the New Deal, but virtually all the substantial organizations of business were officially in opposition, and the Liberty League aggressively presented their point of view. Progressive Republican leaders such as Senators Nye of North Dakota and Couzens of Michigan supported the President, although this phenomenon was not as marked in 1936 as in 1932. More numerous were the conservative Democratic leaders, including ex-Governor Ely of Massachusetts and former Secretary of State Colby, and those who had been active with Alfred E. Smith in the Liberty League, who "took a walk" into the Republican ranks.

The Liberty League had been discredited by public laughter at a highly-staged dinner of industrialists, financiers, and dissident Democrats. Speeches seemed to identify the privileges of big business with liberty, and the presence of twelve members of the Du Pont family did not make the public response more favorable. Possibly because the Liberty League had become a boon for the opposition, the "Jeffersonian Democrats" were widely organized with offices in most cities to continue and expand the work of appealing to conservative Democrats to vote against the administration.

Class lines corresponded to party lines more markedly in 1936 than in 1932, and, as when Jefferson and Jackson were elected, might have justified naming the Democratic Party the Farmer-Labor Party. The press was overwhelmingly favorable to Landon. Together with polls of public opinion which confined their attention to such groups as subscribed to national magazines or owned telephones, this obscured the degree to which farmers and workers were united in support of the President and therefore able to win majorities in practically every state in the Union.

The President conducted a vigorous campaign in which he gave no indication of over-confidence. In August, he visited areas devastated by floods, and made many short addresses besides a long one at Chautauqua, New York, a traditional home of pacifism, strongly condemning war and the forces which were making for war. The plains country was being visited by another season of ruinous drought in the summer of 1936. The President made an extensive tour of the region early in September, in which he sought to demonstrate, and pointed out in frequent speeches, the interest of his administration in the economic problems of the people and its efforts to find solutions for them. He drove home with simple lessons the fact that the country's economy was interdependent. Cattle ranchers of the Southwest were told that cotton growers could buy more beef when the price of cotton was high; industrial workers that farmers could buy more manufactured goods only when they received fair prices for their produce; and the drought was used as an object lesson to show the need for soil and water conservation and regional planning, and the value to other sections of the prosperity of every section. In this way the President sought to allay the antagonisms which frequently separated labor and farm groups in order to strengthen an alliance between them based on understanding of their interdependence.

Conferences with Governors and state officials of the drought states were held by the President. The most important one occurred on September 3 in Des Moines, Iowa, where a meeting with Governor Landon had been arranged. Plans were made for immediate relief to drought-stricken farmers, for aid to enable them to hold out through the winter, and for prevention of future disasters. The drought intensified the problems of farm tenancy and migration, and led the President to ask the Agricultural Committees of Congress to prepare plans to extend federal aid for the purchase of land by tenants and migrants. The Farm Tenant Act of July, 1937, was the result.

Two more Executive actions which were taken as the campaign got under way served to clarify administration policies. Charges that Postmaster General Farley conducted a vast patronage mill in the interest of building a political machine were more common and more convincing than most stock charges of patronage-mongering. The President had advocated a bill to extend the civil service to include many exempted categories of officials, but it was defeated. On July 22, he issued an Executive Order which placed postmasters of the first, second, and third classes under the civil service. This abolition of an ancient field of Presidential and Congressional spoils partially answered campaign critics of the increase of the President's appointive powers which resulted from the increase of administrative agencies. But it was pointed out that since the current incumbents in the post offices were automatically given civil service status, the Order would reduce the spoils only of new administrations in the future. This was true of any extension of the civil service.

On September 25, the last step was taken in the evolution of the administration's money policy from unilateral devaluation to international stabilization. The United States, Britain, and France issued statements in which they agreed to avoid competitive devaluation of their currencies and to use stabilization funds to buy and sell their own currency whenever necessary to prevent fluctuations in their value. France had reached a monetary crisis which threatened to take it off the gold standard. The Stabilization Agreement allowed for devaluation of the franc by about 30 per cent of its previous gold value, but helped to save the gold basis of French currency, and prevented a new cycle of competitive devaluation from being initiated. All countries were invited to adhere to the Agreement, and Belgium, Switzerland, the Netherlands, and others accepted the offer. The hope expressed in the Agreement that no nation would attempt to obtain "an unreasonable competitive exchange advantage" was frustrated by the currency techniques which Germany in particular was carrying to unprecedented lengths in order to win advantages in trade. But the Agreement finally ended the period during which the United States could be said to commit or even to threaten "aggression" on foreign currencies and economies. Its broad significance was recognized in the statement that its success was linked with the development of international trade and the relaxation of quota and

248]

exchange controls. It affirmed the common desire of the three nations to

foster those conditions which safeguard peace and will best contribute to the restoration of order in international economic relations and to pursue a policy which will tend to promote prosperity in the world and to improve the standard of living of peoples.[10]

In more immediate terms the Stabilization Agreement helped to end criticism during the campaign of the administration's devaluation of the dollar.

But the WPA offered a fertile field for campaign material on both sides. Congress had refused to authorize the use of funds for the continuation of the Passamaquoddy Bay tidal electric power project and the Florida Ship Canal on which WPA labor was being used. The abandonment of ambitious plans and the waste of labor and materials brought widespread criticism, so that for many these two fiascos became symbols of the administration's ineptitude. "Boondoggling" became a popular descriptive term for all WPA projects and the subject of innumerable cartoons and editorials. The constructive accomplishments of the WPA were largely ignored. The WPA worker was pictured as entirely lazy and unwilling to work for private industry.

The President perhaps took particular pleasure in discussing the subject of boondoggling when he was inspecting works built by the WPA. He described to an audience in Nebraska an earth dam across a river in Vermont which had cost a million and a half dollars and prevented repetition of the six million dollars worth of damage which one cloudburst had caused:

I said to the Governor of Vermont when he was sitting beside me in the automobile on the top of that dam . . . "Governor, it seems to me that this is a pretty good example of coöperative boondoggling between your State and the Federal Government." [11]

At a new stadium in Detroit, the President said:

Some people in this country have called it "boondoggling" for us to build stadiums and parks and forests and to improve the recreational facilities of the Nation. My friends, if this stadium can be called boondoggling, then I am for boondoggling, and so are you.[12]

The President formally opened his campaign on September 29 with an address which took up one of the main charges of the opposition, that the New Deal was somehow related to communism. This was called a false issue, a "red herring," comparable to the charges made by their political opponents that Washington wanted to make himself king, that Jefferson wanted to set up a guillotine in the manner of the French Revolution, that Andrew Jackson wanted to make himself dictator on the shoulders of a frontier mob, that Abraham Lincoln was a Roman Emperor. The Democratic Party agreed with the Republican Party in its attitude towards communism; they differed in what they did about it. The Republican solution was neglect and evasion of the conditions which bred unrest. The Democratic solution was removal of those conditions through reforms which protected the system of private property and free enterprise by correcting the injustices and inequalities which arise from it. "The most serious threat to our institutions comes from those who refuse to face the need for change. Liberalism becomes the protection for the far-sighted conservative."[13]

The refusal of the Republican Party to advocate repeal of New Deal legislation was called, in a passage which became famous for the mimicry of the accents of the hypocrite:

the smooth evasion which says, "Of course we believe all these things; we believe in social security; we believe in work for the unemployed; we believe in saving homes. Cross our hearts and hope to die, we believe in all these things; but we do not like the way the present Administration is doing them. Just turn them over to us. We will do all of them—we will do more of them—we will do them better; and, most important of all, the doing of them will not cost anybody anything."

But, my friends, these evaders are banking too heavily on the shortness of our memories. No one will forget that they had their golden opportunity—twelve long years of it.

. . . Make no mistake about this: the Republican leadership today is not against the way we have done the job. The Republican leadership is against the job's being done.[14]

In Pittsburgh on October 1, and in several minor speeches, the President defended the policy of deficit financing as justified by the increase in national income which had been brought about through priming the pump of industry with purchasing power:

Suppose I were to say to anybody in this crowd, "If you, by borrowing $800, could increase your annual income $2,200 every year, would you do it?" Well, that, in effect, is what happened in this country. We increased the national debt a net of a little less than eight billion dollars but we increased the annual national income over twenty-two billion dollars.[15]

The charge that the administration was antagonistic to business as a whole was carefully analyzed in an address at Chicago on October 14. The President called the roll of the leading types of enterprise and described the prosperity which had come to each during his years in office:

It was this Administration which saved the system of private profit and free enterprise after it had been dragged to the brink of ruin by these same leaders who now try to scare you.

Look at the advance in private business in the last three and a half years; and read there what we think about private business.[16]

But this was coupled with a sharp attack on certain categories of businessmen and their policies. The Hoover administration had supported not industry, or agriculture, or labor, but a small group of financiers, not even all bankers or corporation executives or multimillionaires, but a minority which believed that

popular government cannot be trusted and, therefore, that the control of business of all kinds and, indeed, of Government itself should be vested in the hands of one hundred or two hundred all-wise individuals. . . .

High finance of this type refused to permit Government credit to go directly to the industrialist, to the business man, to the home owner, to the farmer. They wanted it to trickle down from the top, through the intricate arrangements which they controlled and by which they were able to levy tribute on every business in the land.

They did not want interest rates to be reduced by the use of Government funds, for that would affect the rate of interest which they themselves wanted to charge. They did not want Government supervision over financial markets through which they manipulated their monopolies with other people's money.[17]

Half the corporate wealth of the country had come under the control of less than two hundred huge corporations, which in some cases did not even try to compete with each other, being tied together by interlocking directors, bankers, and lawyers. "This concentration of wealth and power . . . . has been a menace to the social system as well as to the economic system which we call American democracy."[18] By establishing controls over this "menace," the administration had hauled business out of the ditch into which finance had driven it. "The train of American business is moving ahead."[19] The President frequently drew attention to the striking fact that during the previous year not a single national bank had failed—a record unequaled for fifty-five years.

Today for the first time in seven years the banker, the storekeeper, the small factory owner, the industrialist can all sit back and enjoy the company of their own ledgers. They are in the black. That is where we want them to be; that is where our policies aim them to be. . . .

Some of these people really forget how sick they were. But I know how sick they were. I have their fever charts. I know how the knees of all our rugged individualists were trembling four years ago and how their hearts fluttered. They came to Washington in great numbers. Washington did not look like a dangerous bureaucracy to them then. Oh, no! It looked like an emergency hospital. All of the distinguished patients wanted two things—a quick hypodermic to end the pain and a course of treatment to cure the disease. They wanted them in a hurry; we gave them both. And now most of the patients seem to be doing very nicely. Some of them are even well enough to throw their crutches at the doctor.[20]

The "quick hypodermic to end the pain" was one of the few references the President made to the policies favorable to business which had dominated the First New Deal; his campaign was built around the "course of treatment to cure the disease"—the Second New Deal. And the meaning of the "treatment" was simply stated:

The struggle against private monopoly is a struggle for, and not against, American business. It is a struggle to preserve individual enterprise and economic freedom.[21]

The same theme was developed by the President in a radio address on October 23 to businessmen's dinners throughout the nation. He gave point to his attack on "certain" businessmen by describing the campaign of employers who told their employees in pay envelopes only of the employees' contributions under the Social Security Act, and concealed the fact of the employers' contributions. "The real objective of this minority is the repeal of any form of social security to which they themselves have to contribute." [22] This criticism of even an unidentified portion of an audience

[253

in the middle of a campaign address was perhaps without precedent. Listeners were reminded that the great majority of Republican Congressmen had voted for the Social Security Act. This and the fact that the Republican Platform approved the law, as well as its widespread popularity, made the bitter attacks upon it by Republican leaders during the campaign seem impolitic if not irresponsible. The attempt to make capital of the social security issue was the greatest tactical blunder of the Republican campaign. The President accepted the issue with aggressiveness and evident success. He dwelt upon it as an object lesson again and again, and never more bluntly than when—in a speech to Pennsylvania miners —he called the insertion by employers into pay-envelopes of the suggestion that some future Congress would "steal" the funds built up for payments under the Act, a sign of their desperation:

contemptible, unpatriotic. . . . If they really believe what they say in the pay envelopes, they have no confidence in our form of government or its permanence. It might be well for them to move to some other Nation in which they have greater faith.[23]

Wilmington, Delaware, the home of the Du Pont corporations, whose heads were leaders of the Liberty League, was chosen by the President for a brief address on "Liberty." He quoted Abraham Lincoln's surgical analysis:

"With some the word liberty may mean for each man to do as he pleases with himself, and the product of his labor; while with others the same word may mean for some men to do as they please with other men, and the product of other men's labor. Here are two, not only different, but incompatible things, called by the same name, liberty. And it follows that each of the things is, by the respective parties, called by two different and incompatible names—liberty and tyranny." [24]

Liberty for all but the anti-social, and democracy as the

technique of its achievement were main themes of the President's campaign. And the contrast between the state of the nation and its people in 1932 and 1936 was cited as proof that democracy and liberty were meeting and solving the problems which caused despair and dictatorship abroad. Wherever he spoke, the President found a local interest, whether sugar beets or automobiles, Negro education or cattle-raising, whose conditions "before and after" he could favorably contrast. But he never left the subject on its local plane: he always drew out the lesson of interdependence of interests, groups, and sections, and seemed to refute the contention that he set class against class. He told New Yorkers of the farm problem and farmers of their dependence on the prosperity of city workers, and workers of their dependence on the prosperity of business, and businessmen of their dependence on purchasing power. Everywhere he told wayside groups that their faces were cheerier than they had been four years before, that he was pleased to note their share in prosperity, and that "we are on our way." He offered no specific proposals of new legislation for the approval of the electorate, but strove to raise the championing of the principles of the Second New Deal to the level of a popular crusade.

The President did not fail to promise that if he were re-elected new laws would be proposed. In the last address of the campaign, in Madison Square Garden, New York City, he answered a challenge from Governor Landon that he state his specific objectives by declaring that "of course" his administration would continue to seek to reduce the hours of labor, increase wages, support collective bargaining, end child labor, sweatshops, and monopoly in business, stop unfair competition and trade practices; work for cheaper electricity and transportation, low interest rates, sounder home financing, better banking, regulation of securities, reciprocal trade, and abolition of slums; do all in its power to end surpluses which ruined farm prices, improve forestation, land use and conservation of water for drought and flood control, reduce farm tenancy and improve crop insurance; provide work for the unemployed, aid indigent mothers, the crippled and blind, and education for youth; provide unemployment insurance and old-age pensions and protect the consumer; and many other objectives which spelled peace and security at home and abroad: "For all these we have only just begun to fight." [25] This stirring recital left unanswered only the question of method. Laws to achieve several of the objectives had been declared unconstitutional by the Supreme Court, and almost all of them could be so interpreted under its recent decisions. The proposal in the Democratic Platform of a constitutional amendment had been largely ignored during the campaign. This left open the opportunity for opponents of the President's proposal for judicial reform during the next session of Congress to object that the electorate had given no mandate for such action. It was still true that the Madison Square Garden speech, if no other, invited a mandate to fight for objectives which could be achieved only if the barrier of adverse Supreme Court decisions was somehow reduced.

The Republican campaign was weakened by the inconsistency between official concessions to the New Deal and admission that little of it would be abolished, and sweeping condemnations of the New Deal and all its works. However much individual partisans and lesser leaders might condemn the whole New Deal, the responsible leaders of the Party were inhibited from threatening the repeal of any legislation which an important group of voters demanded. In several fields, near-substitutes for New Deal laws were offered. Governor Landon, in his speech to farmers at Des Moines on September 23, attacked the Soil Conservation and

Domestic Allotment Act, but declared that he supported the variation of the domestic allotment plan which George N. Peek had tried to put into effect during the first year of the AAA. Peek himself had resigned from his office as adviser on foreign trade because he opposed the reciprocity trade policy of the administration, and was now supporting Landon. The latter promised to continue and expand other farm policies of the administration, especially crop insurance, aid to tenants to buy farms, and relief for farmers injured by drought. The candidate placed great emphasis on the rehabilitation of "family-type farms," and accused the administration of changing its farm program every year in order to bring out an annual model, like the automobile industry. The President later accepted the simile. He stated that the improvements which new automobile models achieved were also the purpose of his farm policy. But Landon's farm speech could hardly have satisfied opponents of the New Deal. It seemed a simple attempt to outbid the administration for the farm vote, and virtually admitted the value and necessity of the administration's program.

The Governor chose Minneapolis as the place for an attack upon the administration's reciprocity trade agreements. He approved the principle of reciprocity, but said that the negotiation of agreements would be managed to better advantage if he were elected President. Canadian cheese was entering the country, and the farmers of the dairy region might be expected to respond favorably to the Governor's appeal, were it not that the return of general prosperity had greatly expanded the market for their cheese in spite of the imports from Canada. This was an example of the difficulty Republican campaigners found in winning acceptance for arguments that the administration's policies were injuring particular groups at a time when growing prosperity seemed to prove the success of those policies.

In Milwaukee, the Republican nominee made the charge that funds accumulated by the Social Security Board would be spent by Congress as they were loaned to the Treasury in return for Treasury bonds. What should be done with the funds rather than lend them at interest until they were needed to pay benefits was not stated. The unemployment insurance feature of the Act should be left entirely to the states instead of making any attempt to secure compliance by all states, but the old-age pension benefits which were paid under the law should be increased.

On October 1, Alfred E. Smith came out openly for Landon. He called the New Deal a "dismal, dull, dark, and dreary failure," and said the accusation that he had forgotten his fishmarket days to don a silk hat was "silly." [26] A week later Doctor Townsend told his followers in California and several other states where Lemke was not on the ballot to vote for Landon, and to remember that the President was "our sworn enemy." [27] The latter considered his victory in California and the Pacific states assured; he did not campaign farther west than Denver. Landon now decided to include California in his own itinerary.

The Governor made several more major addresses which dwelt upon particular issues. He appealed for the Negro vote, which had largely deserted its ancient allegiance to the Republican Party, by advocating an anti-lynching bill. In Chicago, he promised to balance the budget, remove specters of inflation and bankruptcy, relieve "family incomes" of intolerable tax burdens, and restore business confidence. The budget would be balanced, "not by depriving our needy of relief, not by refusing necessary aid to our farmers, not by swamping the country with taxes," but by cutting out waste, extravagance, and the use of public funds for political purposes. "The spenders must go." [28] Democratic speakers were quick to point out the implication that President Hoover, when he failed to balance the budget even while carrying out a program much less expensive than Landon's, had been guilty of waste and extravagance.

In Cleveland, the Governor called the administration's relief program a "scandal" used to build up "a shameless political machine," and an experimental playground for "foolish fads and pet theories," marked by secrecy to conceal mismanagement and favoritism. If he were elected, no American would ever again have to "sell his vote for bread." But he would continue relief for the eleven million unemployed.[29]

That the President was on the road to dictatorship was the burden of an address in Detroit on relations between government and business. Economic planning, a violation of American ideals, was destroying economic freedom, which goes "hand in hand" with "personal liberty." If elected, Landon would recommend repeal of the "autocratic powers" the President had been given. The recovery which had been achieved was the result not of governmental policies but of industry's own efforts. The prosperity of Henry Ford, who had refused to sign an NRA code, was held up as proof.[30] The next day Henry Ford received the candidate and issued a statement endorsing him for the Presidency.

At Toledo, Landon made his most direct appeal for the votes of organized labor. He warned that the methods of dictatorship under the New Deal were leading to serfdom for labor as had already occurred in Europe. Labor unions and their rights were approved by the Governor, but he recommended that workers follow the advice of Samuel Gompers and refuse to take part in political activity.

With this rather futile gesture towards labor, the candidate seemed to run out of material for his campaign. The remainder of his addresses repeated themes already developed and showed even more plainly the painful indecision of responsible leaders of the Republican Party on how to appeal to specific groups for their support without approving too completely the New Deal policies which were designed for their benefit. The effort seemed to break down in such a speech as the one delivered by Landon in Phoenix, Arizona. He declared that "regimentation of the individual and curb of his liberties underlie every one of the New Deal's plans." Yet he said he did not doubt the humanitarian sincerity of the administration or the necessity for change. But he would himself carry out necessary changes "without destroying the freedom which comes to us from our fathers." [31] The candidate's western trip was generally considered a failure. He made perfunctory appeals to cattle ranchers, offering them better tariff protection than the administration; was cordial to the Townsendites of California to the embarrassment of his conservative supporters; paid tribute to William Randolph Hearst for fighting against a Senate investigation for "freedom of the press"; declared that not those who suffered from the higher taxes on large income and undistributed profits, but the "little fellow," was paying for the New Deal; and he approved the President's Good Neighbor policy.

The Republican candidate's colorless personality and inadequacy as a public speaker, as well as the inability of one whose promises might acquire weight with victory to strike out too violently against the New Deal, led his most eminent supporters to come forward in mid-campaign and take up the burden. During the last weeks Herbert Hoover and Alfred E. Smith overshadowed the official candidate. They and lesser leaders gave the Republican campaign a more uncompromisingly conservative tone towards its close. It was as if the Party leadership had regretted, or given up hope when they foresaw its failure, the strategy of compromise with the New Deal and conciliation of liberal and progressive voters, especially farmers and workers. The apathy and small crowds which usually greeted Landon were in great contrast with the President's receptions. No significant farm or labor organization had been won over. The public seemed amused in the wrong way at the efforts of the campaign managers to dramatize their cause, such as the heroic size of the Kansas sunflowers which Rolls-Royce cars displayed, and the "Victim of Future Taxes" entertainment which the "Landon First Voters League" presented, featuring a young lady whose missing skirt was intended to demonstrate that "Taxes take $5.00 of every $25.00 evening gown." It was perhaps chiefly the conviction that stronger measures were needed to rescue the campaign from their vacillating candidate and platform that determined the leaders to subordinate Landon.

Ex-President Hoover in Philadelphia on October 16 delivered a sharp analysis of the administration's budget practices. He said that its "morals in arithmetic" were intellectually dishonest because it enlarged the deficits of the Hoover years with certain recoverable items which were subtracted from the deficits for New Deal years. This was the first of a series of vigorous assaults which ended on October 30 when the former President asked whether the administration intended to "stuff" the Supreme Court, and called the Statue of Liberty "the forgotten woman." [32] Alfred E. Smith's contribution was chiefly invective. The irony of his approval of the Party and policies he had fought all his life was complete. He made his last effort to discredit his former friend when he associated the President with communism, atheism, and crackpots. [33]

During the last stage of the campaign the attempt to present a positive program was abandoned by the Republicans, and they concentrated on destructive attacks on the New Deal. Heinous labels were attached to it and then vilified. The procedure was carried farthest by Father Coughlin, who called the President "betrayer," "scab," "anti-God," "communist," and "liar," until he was reportedly reprimanded by a superior and half-heartedly apologized.[34] Governor Landon maintained his balance. He closed his campaign with the demand that the President state in detail what his future program would be, and to his own questions reiterated the answer, "No one can be sure." [35] This provided the challenge which the President met in his speech at Madison Square Garden: "We have only just begun to fight."

The 1936 campaign was remarkable for its combination of bitterness and one-sided results. An impression of unquenchable hatred for the New Deal was given by Republicans to the electorate, and in private if not always in public discussion it seemed apparent that a vote for Landon was a vote against labor unions and federal legislation to strengthen them, against federal work relief for the unemployed, against direct aid to the farmers, against federal regulation of business, especially utilities, securities, and banking, against the TVA, tariff reductions, and social security. The compromises with this program which appeared in the Republican Platform and Governor Landon's addresses were perhaps the attraction which brought those farmers, workers, and middle-class voters who were tied by tradition and conservative sentiment to the Republican Party to add their votes to the great majority of businessmen and wealthy individuals who were thoroughly opposed to the New Deal, and swell the Republican vote to 16,682,000. But the failure to capture the "independent" voters belonging to any group except business may explain the failure to win majorities in any states except Maine and Vermont.

The administration appealed to the electorate not as an untried quantity or even as the sponsor of the First New Deal, with its doubtful attractions for liberals and labor, but as the champion of the Second New Deal carrying out exclusively the liberal and progressive policies of small business, farmers, and workers. Republican campaigners frequently excoriated the administration for policies which had been tried and discarded. NIRA and the Bombshell Message to the London Economic Conference were often cited. But probably none of the liberals or labor groups who had condemned the NIRA and economic nationalism considered the possibility of their revival a justification of a vote for Landon. And James P. Warburg, who had broken with the administration because of the Bombshell Message, significantly returned to its support in 1936. The reciprocity and stabilization policies satisfied his faith in international economic cooperation, and he called the Republicans the advocates of economic nationalism.[36] It was clearly the Second New Deal for which the President had just begun to fight, and before and during the campaign he had made strenuous efforts to extend its appeal beyond the limits of its obvious beneficiaries, farmers and laborers, to include middle-class groups, especially small businessmen. Traditional Democrats, whose numbers were evidently little thinned by the defections of conservative Democratic leaders, and the "independent" vote within the great labor and farmer groupings and reaching well into the ranks of the middle class, gave the President his great popular vote of 27,751,000 and spread it through all sections to win a victory in the electoral college which was unprecedented in a contested election.

The largest Democratic majorities were polled as usual in the South, where the average was 94 per cent of the vote cast. The Rocky Mountain and Pacific Coast states gave the President slightly more than 67 per cent of their vote, while the border states from Delaware to Oklahoma gave him slightly under 67 per cent. The East and the Midwest gave him his smallest majorities, about 54 per cent in both sections, but in the six most populous industrial states of the two sections, the Roosevelt majority was 58 per cent. The total popular vote was 60.7 per cent Democratic, and the President won 523 out of 531 electoral votes. His popular majority had been equalled on a few previous occasions, but the electoral majority was greater than any candidate achieved when two parties were supporting two separate tickets.[37] A wit changed the old adage to: "As Maine goes, so goes Vermont." Only Postmaster General Farley, in the course of duplicating and surpassing his organizational feats of 1932, foresaw the results.

The Congressional elections increased the Democratic majorities in both houses, so that in the next session of Congress three-fourths of the Senators and almost four-fifths of the Representatives would be of the President's Party. The consolation of the Republicans was that the Democratic majorities were so large as to be unmanageable. Splits were predicted which would end the President's influence in Congress, and the prognosis was partially correct.

In the meantime, a bartender in Geneva, Switzerland, expressed the feelings of a large part of the world when he invented the "Forty-Eight States Roosevelt Cocktail": ten states of Dutch curaçao for the President's ancestors; ten states of English gin because he glorified the language; eight states of grapefruit juice for the American way of life; eighteen states of French vermouth for America's God-parent; one state of Angostura bitters for Maine; one state of green absinthe for the hills of Vermont. Drink, and see the landslide.

CHAPTER XIII

YEAR OF CRISIS: 1937

PRESIDENT ROOSEVELT was returned to the White House in 1937 as the choice of the majority in every section after four years' trial and a great national debate, and with a majority of his own Party in Congress larger than any other modern President had enjoyed. A development immediately after the election, which was surprising in comparison with the predictions of disaster to business if the President were re-elected, was the spurt forward of recovery. Many corporations announced extra dividends, employment increased, and the prices of stocks on Wall Street made the best day's gain since 1933.[1] The prosperity which had been growing since the summer of 1935 continued through the first half of 1937, and was if anything stimulated by the administration's great victory at the polls.

The President's personal prestige had risen higher than ever with the defeat of the Republican Party and of those who had tried to discredit him and his policies. He was expected to carry out a program which would complete the structure and achieve the objectives of the Second New Deal, and he did not fail to initiate actions which would accomplish these purposes. But within two years the President's support in Congress had declined, the further reform of domestic institutions was suspended for an indefinite time, and the creative period of the Second New Deal, its structure still far from complete and its objectives still far distant, had run its course. This startling reversal constitutes the theme of the remainder of this book.

In his Annual Message of January 6, 1937, the President proposed a series of fields in which Congress should legislate to achieve

the deeper purpose of democratic government . . . to assist as many . . . citizens as possible, especially those who need it most, to improve their conditions of life, to retain all personal liberty which does not adversely affect their neighbors, and to pursue the happiness which comes with security and an opportunity for recreation and culture.[2]

This conception of the meaning of "life, liberty, and the pursuit of happiness" could be realized by solving the problems of housing, farm tenancy, further development of social security, unemployment relief, private employment, reckless overproduction, monopolistic underproduction, speculation, unfair trade practices, minimum wages, maximum hours, and a just return for agriculture. Federal laws to supplement state laws were necessary.

On the all-important question of the barriers which the Supreme Court had raised, the President prepared the way for his specific proposals of a month later. He declared the belief had grown that amendment of the Constitution was not the vital need, but rather

an increasingly enlightened view with reference to it. Difficulties have grown out of its interpretation; but rightly considered, it can be used as an instrument of progress, and not as a device for prevention of action.[3]

He recommended the reading and rereading of the Constitution and of the debates in the Constitutional Convention of 1787. He was convinced that the framers of the Constitution had definite intent and expectation that a liberal interpretation in the years to come would give to the Congress the same relative powers over new national problems as they themselves gave to the Congress over the national problems of their day. . . .

Means must be found to adapt our legal forms and our judicial interpretation to the actual present national needs of the largest progressive democracy in the modern world.[4]

The patriotism and logic was urged of passing new laws consistent with "an historic constitutional framework clearly intended to receive liberal and not narrow interpretation."[5] A comprehensive overhauling of the administrative machinery of the Executive branch to modernize and improve it would presently be recommended, and:

The Judicial branch also is asked by the people to do its part in making democracy successful. We do not ask the Courts to call non-existent powers into being, but we have a right to expect that conceded powers or those legitimately implied shall be made effective instruments for the common good.

The process of our democracy must not be imperiled by the denial of essential powers of free government.[6]

This unprecedented request of the Judiciary, coupled with a warning, seemed to indicate that the President had determined to rely upon a shift of opinion of one or more Supreme Court justices for the validation of laws already enacted and to come. Cases involving the constitutionality of several important acts, particularly the Wagner Labor Relations Act and the Social Security Act, had already been accepted by the Court, and possibly it was hoped that at least the "roving" justices would "follow the election returns."

The only important prepared legislation which was sent to Congress during the first month of the session was the plan to reorganize the Executive branch and a request for renewal of the Reciprocity Trade Agreements Act. Before they could be acted upon, the President had been inaugurated for his second term and had sent a third proposal to Congress which claimed its major attention throughout the long session.

○ In his Second Inaugural Address on January 20, 1937, the President made his famous statement: "I see one-third of a Nation ill-housed, ill-clad, ill-nourished." [7] The purpose of his second term would be to correct this condition. The statement came as a shock to most Americans. It implied that the recovery which had been achieved was superficial, that the measures which the administration had already taken were mild compared with the drastic remedies which would now be applied, and that the famous American standard of living was to a great extent illusory. This latter implication seemed unpatriotic to some, while to others it was a confirmation of facts which were available in the treatises of economists and sociologists. To most citizens it brought a more or less prolonged troubling of conscience, mixed with incredulity and interest in discovering the truth of the matter. The poverty of the most unfortunate groups of society became a topic of current news interest for almost the first time in American history. Knowledge of the lot of the slum-dweller, the migrant, and the sharecropper became widespread. Novels, plays, articles in newspapers and magazines, and topical studies which treated such groups with sympathy and understanding became popular. Women's clubs became interested, a sign of the extremity of public concern. The poor entered the public consciousness as more than an abstraction or an opportunity for private charity. The President had described the condition of the submerged one-third of the nation without reference to recovery or depression: something more fundamental than a depression, at once more shameful and more compelling, less dramatic but more significant, was placed squarely in the center of the administration stage. It remained to be seen whether the one-third of the nation would occupy a similar position for Congress during the new Presidential term.

On February 5, the President sent his momentous proposal for the reorganization of the Judiciary to Congress. The choice of time and method for the solution of the Supreme Court problem was determined in the first place by the decision to make the policies of the administration and not the opinions of the Supreme Court the main issue in the election campaign of 1936. The imminence of new Court decisions on the constitutionality of the major laws of the Second New Deal dictated that the lengthy process of constitutional amendment be avoided. On January 11, the Circuit Court of Appeals in San Francisco had been the latest of the lower federal courts to declare the Wagner Act unconstitutional. Sit-down strikes in the automobile industry and other industries, which had begun in December, had been called because employers refused to engage in collective bargaining, and they became more serious through January, indicating the consequences of failure to enforce the provisions of the Wagner Act. It seemed futile, if not defiant, to propose legislation to complete the Second New Deal while weeks stretched into months and the Supreme Court gave no sign that the liberal minority might become a majority. These considerations seemed to many sufficient to explain the time and the method which were chosen for solution of the Court problem; but the bitterest opponents of the plan were convinced that the President's chief motives were personal, such as the desire for "power," and for "revenge" on the conservative majority of the Court.

In his special message of recommendation, the President carefully reminded Congress of its authority under the Constitution to create judicial offices and formulate the rules of practice and procedure for federal courts; that it had fixed the number of Supreme Court justices during various epochs at five, six, seven, nine, and ten; and that the Constitution enjoined the President to recommend to Congress "such measures as he shall judge necessary and expedient."

Insufficient personnel to meet the business before the courts was now causing overcrowded dockets and complexities, delays and expense to litigants. Delay resulted in injustice and made lawsuits a luxury which only the wealthy or those who had great property interests at stake could afford. A speeding up of justice was necessary to "eradicate the growing impression that the courts are chiefly a haven for the well-to-do." [8] Speedier trials in the lower courts would enlarge the work of the Supreme Court. Already the Supreme Court had denied in one year 87 per cent of the applications for hearings on appeal, without giving its reasons.

A part of the problem of obtaining a sufficient number of judges to dispose of cases is the capacity of the judges themselves. This brings forward the question of aged or infirm judges —a subject of delicacy and yet one which requires frank discussion. . . .

In exceptional cases, of course, judges, like other men, retain to an advanced age full mental and physical vigor. Those not so fortunate are often unable to perceive their own infirmities. [9]

The voluntary retirement law of 1869, still in force, had not proved effective in inducing aged judges to retire. A law had been passed in 1919 under which the President might appoint an additional district or circuit judge when one failed to retire at the age of 70, but it required the President to find that the incumbent was incompetent by reason of mental or physical disability. "No President should be asked to determine the ability or disability of any particular judge." [10] Modern judges needed full energies:

A lowered mental or physical vigor leads men to avoid an

examination of complicated and changed conditions. Little by little, new facts become blurred through old glasses fitted, as it were, for the needs of another generation; older men, assuming that the scene is the same as it was in the past, cease to explore or inquire into the present or the future.[11]

Life tenure of judges was intended to remove them from temptations which might impair their judgments, but

it was not intended to create a static judiciary. A constant and systematic addition of younger blood will vitalize the courts and better equip them to recognize and apply the essential concepts of justice in the light of the needs and the facts of an ever-changing world.[12]

It was therefore recommended that an increase of judges in all federal courts be provided when incumbents over 70 years of age did not retire. The Bill which accompanied the recommendation limited the number of new Supreme Court justiceships to six, and of new circuit and district judgeships to forty-four.

Further proposals were made for temporary transfers of district and circuit judges to courts which were in arrears, for notice to the Attorney General and opportunity for the government to present evidence to a court before it issued a decision, injunction, judgment, or decree involving constitutionality of legislation, and for immediate appeal of cases concerning constitutionality from the lowest federal courts to the Supreme Court, where they should have precedence over all other matters. In these ways the inequality arising from a decision in one district that a law was valid and must be obeyed, while in another district it was called invalid and need not be obeyed, and the uncertainty caused by the long period of litigation during which labor, industry, agriculture, commerce, and even the government itself did not know what would and what would not be called law, would be corrected in large degree. The various reforms would also prevent the Judiciary from becoming a third house of Congress and falling into disrepute.

At the end of his Message, the President declared that reorganization of the Judiciary would make unnecessary any fundamental changes in the powers of the courts or in the Constitution, "changes which involve consequences so far-reaching as to cause uncertainty as to the wisdom of such course." [13]

One effect of the proposal to reorganize the Judiciary was the passage by the end of the month of the Supreme Court Retirement Act, which the President had incidentally approved. Under previous law, Supreme Court justices could resign at 70 on full salary; but they lost their judicial status, which made their salary subject to reduction by Congress (such as Justice Holmes had suffered under the Economy Act of 1933), and their salary also became subject to income taxes. It had been rumored that Justices Van Devanter and Sutherland were ready to leave the bench if these disabilities were removed. Under the new Retirement Act, a justice could retire and maintain his judicial status rather than resign. The measure had been introduced a year earlier, but it was passed now possibly in the hope that several justices would retire and make the Judiciary Reorganization Bill less urgent.

The immediate reception of the court plan as a whole by Congress was not unfavorable. But the stock market fell with the news, and before the first day was out ex-President Hoover had publicly accused the President of wanting to pack the Supreme Court. The first opposition in Congress came from those who would not be expected to support an administration measure, chiefly Republicans. A movement of more than normal opposition was soon afoot. State legislatures began to pass resolutions condemning the proposal.

Many private organizations with names such as the "Committee to Save the Constitution" sprang up. The larger part of the press launched and sustained a comprehensive attack. Bar associations, educators, clergymen, and other groups took sides, with the weight of opinion seeming to be in opposition. The burden of the argument as it reached the popular mind was that the plan would give the President the powers of a "dictator," and that it was "unconstitutional." Letter-writing and telegram campaigns were directed at Congressmen.

The legislators began to show reluctance. The House Committee on the Judiciary worked to split the Bill into separate measures in order to isolate the "packing" proposal from the less controversial sections. This development was stopped after a conference between the President and the Committee members. A number of conservative Democrats joined Republicans in open opposition. These the President might have been willing to lose as unnecessary to pass the Bill. Many Democratic Congressmen, particularly Southerners, who could not be called liberals on the score of their personal philosophies, but who on the basis chiefly of party loyalty and the economic emergency had generally supported the administration, joined the opposition. Senator George of Georgia, who had taken a leading part in writing the Democratic Platform of 1936, accused the President of repudiating that document. The danger sign came when leading liberals declared against the Bill. Senator Wheeler of Montana, a Democrat, campaigned through the country and over the radio on the theme that the Bill would make the Supreme Court subservient to one man, and he became the ardent and skilled leader of the opposition forces. It became the tactic of Republicans to remain in the background while the Democrats split themselves into two warring camps. The Senate, where the main fight took place, seemed divided almost evenly over the issue. The great Democratic majorities in Congress had fallen into disunity within two months after the session began.

Faced by the danger that the Bill would be lost because of the growing success of the offensive which the opposition staged, the President early in March took over direct leadership of the campaign for passage. His purpose was to organize a counter-attack among the vast ranks of voters who had shown faith in him in November. On March 1, it was reported that the Democratic National Committee had begun to organize popular support for the court plan. On March 4, the anniversary of his first inauguration, the President addressed by radio Victory Dinners of Party workers throughout the nation. Only by making political and economic democracy work, he said, could the Democratic Party remain the majority party. "As yet there is no definite assurance that the three-horse team of the American system of government will pull together." [14] The Supreme Court had "assumed the power to veto" leading measures of the New Deal. Court injunctions had paralyzed the enforcement of the Wagner Act and encouraged great corporations to defy it. While flood and drought swept the country, injunctions by lower federal courts paralyzed the TVA. In a dramatic peroration, the President pointed to strikes, child labor, and many other problems which demanded immediate action: "If we would keep faith with those who had faith in us, if we would make democracy succeed, I say we must act—*now!*" [15]

This address called upon the rank and file of the Party workers to enter the fight and organize voters to force the Party leaders in Congress to close their ranks and support the Judiciary Reorganization Bill. On March 9, the President amplified his appeal and his audience in a fireside chat to the nation. The Supreme Court was directly attacked as usurping a legislative veto, and dissenting opinions of the Court itself were quoted to prove the charge. Listeners were reminded of Chief Justice Hughes's statement that the Constitution is what the judges say it is, and the conclusion was drawn: "We must take action to save the Constitution from the Court and the Court from itself." [16] The President boldly faced the charge that he intended to pack the Court:

If by that phrase "packing the Court" it is charged that I wish to place on the bench spineless puppets who would disregard the law and would decide specific cases as I wished them to be decided, I make this answer: that no President fit for his office would appoint, and no Senate of honorable men fit for their office would confirm, that kind of appointees to the Supreme Court.

But if by that phrase the charge is made that I would appoint and the Senate would confirm Justices worthy to sit beside present members of the Court who understand those modern conditions, that I will appoint Justices who will not undertake to override the judgment of the Congress on legislative policy, that I will appoint Justices who will act as Justices and not as legislators—if the appointment of such Justices can be called "packing the Courts," then I say that I and with me the vast majority of the American people favor doing just that thing—now.[17]

The President pleaded with the liberals who were in opposition to leave their "strange bed-fellows," who intended to "sabotage" all reform. He concluded with an appeal for confidence in his own intentions:

This proposal of mine will not infringe in the slightest upon the civil or religious liberties so dear to every American.

My record as Governor and as President proves my devotion to those liberties. You who know me can have no fear that I would tolerate the destruction by any branch of government of any part of our heritage of freedom. . . .

You who know me will accept my solemn assurance that in a world in which democracy is under attack, I seek to make American democracy succeed.[18]

An energetic campaign of speeches was conducted by Secretaries Ickes and Wallace, Senator Guffey, and other leaders, and these spared their criticisms of the Court even less than had the President.

But the popular response was not impressive. It was rumored that Postmaster General Farley was unwilling to exert to the full his ability to rally Party support and unity. The opposition assiduously cultivated respected groups and public leaders, and spent many weeks in bringing their arguments before the Congressional Committees. Liberal opinion throughout the country seemed more or less evenly split. And the great interests which had re-elected the President, farmers and laborers, failed to respond vigorously to the President's appeals. The traditionally conservative South was apathetic or opposed to the Bill. Farmers' organizations gave it only perfunctory support. But the most extraordinary development in the struggle was the series of Supreme Court decisions which made labor and, to a lesser extent, farmers lose a part of their obvious immediate interest in the appointment of new liberal Supreme Court justices.

On March 29, the Court handed down its decision on the constitutionality of the Washington State Minimum Wage Act, a law which raised the same issues as the New York measure the Court had found invalid in 1936. That decision was now reversed by the simple act of Justice Roberts abandoning the conservative justices and joining the liberals. The contention of the minority in 1936, that a minimum-wage regulation for women did not violate their freedom of contract, but was a reasonable regulation with due process of law adopted for the protection of the community against evils menacing the health, safety, morals, and welfare of women, became the decision of the majority in 1937. Chief Justice Hughes in the ruling opinion seemed to hold out the possibility that other varieties of labor legislation would also be sustained in the future:

The community may direct its law-making power to correct the abuse which springs from [employers'] selfish disregard of the public interest.[19]

On the same day the Court decided unanimously that the new Frazier-Lemke Farm Mortgage Act, which had been passed after the earlier law had been found invalid, was constitutional. The decision was not a reversal, for the new law had corrected certain objectionable clauses of the former one, but it indicated a willingness to permit a fairly liberal interpretation of the due-process clause. Its political effect may well have been to take the edge off any resentment farmers felt against the Court.

These decisions were remarkable enough, but on April 12, the Court astonished the country by finding the Wagner Labor Relations Act constitutional. A favorable verdict was given in five cases which raised the main constitutional questions concerning the Act, and the decisions were at once a great victory for the New Deal and a crushing blow to the Judiciary Reorganization Bill. Three of the cases involved manufacturing enterprises the relations of which to interstate commerce might seem to be only "indirect." But Justice Roberts joined the liberals to form a majority which interpreted interstate commerce so broadly as to create a general expansion of the government's power. Factories which obtained their raw materials and sold their products across state boundaries were declared to be engaged in interstate commerce. The right of employees to organize a union was said to be as clear as the right of employers to organize their business, and essential in order to "give laborers opportunity to deal on an equality with their employer." [20] But employers had no right to interfere with their employees' union activity, for "such collective action would be a mockery if representation were made futile by interference with freedom of choice."[21] The right of employers to intimidate, coerce, or discharge their employees for union activities was denied. If the Act restrained abuses by employers and failed to restrain abuses for which employees or unions were responsible, Congress had the power to correct such evils by further legislation. The use of labor spies by an employer was found to be an unfair labor practice, tending to cause unrest and disturbance injurious to interstate commerce. When a majority of his employees demanded it, an employer was required to bargain collectively with them or their freely chosen representatives, because collective bargaining is often

an essential condition of industrial peace. Refusal to confer and negotiate has been one of the most prolific causes of strife. This is such an outstanding fact in the history of labor disturbances that it is a proper subject of judicial notice.[22]

The decision of a case involving the Amalgamated Clothing Workers Union and a Southern employer pointed out how great strikes obstructing commerce had preceded the recognition of the Union by Northern employers, and how subsequent collective bargaining had brought peace to the industry. Employers who established clothing factories in the South to escape the Union and pay lower wages were not to be allowed to revive labor strife in the industry, but were required to deal with the Union under the provisions of the new law. The fourth case had been brought by the Associated Press, on the ground that preventing the discharge of an editorial employee for reason of his membership in a union violated the freedom of the press. The new majority of five justices agreed that the Wagner Act did not violate the freedom of the press because it did not require the Associated Press to employ any particular person, or to retain any incompetent employee or one who failed faithfully to edit the news without bias and in accord with the employer's wishes. Only the discharge of an employee for union activities was forbidden. The procedure which the law established for determining the true reason for an employee's discharge guaranteed to both sides the right to present evidence before decision by the National Labor Relations Board and the right of review of the Board's decision by a federal court, thereby satisfying the requirements of due process of law. The fifth case involved a bus company the business of which was obviously interstate, so that the nine justices decided unanimously in favor of the law.

These historic decisions assured the validity of the most favorable law which American labor had ever won. Their immediate effect on the struggle over the Judiciary Reorganization Bill was to reduce support for reform of the Supreme Court, and for this reason the decisions were welcomed in circles which were ordinarily opposed to the Wagner Act. The President pointed out to reporters, off the record, that the *New York Herald Tribune* on September 21, 1935, had written an editorial completely approving the unanimous opinion of the National Lawyers' Committee of the Liberty League that the Wagner Act was unconstitutional; and that on the day after the Supreme Court's decision the same newspaper published an editorial in an opposite sense, entitled "A Great Decision." [23] Employers who had disobeyed the Wagner Act on the advice of the Liberty League lawyers, and now found themselves liable for the penalties of the Act, such as the payment of back wages and re-employment of workers discharged for union activities, perhaps could not be expected to follow the strategy of the opponents of the Judiciary Reorganization Bill, but to the latter the Supreme Court's decisions were a boon and deserving of high praise as an example of judicial statesmanship.

On May 18, Justice Van Devanter, who had been staunchly conservative in his opinions, announced his retirement to take effect on June 1 under the new Retirement Act. The irony of this action was not lost on observers, and it was possibly doubled for the President by the fact that Senator Robinson of Arkansas, Democratic floor leader and organizer of the fight for the court plan, hoped to be appointed Justice and would probably revert in the security of that position to the conservatism out of which he had been drawn, like so many Southerners, chiefly by loyalty to his Party and its leader. Nevertheless, supporters of the court plan began to ask that a compromise be arranged.

The movement for compromise grew stronger when the Supreme Court validated the Social Security Act on May 24. Three decisions declared that state unemployment-insurance tax laws under the federal Act did not violate due process of law but served the public interest; that the provision of rebates to states which passed unemployment insurance laws in conformity with the Act did not constitute coercion or unconstitutional surrender of state powers, because offering a motive or a temptation was not equivalent to coercion; and that the federal tax on employees and employers for old-age pensions was a valid exercise of the power to tax for the general welfare. Businessmen who argued that the Act was paternalistic found the argument turned against their own interest in tariff protection:

Counsel for respondent has recalled to us the virtues of self-reliance and frugality. There is a possibility, he says, that aid from a paternal government may sap those sturdy virtues and breed a race of weaklings. . . . One might ask with equal reason whether the system of protective tariffs is to be set aside at will . . . whenever local policy prefers the rule of *laissez faire*.[24]

In two of these decisions Justice Roberts once more made the liberals the majority. Justices Sutherland and Van Devanter also joined the liberals in the third decision which validated old-age pensions under the general welfare power.

The Supreme Court had now validated, in effect, the Second New Deal. Liberal interpretations of state authority to enact labor legislation and of federal authority to enact reforms favorable to labor and farmers under the interstate commerce and general welfare powers opened the door to completion of the program which the President had most recently formulated in January. On the day of the validation of the Social Security Act, the President for the first time sent a specific recommendation to Congress that a wages-and-hours law be passed. But he also continued the fight for the Judiciary Reorganization Bill.

The considerations which had led Justice Roberts to join the liberal justices excited keen speculation. To some it seemed that an act of judicial statesmanship and of respect for the election returns had inspired his action. Others credited him with the intention of frustrating the President's court plan by removing the immediate motives for it. Some believed that Chief Justice Hughes, for whom the independence and prestige of the Court were paramount, had been the master strategist, first joining the liberals himself, and then convincing Justice Roberts of the wisdom of ending the "blockade" against the New Deal. In any case it was not doubted that the liberal decisions of the Court contributed to the defeat of the Reorganization Bill. The Senate had been evenly divided on the issue with eight or ten members undecided. Now the waverers joined the opposition, believing that the necessity for the Bill had passed, and even the ranks of its supporters showed signs of breaking. The public debate matched that of an election campaign. Charges were freely made of the use of patronage by the administration, while supporters of the Bill accused wealthy persons and groups of financing a vast propaganda directed not merely at defeating the Bill but also at splitting the Democratic Party in order to rob the President of his election victory and frustrate the further development of his program.

The majority report of the Senate Judiciary Committee was unfavorable and framed in strong terms of denunciation. The Committee declared that the Bill had as its object "a change in the decisions of the Court—a subordination of the views of the judges to the views of the executive and legislative."[25] The debate which followed seemed to show that the majority of Senators opposed the Bill. Supporters made an attempt to save its principle by introducing a substitute which would allow the President to appoint a maximum of one new Supreme Court justice per year, and to supplement an incumbent only after he reached the age of 75. But the opposition lost no strength so long as the "packing" principle was at stake, in spite of rumors that the administration would make reprisals with patronage.

In the midst of the intense struggle now being dragged into its sixth month, Senator Robinson was found dead in his apartment. Many believed that he was the victim of overwork for the Bill. Senator Barkley of Kentucky was elected floor leader, and received a note from the President recommending that the Bill be passed in whatever form the Senate desired. By this time, the strength of the opposition by liberal supporters of the President had been shown by such defections as that of Governor Herbert Lehman of New York. Fear of an irrevocable split in the Democratic Party in which many liberals would unite with conservatives against the administration had caused strong pressure for retreat.

Vice President Garner, evidently motivated chiefly by considerations of Party unity, took the lead with Senator Barkley in meeting with Senator Wheeler to write a bill which would be approved by all Democrats. Appointment of new justices and judges was entirely abandoned, but most of the procedural reforms recommended by the President were adopted. Opportunity for the Attorney General to take part in any case in a lower federal court involving constitutionality of legislation was provided; speeding up of such cases was made possible by appeals directly to the Supreme Court from the lowest federal courts; injunctions against the enforcement of federal acts on the ground of unconstitutionality were forbidden, except that stays of sixty days might be granted by special courts of three judges; and provision was made for shifting of judges to busy courts to speed their work. This Judicial Procedure Reform Act was easily passed, and was signed on August 24. The President upon signing it declared that the original bill was still needed, and that it was still recognized as desirable by most citizens. Amid the comment on the President's first important defeat by Congress, it was generally ignored that the Act which did pass installed reforms that would make virtually impossible repetition of such a situation as had made the constitutionality of the Wagner Act doubtful for two years while employers defied it and lower federal courts encouraged them. On the other hand, it was obvious that, as the President later said, the "war" had been won by the Supreme Court's reversal of its earlier decisions, and only a "battle" had been lost by the defeat of the "packing" Bill.

In another sense, victory in the "war" was doubtful. The fight over the court plan substituted for the high degree of unity within the Democratic Party which had prevailed during the President's first term a division on domestic policy which was never corrected beyond the return of most of the liberals to support of the administration. Conservative Democrats, chiefly Southerners, henceforth were quick to repudiate loyalty to their Party and its leader when they found liberal-progressive measures not to their liking. By the end of 1938, with the increase of Republican strength in Congress after the November elections, conservative Democrats held the balance of power between liberals and conservative Republicans, and they used it to prevent completion of the structure of the Second New Deal.

The President seemed to rebuff efforts at conciliation between the groups within his Party after the court fight was ended. His nomination of Senator Hugo L. Black of Alabama to the Supreme Court in Van Devanter's place was interpreted as a refusal to conciliate conservative Southerners. Southern Democrats could be called "liberals" only in the ancient sense that they supported agrarianism against industrialism and states' rights against federal power, but Senator Black was that rarity among them, a liberal in the modern sense that he favored broad use of federal power to redress the balance in favor of submerged groups, especially labor. He was chiefly known as the sponsor of wages and hours legislation for labor which was introduced in Congress seven times before it passed as the Fair Labor Standards Act of 1938. Such legislation was bitterly opposed by Southern conservatives, who feared that it would end the low-wage and labor conditions in the South which were attracting the migration of Northern factories and capital to their section. A Southerner could hardly have been chosen for the Supreme Court who was less acceptable than Senator Black to the majority of Southern Democrats. Nevertheless, by the traditional rule of Senatorial "courtesy" whereby its members were invariably approved for high office, the Senate could not well refuse him a seat on the Court.

By a refinement of irony, the only important objection to Black's appointment which the Senate could unearth was a charge that he was a member of the Ku Klux Klan, and this objection was not one which Southern Senators would find serious. Black was understood to deny that he was a member, and his appointment was approved on August 18. Later, while he was in Europe, a sensation was created by the publication in the Pittsburgh *Post-Gazette* of proofs that Black held a life membership in the Ku Klux Klan. The fitness of a Supreme Court justice, who belonged to an organization which was hostile to three groups of citizens, Catholics, Jews, and Negroes, to interpret a Constitution which admitted of no such prejudices, was widely denied. Justice Black was relentlessly pursued by newspaper reporters for a statement until he made a nation-wide radio address on October 1. He declared that he had once belonged to the Klan, but that he had resigned and never considered the unsolicited card which was given to him as a renewal of his membership. He said that the affair was being dwelt upon to stir the flames of racial and religious prejudice, and denied that he harbored any intolerance. This denial was borne out fully by Justice Black's decisions and votes as a member of the Supreme Court.

A more immediate and significant consequence of the bitter fight over the court plan was the failure of Congress to pass important laws which the administration advocated as parts of the program for which it had "just begun to fight." Such a result would have seemed impossible when the 1937 session of Congress opened. The Executive Reorganization Bill which the President submitted in January was the product of a committee that had studied the unsuccessful attempts of Presidents Theodore Roosevelt, Taft, Wilson, and Hoover to rationalize the crazy quilt of Executive agencies grown unmanageable as a result of planless accumulations. The Bill seemed to give little room for controversy, since leaders of both Parties had long agitated for Executive reorganization to end the bureaucracy and waste for which each succeeding administration for decades had been more se-

[285

verely criticized. The President pleaded "guilty" to the charges in the Report of his Committee on Administrative Management that he was unable to handle adequately his responsibilities, that he was overworked, and that it was humanly impossible to carry out fully his duties because he was overwhelmed with minor details and needless contacts arising directly from the bad organization of the government. Over one hundred separate departments, boards, commissions, corporations, authorities, agencies, and offices produced an administrative chaos in which overlapping, duplication, and contradictory policies were inevitable. The Executive Reorganization Bill proposed five changes: a group of non-political, "anonymous" administrative assistants to the President who should establish close liaison with all activities of the Executive departments; strengthening of managerial agencies, especially those dealing with the budget, efficiency investigations personnel, and planning; extension of the civil service merit system "upward, outward, and downward," to include all jobs except those which were temporary or carried policy-making responsibility—a reform which would bring 250,000 more positions under the civil service immediately; location of the great majority of the independent agencies under one of the Cabinet departments, to which should be added the two new departments of Social Welfare and Public Works; and restoration of Executive responsibility for accounts with provision of an independent post-audit of all fiscal transactions. The President stated:

I realize that it will be said that I am recommending the increase of the powers of the Presidency. This is not true. The Presidency as established in the Constitution of the United States has all the powers that are required. . . . What I am placing before you is the request not for more power, but for the tools of management and the authority to distribute the work so that the

President can effectively discharge those powers which the Constitution now places upon him.[26]

During 1937, the Executive Reorganization Bill was not passed largely because conservative Democrats and Republicans opposed it as the twin of the Judiciary Reorganization Bill and another attempt of the President to obtain "dictatorial" powers. The counter-charge, that its expansion of the civil service and consequent loss of patronage by Congressmen was the more important reason for opposition, had little effect.

The Black-Connery Wages and Hours Bill had been introduced once more when the 1937 session of Congress opened. Debate revealed that the Bill was opposed chiefly by Southerners who desired a differential which would permit lower wages to be paid in the South than in the rest of the country. Senator "Cotton Ed" Smith of South Carolina declared that "any man on this floor who has sense enough to read the English language knows that the main object of this bill is, by human legislation, to overcome the splendid gifts of God to the South." [27] The special message of the President on May 24 recommended a Fair Labor Standards Bill embodying somewhat more flexible provisions as a substitute for the Black-Connery measure. He said that Congress and the administration were pledged

to take further steps to reduce the lag in the purchasing power of industrial workers and to strengthen and stabilize the markets for the farmers' products. . . . Our Nation so richly endowed with natural resources and with a capable and industrious population should be able to devise ways and means of insuring to all our able-bodied working men and women a fair day's pay for a fair day's work. A self-supporting and self-respecting democracy can plead no justification for the existence of child labor, no economic reason for chiseling workers' wages or stretching workers' hours. Enlightened business is learning that competition ought not to cause bad social consequences which inevitably react upon the profits of business itself. . . .

The exponents of the theory of private initiative as the cure for deep-seated national ills want in most cases to improve the lot of mankind. But, well intentioned as they may be, they fail for four evident reasons—first, they see the problem from the point of view of their own business; second, they see the problem from the point of view of their own locality or region; third, they cannot act unanimously because they have no machinery for agreeing among themselves; and, finally, they have no power to bind the inevitable minority of chiselers within their own ranks.[28]

The Fair Labor Standards Bill provided for a Board which should have power to fix wages and hours at its discretion but aiming at a "floor" under wages of forty cents an hour and a "ceiling" over forty hours of work per week. An employer who required more hours per week than the standard would pay time and a half for overtime. Child labor would be outlawed. Southern criticism of the Bill became a storm when Senator Copeland of New York added an amendment to penalize local law-enforcement agencies which permitted lynch mobs to obtain possession of prisoners. Senator Vandenberg of Michigan offered an amendment to forbid "unfair labor practices" by labor groups, and this permitted revival of the debate over the Wagner Labor Relations Act. Senator Lodge of Massachusetts wished to add amendments for quota restrictions on foreign imports manufactured under inferior labor conditions. All of these attempts to raise other issues were defeated. Republican Senators declared the Bill would lead to fascism, and supporters of the measure raised the question whether this was the reason why businessmen opposed it. The attempt of the administration to show that higher wages for labor would create a larger market for farmers was offset by a campaign on the part of manufacturers' associations to prove to farmers that the prices of goods they purchased would rise if the Bill were passed. The opposition to the Bill by Southern Democrats and Republicans was not sufficient to prevent its passage in the Senate on July 31, but effectively blocked it in the House.

On June 3, the President recommended to Congress that it establish seven regional authorities, which, with the existing Tennessee Valley Authority, Columbia Valley Authority, and the Mississippi River Commission, should cover the nation with agencies "to conserve and safeguard the prudent use of waters, water-power, soils, forests, and other resources of the areas entrusted to their charge." [29] This "seven TVA's" proposal was looked upon by the administration as the ultimate solution for a multitude of problems which had been met thus far only by palliatives. The most important of these problems were drought and flood, waste of hydroelectric resources, and soil depletion. Senator Norris made efforts to secure favorable action on preliminary planning machinery, but Congress was largely hostile to the program, and it was never taken out of committee. The inadequacy of the Soil Conservation and Domestic Allotment Act to achieve the objectives of the original AAA, and the new liberalism of the Supreme Court, led the President to propose on July 12 that a new AAA be established, but this, too, received little attention from Congress.

Only two important new laws were passed during 1937. On February 16, the President submitted the Report of the Special Committee on Farm Tenancy, and drew special attention to its proof that:

The American dream of the family-size farm, owned by the family which operates it, has become more and more remote. The agricultural ladder, on which an energetic young man might ascend from hired man to tenant to independent owner, is no longer serving its purpose. [30]

Instead, the equity of owners in their own farms was on the

average only 42 per cent, and they were being forced into the tenant class, which had increased in fifty years from 25 per cent of the total number of farmers to 40 per cent. Congress was not told what other authorities made clear, that the first AAA had contributed to the growth of tenancy and of the migrant farm labor class at the bottom of the ladder.[31] It was, therefore, to some extent to correct the effects of the farm program of the First New Deal that the President recommended that the "present intolerable condition of the lowest income farm families"[32] be improved. Congress accordingly passed the Bankhead-Jones Farm Tenant Act which was signed on July 22. It established the Farm Security Administration and provided ten million dollars for loans at low interest and repayable in small installments over a period of forty years to tenants who would purchase farms and whose applications were approved by committees of local farmers. Rehabilitation loans for operating expenses and educational assistance to establish the families as successful farmers were also provided. Aid to migrants in the form of sanitary camps, medical and other relief, and employment service which would diminish the extreme exploitation of these workers were gradually developed under the FSA. The Resettlement Administration was placed under the new agency.

Prior agreements on hours and wages with employers of migrant workers, and regulation of the supply of migrant laborers so that a surplus should not continue to make their bargaining efforts futile, made the FSA extremely unpopular with the owners of the increasingly large fruit and vegetable "factories in the fields," many of whom had been accustomed to exploit a peculiarly helpless class of workers without restraint. Southern landowners who found that the FSA gave the best of their sharecroppers an alternative to unattractive conditions on their farms, and those who resented the use of rehabilitation loans by poor whites and Negroes to pay poll taxes, became equally opposed to the new program. Sporadic campaigns against the FSA were conducted in Congress chiefly by Southern members, and while they never succeeded in abolishing the agency, they prevented its appropriations from becoming large enough to expand the work to a scale commensurate with the size of the problem. This was in spite of the fact that the loans made by the FSA were being repaid by 1939 at a rate faster than the contracts required.[33]

The Wagner-Steagall Housing Act of September 1 was the product of experiments with slum clearance which had begun in 1933 under the PWA. Experience had shown that housing could be provided at rents low enough to meet the needs of slum-dwellers only if extraordinary measures of federal aid were undertaken. The new law established the United States Housing Authority as a corporation under the Department of the Interior and gave it power to lend money, obtained by bond issues, at low interest for periods up to sixty years to local agencies which provided at least 10 per cent of the cost of projects. Low maximum costs of construction and rentals were enforced. When low rentals could not be established even with the aid of federal loans, the USHA was empowered to make outright annual gifts of money appropriated by Congress if a gift from a local government equal to 25 per cent of the federal gift could be obtained. Earlier federal housing projects were all brought under the USHA, and efforts were made to lower their rental charges. To ensure that the lowest income groups should benefit by the new federal projects, only families whose net incomes were not above fixed maximums were accepted as tenants. The new law, by combining local and federal funds and joining loans with gifts, made possible the first housing projects in which the actual slum-dwellers whose tenements had been cleared could rent space. Slum clearance was presently underway on a wide scale, and by the end of 1940 almost 350 projects were completed or under construction.

The Farm Tenant Act and the Housing Act added important new elements to the Second New Deal by adding to its beneficiaries two groups which were extremely vulnerable to private exploitation. The remainder of the laws passed in 1937 were renewals or revivals of earlier enactments. The Reciprocity Trade Agreements Act was renewed for another term of three years on March 1. Some of the opponents of the Act had lost their seats in Congress, and the verdict of the elections clearly favored renewal. Hearings and debate demonstrated wide approval of the purposes of the Act as well as satisfaction with the agreements already negotiated under it. Effective testimony was offered by Assistant Secretary of State Francis B. Sayre to prove that the agreements had benefited many specific products by increasing their exports, and had injured American products only in a minor way by increased imports. His testimony won the approval of many Republicans. The chief objection to the Act came from those who were dissatisfied with the hearings on agreements which were conducted by the State Department, and wanted Congressional hearings and Senate ratification of agreements in order to permit better opportunity to bring pressure to bear in favor of special interests. These arguments were answered by pointing out that the interests of the nation as a whole, political as well as economic, should prevail over particular interests, and that the existing procedure secured precisely that end. The resolution for renewal easily passed both houses.[34] This was a significant victory for the Second New Deal policy of international economic coöperation.

The Guffey-Vinson Bituminous Coal Act of April 26 revived all the main provisions of the law which the Supreme Court had invalidated except the hours-and-wages clauses of the code of fair competition. Price regulations and the guaranty of collective bargaining were expected to result in satisfactory labor conditions. Constitutional objections were met by exemption of producers of coal which did not enter interstate commerce. The Railroad Retirement Act of June 24 and the Carriers' Taxing Act of June 29 organized the pension system for railroad employees which the companies agreed upon voluntarily, and superseded the legislation of 1935. The Revenue Act of August 26 plugged loopholes in the income-tax laws which had permitted personal holding companies and foreign and domestic property trusts to be used for avoidance of tax payments. The law was proposed by the President when it became apparent that tax collections were being materially reduced by these devices, and officials of the Treasury Department worked closely with Congress to demonstrate to it the methods and cure of tax avoidance.

The 1937 session of Congress was considered to be a sharp defeat of the administration in spite of the two important new laws which were passed. At its close, the President made a coast-to-coast tour, during which spectacular popular support, exceeding that of campaign tours, was demonstrated in contradiction of the prognoses of political experts. Many Democratic Congressmen who had voted against the administration program, especially the Judiciary Reorganization Bill, made haste to show their loyalty by rousing speeches and eager jostling for place at the President's side and a word of approval from him when he appeared before their constituents. The President's conviction that the majority of the people approved his policies led him to call a special session of Congress for November 16 in hope of obtaining enactment of legislation which had been refused during the regular session. He did not revive the court "packing" issue which had disrupted the regular session. He had declared the defeated parts of the Judiciary Reorganization Bill to be still necessary when the Judicial Procedure Act was signed in August, but now the question was allowed to die. Besides the laws on executive reorganization, hours and wages, the seven TVA's, and the new AAA, the President asked for a new antitrust measure and liberalization of the Housing Act. During a five-week session Congress advanced most of these several stages towards enactment, but nothing final was accomplished. The year ended with the defeat of the administration by Congress still the outstanding feature of the political situation, and the split in the great Democratic majority in Congress only partially repaired.

The outstanding economic development of 1937 was the "recession" which began during the summer. Since the administration had claimed credit for the great recovery which had set in with the launching of the Second New Deal, it was inevitably blamed for the decline, particularly by those who had denied that administration policy was responsible for recovery. Late in 1936 and early in the next year, the steady movement of recovery which had begun in 1935 threatened to develop into a full-fledged boom. Prices rose very rapidly. Many speculative activities typical of a boom period began, even though new federal controls restricted the possibilities. Buying of commodities before they were needed in anticipation of higher prices became widespread. Some observers declared that the deficit-financing policy of the administration was causing an inflationary debauch.

Administration authorities began to fear that a runaway boom of the 1928–1929 variety was beginning, and, if allowed to grow unchecked, would end in another disastrous crash. It was therefore determined that in the interest of stabilization certain corrective measures should be taken. By taking account of increased revenues and drastically reducing the number of workers on WPA rolls, the administration planned to balance the budget within a year. WPA rolls had been considerably reduced late in 1936, and early in 1937 the policy was announced of discharging about half of those remaining. By August only one and a half million persons were still employed by the WPA. This reduction of "pump-priming" was considered by some economists to have been too drastic and a direct cause of the recession. New rules for loans to local governments for PWA projects brought this form of pump-priming virtually to an end. The Treasury no longer needed to borrow funds as heavily as in former years, and it did not object when the Board of Governors of the Federal Reserve System used its discretion to increase the reserve requirements of member banks by 50 per cent during the first half of the year. The effect of this action was to dry up sources of credit which might have been used for the expansion of industry as well as for speculative purposes. Again critics believed that the action was too drastic and not only prevented a runaway boom but led to the recession. During April, when the recovery reached its climax, the administration called for reduction of expenditures by executive agencies.

Conservative opponents of the New Deal no doubt approved economy and the deflationary actions of the government especially reduction of WPA. When the recession occurred, they blamed the "anti-business" policies of the administration. The undistributed profits taxes and the high personal income taxes were said to discourage business expansion, reduce the incentive of profits for investors, and cause too much capital to be left idle in banks and to be sent out of the country. The labor policies of the administration were declared to be unsound, particularly as they encouraged the organization into unions of the workers in mass-production industries. CIO unions had been successful in a series of sit-down strikes, and were beginning to win contracts from such traditionally anti-union corporations as United States Steel.

This, and the validation of the Wagner Act with the prospect of paying the penalties which many corporations had incurred by disobedience of the law, led to a loss of confidence by businessmen. The struggle of the administration to "pack" the Supreme Court was pointed to as an outstanding example of political activities which unsettled business. And the multitude of new regulatory laws with which businessmen had to contend, aggravated by the inexperience and anti-business attitude of the officials who enforced them, were said to discourage that aggressive spirit of enterprise which was a prime requisite of a healthy economy.

Counter-charges were made by supporters of the administration. The recovery of 1935–1937 was proof that the policies of the administration were not incompatible with vigorous private enterprise and prosperity. Businessmen wanted more than an opportunity to develop a sound recovery. They wanted an unregulated speculative boom of the kind which had ended, even under the friendly administration of President Hoover, in disaster. Business fears of excessive deficit financing and inflation had been met by reduction in government spending and deflationary action by the Federal Reserve. But the 1937 decisions of the Supreme Court which had assured the permanence of the Second New Deal, and the efforts of the administration to complete its structure, had led businessmen to engage in a "political strike of capital." This was the basic cause of the recession. Businessmen refused to invest new capital, for which opportunities abounded, and reduced employment as a deliberate demonstration intended to discredit the administration and, in conjunction with the new coalition of conservative Democrats and Republicans in Congress, frustrate the completion of the administration's program.

Cooler observers were inclined to believe that the administration was able at best merely to mitigate with its new controls the excesses of speculation and the degree of depression without eliminating the basic factors which produced the business cycle. After more than two years of steady recovery a reaction was inevitable. The country was fortunate that the recession was no more severe than the boom had been excessive; for their minimization the administration could legimately claim some credit.

Whatever were its causes, the effects of the recession were serious but short-lived. The index of industrial production fell from 117 in August, 1937, to 76 in May, 1938. Thereafter it staged a rapid recovery to 104 in December, 1938.[35] Wholesale prices fell from the index of 87.9 in August, 1937, to 78.1 in May, 1938; during the same period farm prices fell from 123 to 92.[36] Employment in manufacturing industries reached the index of 112.3 in August, 1937, and dropped to 84.7 in July, 1938. Pay rolls were 108.7 in August, 1937, and fell to 71.1 by July, 1938.[37]

The recession of 1937–1938 undoubtedly caused a loss of prestige by the administration. It was placed on the defensive, its situation to a distressing extent analogous to that of the Hoover administration. The claim of exclusive ownership of policies conducive to prosperity has been made by almost all administrations, and has been turned against them with political effect when prosperity lapsed. Combined with the split in the Democratic Party between liberals and conservatives and the failure of a large part of the administration's program in Congress, the recession made 1937 the year of crisis of the Second New Deal. That it came so hard on the heels of the great electoral victory of November, 1936, underlined the misfortune.

At the same time, war in Europe and Asia, still confined to Spain and China, was threatening to engulf the world, and produce in the United States the retreat from domestic reform which is the classical route to unity in face of foreign dangers. But one more year remained while war came no closer than the horizon, during which the President could attempt to rescue the country from depression, his Party from disunity and reaction, and his program from defeat.

CHAPTER XIV

END AND BEGINNING: 1938

THE President's Annual Message of January 3, 1938, opened with a warning that the nation's defenses must be strengthened. By the end of the year this theme had superseded all others. But domestic issues were still paramount in January, and the President's chief proposals were for the passage of legislation which had failed to be enacted in 1937. The recession was minimized. No revival of "pump-priming" was announced. A careful distinction was made between the "minority" of businessmen whose practices were censurable, and business in general and the capitalist system of private enterprise, which the President declared it was "deception" to accuse the administration of opposing or attacking. Government would coöperate with business "provided the component parts of business abandon practices which do not belong to this day and age, and adopt price and production policies appropriate to the times." [1] The proviso seemed to echo current charges that responsibility for the recession lay with the policies of business.

Nevertheless, for three more months the President gave trial to the thesis of conservatives that governmental economy rather than expenditures to increase purchasing power was the best contribution which he could make to ending the recession. The long-range objective of the administration was described as a national income of from ninety to a hundred billion dollars, which would permit balancing of the budget and reduction of the debt. Further curtailments of public works and of relief activities were recommended in the Budget Message.

If the President was offering an olive branch to business in hope that it would reverse the downward spiral of recession, his expectation was disappointed. Production and employment declined rapidly during the first quarter of the year. Therefore, on April 14, the President sent a special message to Congress and addressed the nation in a fireside chat which announced the revival of the policies which had brought recovery in 1935, and had been reversed just prior to the beginning of the recession. A new appropriation of $1,250,000,000 for the expansion of WPA employment was proposed as "ammunition of the highest grade for attack on recession." [2] Additional appropriations for the PWA, FSA, CCC, NYA, USHA and other agencies brought the total recommendation for expenditures and loans to slightly more than $3,000,000,000. Congress very largely approved these appropriations. Besides the revival of direct "pump-priming," the Treasury Department "desterilized" $1,400,000,000 of its gold by issuing paper against it to increase bank credits, and the Federal Reserve Board reduced its reserve requirements for banks. Both of these actions inflated credits available for use by business, agriculture, and commerce.

Renewal of "pump-priming" and expansion of bank credit undoubtedly were influential in ending the recession during the summer of 1938. This did not prevent the national income from declining during 1938 for the first time since the administration came to office. In 1937, the high level of 71 billion dollars had been reached; in 1938, the national income fell to 63 billions; and in 1939, recovery only to 69 billions was achieved. The prospects which had seemed so bright in 1936, that unemployment would virtually disappear while a new era of prosperity would be stabilized by the reform and regulation of capitalism, were disappointed, and

300]

this constituted one of the most important factors in future discussion of the experiments of the New Deal. The conclusions which were drawn would vary with the preconceptions of the analyst. To the conservative, the failure of the New Deal to provide permanent prosperity was proof that its reforms were unsound. But mere objection to the attempts of the Roosevelt administration to solve profound economic and social problems seemed to offer nothing better as an alternative than repetitions of the cycle of boom and depression which had steadily intensified until the greatest crash occurred under the Hoover administration—when the policies of business were most thoroughly supported by government. To the liberal, the failure of the New Deal to provide permanent prosperity was proof that its policies had been pursued too timidly. The inducement of prosperity through government expansion of purchasing power and credit required action which was at once more daring in scope and more closely adjusted to expansion and contraction of industrial production and private employment. Government regulation of business practices, especially investment, required greater encouragement of productive activity at the same time that speculative production and trading were more thoroughly eliminated. Whether these fine balances could be established more easily during future periods of peace because of the experience gained under the New Deal, as liberals hoped, or whether they would require an intolerable expansion of bureaucracy which would only destroy all private initiative, as conservatives feared, was a question which would trouble the architects of policy at the end of the Second World War, for that conflict, with its "unnatural" accompanying prosperity, proved too much about the efficacy of government spending as the route to prosperity, and only postponed without solving the problem.

In 1938, the revival of the spending policy brought the

charge that the administration had adopted it with a particular view to the November Congressional elections, but the defeats which it suffered in those elections took the sting out of the argument. The only significant objection made in Congress to the extra appropriations was to the items for the FSA. The continued disaffection of conservative Southern Congressmen was emphasized by their refusal to permit extension to white and Negro tenants, sharecroppers, and migrants of aids which would reduce the dependence of these classes on landowners and other dominant groups. The additional appropriation of $100,000,000 for loans to purchase farms was refused, and the regular appropriation was reduced to $25,000,000, so that the effectiveness of the FSA program was frustrated in great degree.

The first important new legislation passed by Congress was the Agricultural Adjustment Act of February 16. The need for the law had been emphasized by the severe decline of farm prices, resulting not only from the decline of purchasing power during the recession, but also from the failure of the Soil Conservation and Domestic Allotment Act to prevent production of unmanageable surpluses as a result of a superior crop year free of drought in 1937. The new liberalism of the Supreme Court, confirmed by a number of minor decisions during the new term and the opening made for another appointment by the retirement of Justice Sutherland on January 18, encouraged passage of an act which revived and modified the original AAA and superseded the Soil Conservation and Domestic Allotment Act.

The objective of direct control over farm surpluses had been attained under the first AAA by payments of benefits out of processing taxes under contracts with farmers not to grow crops on a portion of their acres. This objective was revived as the primary purpose of the second AAA, but it was obtained by improved means. Whenever an export crop threatened to create a surplus which would break the price, a marketing quota would be fixed by the AAA. A referendum would be held among farmers who had planted the particular crop, and if two-thirds of them agreed, acreage allotments would be made to each farmer. He was not required to keep out of production or "plow under" the surplus acres, but if he marketed more than the product of his allotted acres during a period when a surplus was being produced, he was subject to a fine. The Commodity Credit Corporation would offer loans to farmers on their surplus crops, and they would be stored under government seal until a shortage developed in a subsequent period of scarcity. A "parity price" would be fixed by the AAA which represented the average purchasing power of a unit of the crop during the years 1900 to 1914. Loans on surplus crops would be made to an amount slightly below the parity price. The farmer would repay the loan and sell the surplus crop only when the market price was at parity or above, and gave him an advantage in so doing. Such sales would in turn prevent the market price from ever rising very far above parity. Thus, in effect, crops would be stored in years of surplus without the farmer losing the income, and they would be available in years of shortage from drought or any cause, while prices would remain always very close to parity levels. This ingenious system of the "ever-normal granary" was credited largely to Secretary Wallace, and represented a solution of the problem of farm surpluses and prices which was not open to the objection that it required destruction or waste of nature's bounty and of the farmer's faith in his art. It substituted the economics of abundance for scarcity economics. Its cost to the government or other groups was only slightly more than that of administration, for the farmer was not "paid for not working." If the yield of acres which the farmers were permitted to market at the end of a crop year was larger than expected and the price fell materially below parity, farmers were allowed "parity payments" to make up the loss of income. But experience with the system made the promise of parity payments a guaranty rather than continuous expense of the new system. It was charged that the system "subsidized" agriculture as well as regulated the farmers' activity. But the regulations were undertaken only when farmers voted for them to solve the problem of a particular year, the subsidies were only guaranties against the farmers being penalized for producing abundant crops, and their income remained proportionate to their efforts and the varying behavior of the weather. The parity-price and ever-normal granary plan met with wide approval during the short period of trial before the Second World War, and, after the War created extreme need for abundant crops, the system continued to operate, but as a powerful instrument against inflation of farm and food prices, successful to the extent that Congress resisted demands of farmers to raise the parity price levels.

The special problems of the Dust Bowl were provided for in the new AAA by a Federal Crop Insurance Corporation which accepted wheat in payment of premiums on insurance policies taken out by farmers against loss of their crops from unavoidable causes, particularly drought. The new law continued the soil conservation activities of the previous measure, but without the former emphasis on substitution of other crops for the export staples. The objectives of increasing benefits paid to the poorest farmers and limiting those paid to the largest landowners and farm corporations were apparent in the provisions that payments for soil-conserving activities should not be smaller than $200 or larger than $10,000, and in the requirement that payments be divided between landowners and tenants under the direct supervision of the Secretary of Agriculture.

The second AAA completed the structure of the farm program of the Second New Deal. Only the inability of the administration to obtain adequate appropriations for the FSA prevented that program from benefiting the poorest farm groups comparably with the larger farmers and farm corporations. In this respect also, the Second World War, with its great expansion of employment opportunities, brought a unique prosperity without solving their basic problems to groups which had benefited least under the New Deal.

The Fair Labor Standards Act of June 25 was the other most important law passed in 1938. It was the last major enactment of the Second New Deal. The President had not advocated a specific wages-and-hours bill until May, 1937, but he repeatedly called public attention to the need for one and often pressed it on Congress thereafter. The Fair Labor Standards Bill which he recommended to Congress substituted flexible provisions for the rigid standards of the Black-Connery Bill, but this was not enough to secure its approval by Congress. Seventy-two amendments were introduced to restrict the application of the law, exempt particular industries, and establish a sectional differential to permit lower standards in the South. A final effort to defeat the Bill was made by Chairman John O'Connor of New York, who led in a manipulation of parliamentary devices by the Committee on Rules to prevent the measure from coming to a vote. The President wrote an open letter to another member of Congress drawing attention to this frustration of the "democratic legislative process," [3] and the Bill was voted. Most of the final opposition in Congress came from the South, and the South won the most important concessions.

The law in its final form applied to enterprises which were engaged in, or which affected, interstate commerce; its broad scope was clearly dependent on liberal interpretation of the commerce power by the Supreme Court. Many occupations were specifically exempted, of which the most important were farm laborers, employees in intrastate retail and servicing establishments, domestic servants, professional and administrative workers, seamen, fishermen, and employees of small newspapers and local food-processing plants. The most important concession obtained by Southern Congressmen was the admission of a sectional differential to provide general exceptions and preserve the cheap labor market in the South. Aside from statutory and administrative exceptions, the law had as its objective a minimum wage of 40 cents an hour and a maximum of 40 hours of work per week. The fact that $16 per week was not a living wage for even a small family did not prevent charges that the administration was coddling labor. And the Act provided that these wage-and-hour objectives should be achieved only gradually: respectively within eight years after beginning at 25 cents an hour and within three years beginning at 44 hours per week. It came as a shock to many that over 750,000 workers received wage increases when the law first went into effect in August, 1938. About 1 per cent of the workers coming under the law was thrown out of work presumably because employers could not meet the new standards and stay in business. Most of the shut-downs occurred in the South in such industries as pecan-shelling, tobacco manufacture, bagging, clothing, and lumber. But it could be argued that employers who could not afford to pay wages of $11 for a 44-hour week, even when they were no longer faced by competition from enterprises which paid less, were too inefficient, if not too eager to sweat labor, to be mourned. On the other hand, the hours of 1,500,-000 workers were shortened when the law went into effect, and a general increase of employment because of this, and the increased purchasing power of those whose wages were raised were pointed to as proof of the beneficial effects of the new law.[4]

Time and a half for overtime was required to be paid by

an employer when more than the maximum hours were worked. Labor by children under sixteen was forbidden, and it was restricted to non-hazardous occupations for those under eighteen. Special exemptions for apprentices and handicapped workers were made. Upon the recommendation of committees representing particular industries, exceptions to lower or raise standards might be made by the administrator of the Act. The many elements of flexibility in the law helped to weaken the opposition to it, not only in Congress but also among the public, which had been told in advertising and other campaigns that its provisions were immoderate. The constitutionality of the law was upheld on February 3, 1941, by the Supreme Court in a decision reversing many previous rulings.

The struggle for federal action to outlaw child labor had begun with laws of the Wilson administration which the Supreme Court had invalidated, continued with Section 7A of NIRA, and the efforts which the President had supported for an amendment to the Constitution. With the validation of the Fair Labor Standards Act, the fight was finally successful. And the struggle for a federal regulation of the hours and wages of adult labor had been only slightly less prolonged when the Supreme Court put its final approval on the 1938 Act.

The law abolished the worst abuses of sweatshops and child labor, and took a long step towards extending the "American standard of living" to the largest sector of workers, who were not organized in labor unions and therefore could not benefit from the Wagner Labor Relations Act. The inability of the labor movement to organize more than about one-fourth of all industrial workers, even after the great gains made by both the CIO and the AFL during the NIRA period and under the Wagner Act, made hours-and-wages legislation the only means of improving the status of the worst-exploited laborers in the country. The laws which many states had passed were no longer being invalidated by the Supreme Court. Other states which made a practice of attracting sweatshops inside their borders could do so after the passage of the federal law only within the limits of intrastate commerce or specially exempted fields.

With the Social Security Act and the Wagner Act, the Fair Labor Standards Act completed the main structure of labor legislation under the Second New Deal. They and their history summed up the largest part of the significance of the New Deal and of its ardent support by labor and opposition by business, as they were probably its most important additions to the permanent institutions of the nation.

The Food, Drug, and Cosmetic Act of June 24 superseded and amplified the famous law which had been passed in 1906 by the Theodore Roosevelt administration as a first result of modern reform agitation. The new law had been intended by the administration to include provision for grade labeling of many commodities, but only cosmetics were added to the products previously controlled. Many varieties of deception and fraud by manufacturers of food, drugs, and cosmetics were forbidden, and statements of ingredients on labels were required. The Act served to expand in a vital field the administration's policy that freedom of enterprise was limited by considerations of the public welfare, and its formula that the seller as well as the buyer was responsible for the abolition of fraud.

The long-promised campaign against business monopoly, which would complete the reversal of the business policy of the First New Deal, was inaugurated in 1938 by the passage of the Monopoly Inquiry Act of June 16. In a special message on April 29 the President called attention to the ever-growing concentration of financial and industrial power in the hands of a few. The recession had increased public concern with the policies of the nation's economic leadership:

Examination of methods of conducting and controlling private enterprise which keep it from furnishing jobs or income or opportunity for one-third of the population is long overdue on the part of those who sincerely want to preserve the system of private enterprise for profit.[5]

A democratic people would not tolerate unemployment and a low standard of living when their capacity to produce was obviously unused:

The power of a few to manage the economic life of the nation must be diffused among the many or transferred to the public and its democratically responsible government.[6]

But the administration was not embarking on a "trust-busting" campaign with the fanfare, the poorly-considered attacks on mere bigness, and the small results which had characterized campaigns early in the century. The message recommended chiefly that a comprehensive study of monopoly be made by the Federal Trade Commission, the Department of Justice, and the Securities Exchange Commission. Objection was made in Congress that the inquiry would be under auspices too closely associated with the Executive branch. The law which was passed provided for a Temporary National Economic Committee, half of whose members were drawn from Congress and the remaining half from Executive departments and commissions. The causes of monopoly, its effect on the price system, trade, employment, profits, investment, savings, and consumption, and the effects on monopoly of taxation, patents, and other government activities were placed within the scope of the Committee's investigations. It was given the power of subpoena and an appropriation of $500,000. When the TNEC Reports began to be issued in 1939, they were generally admitted to be the best available objective studies of the American economic system, and of extraordinary value to makers of policy and citizens generally. They paved the way for far-reaching legislation which was perhaps only postponed by the outbreak of the Second World War. The revelations which came with the War of the scope and significance of the international patent cartels into which many American corporations had entered added new importance to the anti-monopoly campaign which was launched in 1938, and even revived the issue in the midst of the War as one which could not be ignored in planning for the peace.

In 1938, the President also appointed Professor Thurman Arnold of the Yale Law School as Assistant Attorney General in charge of enforcement of the antitrust laws. Arnold was unwilling to launch a suit until he had made a thorough study not merely of the legal but also of the economic and social effects of the alleged monopoly, and his prosecutions were undertaken as test cases to explore the legal status of various business policies rather than as punitive expeditions. He was willing to prosecute AFL building-trade unions as well as contractors for collusion in holding up prices of labor and materials which restricted construction of low-cost housing; he was interested in promoting efficiency rather than penalizing it. The cautious procedures of the President's anti-monopoly campaign did not make for spectacular results, but they had the more valuable effect of attacking the difficult problem, which had been approached under the NIRA, of discriminating between social and antisocial forms of competition as well as monopoly. The implications for future relations between government and business were profound.

The administration obtained no other important part of its program from Congress during 1938. The split which had developed within the Democratic Party in 1937 caused concessions to conservatives even in the laws which were passed during 1938, and produced some legislation the administration did not want and a refusal to pass other laws in any form. The Revenue Act of 1938 was a victory for Republican and Democratic opponents of the administration. The steeply graduated tax on undistributed profits of corporations which had been passed in 1936 was repealed. This was the first casualty of a New Deal law in the growing conservative offensive against which rear-guard action was forced on the administration as it lost leadership in the formulation of domestic policy. Instead of the undistributed profits tax, Congress imposed a tax of 19 per cent on incomes of corporations if they earned more than $25,000. A trivial remnant of the former tax was retained as a concession to the strong opposition of the administration—receipt of such a favor being an extraordinary new experience for the leaders of the New Deal. The concession took the form of a credit of 2½ per cent of the amount a corporation paid out in dividends up to 2½ per cent of all income. The new law lowered the taxes on the earnings of the largest corporations, and increased them to some extent on middle-sized enterprises. Taxes on capital gains, estates, and gifts were slightly lowered. Excise taxes on certain necessities and luxuries were removed.

Senator Pat Harrison of Mississippi, speaking for the Democrats who had voted for the law, declared that concessions to business were necessary in order to encourage new investment and recovery. The anomaly that his own state was the poorest per capita in the Union, and that its corporations would be more heavily taxed under the law, was not discussed by the Senator. The President declared in a public address that the improvement of tax laws to increase incentive for productive investment was very necessary, but that the law which Congress had passed merely gave "an infinitely greater tax concession to the man who makes a very great profit than to the man who makes a comparatively

[311]

small profit. It helps the very few, therefore, at the expense of the many." [7] The measure abandoned the principle of corporation taxes according to ability to pay. The President therefore refused to sign it, but allowed it to become a law without his signature on May 27. This was the first defeat by Congress of a significant New Deal principle which had already been established.

The most direct setback to his leadership which the President suffered was the defeat of the Executive Reorganization Bill. He had asked for it twice in 1937, and again in 1938. The Senate passed the Bill in March after weakening it considerably by refusing to permit quasi-judicial commissions to be placed under Executive departments, by subjecting to a veto by two-thirds of Congress any reorganization which the President might carry out, and by other changes. The major struggle against the Bill, even in the form it left the Senate, occurred in the House, and recalled the intensity of the fight over judicial reorganization. Many organizations which had stirred up opposition to the court plan functioned again. A number of Congressmen said that their answers to petitions against the Bill were returned because signers' addresses were non-existent. The main argument against the Bill was that by it the President intended to make himself a "dictator."

This charge reached the public in such broad and reiterated form that the President undertook to refute it on March 29 in a letter which he made public. He first gave three reasons why he was opposed to becoming a "dictator":

A: I have no inclination to be a dictator.
B: I have none of the qualifications which would make me a successful dictator.
C: I have too much historical background and too much knowledge of existing dictatorships to make me desire any form of dictatorship for a democracy like the United States of America. [8]

Then he pointed out the earlier general admission by its present opponents that efficiency required reorganization, and declared that the opposition to the Bill had been created out of whole cloth for partisan purposes. It was ironic that a measure which had been advocated in similar form by so many previous Presidents, Republican as well as Democratic, should have been singled out as "unprecedented" and "dictatorial." Later the President wrote:

Some radio orators, demagogues, a large part of the press and many of the pernicious Congressional lobbies served to deluge Congressmen with telegrams. What these people were really seeking to accomplish was not so much to block this particular legislation, as to try to discredit the administration so as to block any further thought of social reform, and, incidentally, reduce the effectiveness of its reform program by preventing efficiency generally in government.[9]

It was also ironic that an administration which was so widely accused of inefficiency, waste, and spoils-mongering should have been refused a law which would assist in their reformation. But the charge of dictatorship was difficult to combat because a strong and effective Executive was so easily identified with the word even if the purpose were to strengthen rather than weaken democracy. It was as if opponents of the administration wished the people to believe that democracy was compatible only with weakness and inability to meet modern needs and conditions, that they could not have both liberty and the New Deal.

Congressmen had a special interest in refusing to strengthen the civil service and thereby lose influence over patronage. The House passed further amendments to weaken the Bill and then by a close vote sent it back to committee on April 8. This ended hope of passing the Bill in any form in 1938. A year later a Reorganization Act was passed and signed which provided that minor consolidations of agencies could be effected and authorized six administrative assistants to the President. Like the Judicial Procedure Act of 1937, it was an admission that the wholesale condemnations of the President's original proposals had been unduly partisan and had obscured the need for at least a minimum solution of the problems with which the President had been concerned.

A few days after the defeat of the Executive Reorganization Bill in 1938, the President sent to Congress the recommendations which various groups had made to him for improvement of the situation of the railroads. They were in serious difficulties as a result of the recession, and most experts agreed that permission to unify roads and a unification of governmental agencies dealing with transportation were necessary. The Interstate Commerce Commission was exempted from the unification plan, but Congress rejected both suggestions, until 1940, when the Transportation Act authorized railroad unification and minor changes, but left governmental authority over transportation scattered in a congeries of agencies.

Two events early in 1938 posed in dramatic form the basic political problem of the administration. Events at home and abroad were precipitating the question whether the rise of opposition to the administration's domestic program or the rise of aggression by Germany, Italy, and Japan presented the greater threat to American democracy. The President had said that the forces which opposed democracy at home and abroad were the same. But in the practical matter of obtaining legislation from Congress in favor of domestic reform and collective security the situation was not so simple. Most Republicans in Congress opposed both policies, but they were a helpless minority without the coöperation of one or another group of Democrats. Within the Democratic ranks those who opposed collective security were on the whole a distinct group from those who opposed domestic reform. The latter were chiefly Southerners, but Southerners were at the same time among the strongest advocates in Congress of collective security. On the other hand, Western Democrats were on the whole progressive on domestic issues, but they were at the same time ardent advocates of isolationism.

Eastern Democrats were the only sectional group upon whom the President could usually depend for support of both his domestic and foreign policies, reform, and collective security. Majorities sufficient to pass legislation could be secured by uniting East and South on foreign issues and East and West on domestic issues. But it was increasingly apparent in 1937 and 1938 that the tensions which such a technique set up were reaching the breaking point. The danger was that the South would revolt against the administration's foreign policy if it became too aggrieved against its domestic reforms; or that the West would revolt against the administration's domestic policy if it could not have its way on foreign policy.

Until 1938 the President accepted the policy of the West on neutrality, which prevented effective action for collective security, and pursued domestic reform as his main object. But reform was deepening the antagonism between the administration and the Southern Democratic leaders by 1938, when their support was becoming indispensable to prevent the isolationism of the West, which in its turn was feeding on the rise of aggression abroad, from destroying all hope of developing the policy of collective security.

The struggles over the Ludlow Amendment and the Anti-Lynching Bill early in 1938 suggested the alternatives between which the administration would ultimately be forced to choose. The Ludlow Amendment required a popular referendum before Congress could declare war except in case of invasion. It was intended to appeal to all varieties of pacifist sentiment, but it was chiefly supported by those who believed isolation rather than collective security was the best way to keep the country out of war. It seemed about to pass in the House when the session opened. The President sent a letter to Speaker William B. Bankhead declaring that the proposed Amendment would be "impracticable in its application and incompatible with our representative form of government." Furthermore, it "would cripple any President in his conduct of our foreign relations, and it would encourage other nations to believe that they could violate American rights with impunity." [10] The President had already made clear, in his "Quarantine the Aggressors" speech of the previous October, that "American rights" were bound up with the security of international treaties and of peaceful nations against aggression.

On January 10, the House voted against consideration of the Amendment by the narrow margin of 209 to 188. Three-fourths of the Republican members voted for consideration, as did the great majority of Democrats from the West. But Southern Democrats voted 92 to 24 against consideration, and it was the South that defeated the Amendment, along with the Northeast.[11] Thus it was clearly demonstrated that if the Southern Democratic revolt against the administration should develop much further, the policies of extreme isolationism would be forced on the administration.

During the same month, the Anti-Lynching Bill to penalize local authorities who allowed a prisoner to be taken away from them by a mob and lynched, which had been before Congress during the previous session, was again debated. This time it was apparent that a majority of Northern and Western liberals and progressives of both parties was ready to pass the Bill. Southern Senators filibustered for more than thirty days to prevent it from coming to a vote. They made it clear that they would not stop short of complete revolt against the administration if the Bill were forced on the

South, and many of their threats were even less restrained. Supporters of the Bill hoped that the President would make a statement as he had often done in similar situations, or otherwise bring pressure to bear in favor of cloture to stop the filibuster and permit the Bill to be voted. But no word was forthcoming from the White House. In return for ending the filibuster, Southern Senators obtained a promise that the Anti-Lynching Bill would be dropped.

One recourse was open to the administration to rescue both its foreign and domestic policies from dependence on Southern conservatives. That was to alter the composition of the leadership of the Southern Democracy by substituting liberals for conservatives. The few Southern liberals in Congress, such as Senators Lister Hill of Alabama and Claude Pepper of Florida, demonstrated that an increase of like-minded representatives of their section would solve the crisis over domestic policy, heal the split in the Democratic Party, and at the same time end the dependence of the administration on disaffected conservatives for a broadening program of collective security.

Over and above specific and sectional questions, the vista was opened to the President of encouraging an adjustment of party lines which would make party labels correspond with political philosophies, of making his own Party an organization exclusively of liberals, and the Republican Party one exclusively of conservatives. The necessity of uniting a coalition of sectional-class interest groups to win national elections had always precluded this dream of many who had longed for more logic and cohesion in American political parties. But it seemed possible that the time had come when the spread of industry into sections beyond the Northeast, and the unity of farmers and laborers in support of liberal reform, as evidenced in the elections of 1936, made the attempt of the Democratic Party especially to hold the loyalty of a dissident wing anachronistic. In short, if conservatives of the Southern Democratic variety could be exchanged for liberals of the Western Republican variety, the trade would wonderfully clarify the philosophic meaning and responsibility of American political parties as well as be highly advantageous to the administration. It would extend to the rest of the country the process which had already largely occurred in the East, where conservative "Democrats" had voted Republican in 1936, and liberal "Republicans" such as Mayor La Guardia of New York supported the administration.

Such was the purpose of the President's participation in the 1938 Congressional election campaign which his opponents promptly labeled a "purge." In a fireside chat on June 24 he expressed the hope that every voter would "consider the fundamental principles for which his party is on record."

An election cannot give a country a firm sense of direction if it has two or more national parties which merely have different names but are as alike in their principles and aims as peas in the same pod.[12]

But it was actually not to be expected that in the critical section, the South, conservative leaders and voters would abandon the Democratic Party and join the Republicans so long as white supremacy remained the most important of all issues and the Republican Party was associated even remotely with Negro rights. Only by the nomination of liberal candidates in the Democratic primaries could the President's purposes be achieved. Traditionally the national leadership of the major political parties observed a formal neutrality among the candidates for nomination in the primaries. In practice it was equally traditional for the national leadership to exert influence in ways which were not too obvious to the electorate or offensive to the candidates who were not favored. In 1938, the President resolved to abandon delicacy and campaign actively within selected districts in support of liberals. This frank procedure would no doubt be resented by many leaders, but the President believed it was justified by the responsibility of the administration to carry out the promises of the Party Platform and its inability to do so when Democratic Congressmen, having been elected after assuring voters that they supported the Party leader and Platform, opposed them both.[13] The flaw in the plan was that the very groups in the South to whom the President's policies would most appeal, the poorer whites and the Negroes, were largely disfranchised, the former by state poll taxes, and the latter by discriminatory enforcement of literacy qualifications and "white primary" rules as well as by poll taxes. In the Southern states, where only 4 to 15 per cent of the electorate voted, as compared with 40 to 75 per cent in other sections,[14] the President would be appealing to the natural opponents of his domestic policies to elect Congressmen who would support them. The enfranchisement of the submerged groups of the South would seem to have been the necessary pre-condition of success in the campaign to liberalize its Democratic leadership. But the President had never suggested or supported the numerous proposals for repeal of the poll taxes by federal enactment, or any other reform which might reduce the supremacy of the "Bourbons."

Instead, he appealed to the restricted group of Southern voters to nominate candidates for Congress who would support a program of rehabilitation of the South which should benefit all groups without disturbing white supremacy. He made a cautious appeal to reason and the self-interest of the voting groups, and carefully avoided any suggestion that his program implied a change in the relations among classes or races. The object was to convince Southern voters that they as well as the less fortunate inhabitants of their section needed the Second New Deal and should elect Congressmen who would support it and help to extend it to the South.

The usual charge that outsiders could not understand the problems of the South was avoided by calling a Conference on Economic Conditions in the South composed of leading Southern educators, publishers and editors, bankers, businessmen, farmers, and laborers, under the auspices of the National Emergency Council, which placed at the disposal of the Conference the research and statistical services of various governmental departments and agencies. The Conference met in Washington on July 4. Its report was issued on August 12 when the President was personally campaigning in Georgia against Senator Walter F. George.

The "Report on Economic Conditions in the South" described the exploitation of a section and the inability of its people to find the road to equal progress with other sections. The human and natural resources of the South were not inferior to those of other regions. But the average income of its farmers, even in a good year like 1929, was $186 compared with $528 for farmers in the rest of the nation. A system of large landholdings had been inherited from slavery days. The mechanization of large plantations was increasing farm tenancy and rural unemployment. Many tenants lived in "poverty comparable to that of the poorest peasants in Europe." Many farm laborers were paid 10 cents a day. Industrial wages were the lowest in the country, common labor receiving 16 cents less an hour than in other sections. A large proportion of the industries and resources of the South was owned by outsiders, so that the average dividends per capita were $17.55 compared with $68.97 for the rest of the country. Yet outside capital was invited into the section with promises of low wages, docile laborers, and tax laws which exempted profits taken out of the section and placed a greater burden on consumers by means of sales taxes than in any other section. The climate of the South was as healthful as that of any other section for those who could afford a proper diet and medical care, but poverty made it the most disease-ridden area in the country. Malaria, pellagra, hookworm, syphilis, and typhoid fever were directly traceable to low average diet, lack of sanitary facilities, and inability to pay for public health and private medical services. Controlled tests had shown that the productivity of labor in the South rose in proportion to the improvement of diet and the eradication of disease: no inherent qualities of any class or race could be blamed for the "laziness" and backwardness of the poorer people of the South. Illiteracy was higher than anywhere in the Union. But the inferiority of Southern schools and other social services was not the result of unwillingness to pay for them. The states of the South paid a larger percentage of their income per capita for schools than did other states, but the income of the people was so small that the result was an expenditure of half as much per child as in other regions. Low wages for men produced the greatest amount of child and woman labor in the country. The least skilled industrial work was carried on in the South because of the ignorance and inefficiency of its laboring classes. Wage rates in industry were kept low by the over-supply of workers constantly moving into towns from farms. On the other hand, many of the most intelligent and ambitious young people of the South moved into other sections to find wider opportunities.

Farming in the South was financed by outside capital, for which high interest was charged because of the uncertainty of crops grown on depleted soil. Landlords who were financed by banks were forced to plant cash crops, chiefly cotton and tobacco, which further depleted the soil. Tenants were allowed to use very little land or none for vegetables which would improve the standard diet of fat-back and corn meal. Four-fifths of the food and clothing of the section was imported. The people of the section had average bank deposits of $150 as compared with $471 in the other sections. Landlords who oppressed their tenants were themselves often forced to pay 20 per cent interest on the money they borrowed. The natural resources of the section were being ruthlessly exploited. The insistence on cash crops and the lack of interest of tenants made soil conservation impossible: erosion and barrenness were rapidly destroying the Southern land. Hydroelectric power, natural gas, iron, coal, limestone, bauxite, and sulphur, in which the region was very rich, were largely absentee-owned, and the South received only the low wages of her laborers in exchange for the plundering of her wealth.

The South was the greatest potential market in the country. Its people wanted to buy and had goods and raw materials to exchange, but the exploitation of the section by outside owners left them without purchasing power. The economic and social backwardness of the South could be solved only by the increase of purchasing power of her people. This solution would benefit her most depressed classes, the owning groups, and the prosperity of the nation as a whole.[15]

This Report was perhaps the most concise, penetrating, and authoritative analysis of the problems of the South which had ever been published. Its undoubted accuracy, and its sponsorship by Southern leaders, made it transcend the heated context of a political campaign which inevitably became entangled in personalities and partisan animosities. But even on its own ground, the Report was not without limitations. The authors failed to consider whether the backwardness of the South was not attributable to the disfranchisement and exploitation of the poorest groups by the dominant class at least as much as to the exploitation of the whole region by absentee owners and bankers. Southern "patriots" no doubt enjoyed hearing that the ills of their section were the fault of Northerners, but that did not convince them that they should end their practical coöperation with outside interests, for which they received the consideration due poor relations, and encourage the poor white and the Negro to achieve political, social, and economic reforms. The President had often told businessmen in the country as a whole that the increase of purchasing power would benefit them by increasing the prosperity of industry, and that liberal reforms would preserve rather than injure the system of private enterprise. The arguments had no appreciable effect in winning business support for the New Deal. But outside the South the President did not depend upon the "enlightenment" of businessmen to win elections, rather he encouraged the groups, especially laborers and farmers, who would benefit most directly from his program, to win an improved position in society for themselves by militant assertion of their economic and political rights and power. In the South he did not appeal for such militancy by the submerged groups. But cautious refusal to raise the delicate issues of the Southern racial and class system won no more favorable hearing for the appeal to "enlightened conservatism" in the South than such appeals had received in the rest of the country. The campaign to liberalize the Southern Democratic Party failed, as a cynic without faith in the power of reason to overcome class interest would have predicted in the first place.

The most dramatic scene in the campaign occurred on August 11 at Barnesville, Georgia. Senator George sat on the platform a few feet from the President while the latter declared that the Senator was his personal friend, "beyond any possible question, a gentleman and a scholar," but could not be classified as a liberal, and was, in fact, identified with the "dictatorship of a small minority of individuals and corporations . . . . which has enslaved many of our fellow citizens for more than half a century." [16] As justification for his opposition to Senator George the President declared that the problems of the South as analyzed in the Southern Report required vigorous support in Congress of the administration program.

It is my conviction that the South presents right now the Nation's No. 1 economic problem—the Nation's problem, not merely the South's.[17]

Obvious needs which ought to be attained quickly were the reduction of discriminatory freight rates, a definite floor under industrial wages, and continued raising of the purchasing power of farmers. If the people of Georgia wanted action they had to send to Congress leaders who were

willing to stand up and fight night and day for . . . laws with teeth in them which go to the root of the problems; which remove the inequities, raise the standards and, over a period of years, give constant improvement to the conditions of human life in this State.[18]

The President's campaign did not go unopposed by critics within as well as outside his Party. The label "purge" implied similarity with the purges of party dissidents in the fascist countries and currently in the Soviet Union. The implication served to continue the argument that the President was intent on making himself a dictator. The obvious facts that would-be dictators did not stop with verbal persuasions or permit voters to elect their opponents were not mentioned when the purpose was to avoid discussion on a rational plane. At any rate, the results of the "purge" were unique in the annals of modern politics, for it failed. Those who had been fearful perhaps considered this a demonstration of the truth of the President's statement in March that he had none of the qualifications which would make him a successful dictator, and were comforted. The two Senators whom the President had opposed most actively, Tydings of Maryland and George, were renominated and re-elected. None of the Senators or Representatives who had been singled out as a conservative was defeated except Representative O'Connor of New York, who lost as Democratic candidate for renomination, and again after the Republicans had rewarded him with their nomination. O'Connor's experience was a complete example of the proper party and fate of a conservative Democrat, but the case was in all respects unique, unless the re-election of several liberal Senators, including Barkley of Kentucky, whom the President publicly supported, be accounted further successes of his campaign.

Equally important with the almost total failure of the primaries campaign was the first increase of Republican Congressmen since 1928. Most of the new members had campaigned on thoroughly anti-New Deal platforms, and their victory was taken as the voters' answer to the President's invitation to realign the parties into exclusively liberal and conservative organizations, and then to elect liberals to office. The conservative block in the next Congress was to be much strengthened by the victories of the Republicans as well as anti-New Deal Democrats. The former gained 7 seats in the Senate and 80 in the House of Representatives. The meaning of these results was unmistakable: after eight years of increasing liberalism, as measured by Congressional elections, the country had begun to turn once more towards conservatism. The opposition to the administration which had begun during the fight over the Judiciary Reorganization Bill had taken root in the electorate, which thereupon further strengthened the ranks of opposition in Congress.

In 1939, for the first time since the administration had come to power, no new reform legislation was recommended to Congress. The Fair Labor Standards Act of 1938 turned out to be the last addition to the structure of the Second New Deal. Henceforth efforts on the domestic front were limited to minor improvements of existing laws and their defense against the rising tide of conservative opposition in Congress. In both fields the administration was only partially successful, although none of the major laws of the Second New Deal was repealed, nor was their enforcement compromised by the administration. The essence of the administration's policy on domestic reform during the new period was stated by the President in his Annual Message of January 4, 1939: "We have now passed the period of internal conflict in the launching of our program of social reform. Our full energies may now be released to invigorate the processes of recovery in order to *preserve our reforms. . . .*" [19]

The new strength of conservatism in Congress did not by itself preclude the completion of the Second New Deal and dictate the decision to go over from the offensive to the defensive on the domestic front. That strategy was voluntarily adopted because the administration did not intend to risk defeat of its foreign policy by Southern and Republican retaliation against aggressive pursuit of new domestic reforms. The decision was predicated on the conception that Axis aggression had replaced domestic reaction as the greater threat to American democracy. The creative period of the New Deal was brought to a close in order to reduce domestic tensions and consolidate national unity for purposes of collective security and national defense.

A brief review of events in the foreign sphere since 1935 will reveal the significance of the administration's new strategy.

The Neutrality Act of 1935 was the most important law in the field of foreign policy during the period of the Second New Deal. Isolationists in Congress had several times been discouraged by the State Department from imposing legislation on the administration which would force it to forbid traffic in arms with aggressor nations and their victims alike. In August, 1935, the threat of Mussolini to conquer Ethiopia led the State Department to recommend to Congress adoption of a resolution giving the President power to embargo an aggressor while permitting the victim to buy arms. But the Senate leaders of the Munitions Investigation Committee threatened to filibuster against domestic legislation unless a neutrality law was passed to make an embargo on both aggressors and victims mandatory. In the House, support of the administration seemed stronger, but to prevent an impasse and loss of the important group of reform laws which were about to be voted, the administration consented to a "compromise." This merely limited the term of the law to February 29, 1936. Besides the arms embargo, American ships were forbidden to carry arms to belligerents, and the President was given power to forbid travel by American citizens on belligerent vessels and in designated regions. When the President signed the Neutrality Act on August 31, he criticized the mandatory embargo feature because its "inflexible provisions might drag us into war instead of keeping us out." [20]

In October when the Italian invasion of Ethiopia began, the President invoked the new law and imposed an arms embargo on both nations. In conformity with the law, only materials used exclusively for war, and airplanes, were embargoed. But Mussolini had little need of arms or munitions: he needed oil for his war machines, and this the United States continued to supply him. The Ethiopians, whose arms were absurdly inadequate, were unable to obtain them. The League of Nations imposed similar ineffective sanctions on Italy, which succeeded in antagonizing but not weakening the fascist leadership. The League members argued that if they refused to sell oil to Mussolini, American corporations would willingly assume the additional burden.

The administration recommended in January, 1936, that Congress pass a law under which the President would be empowered to limit to peacetime "normal quantities" the export of articles other than arms which were used in the conduct of war, such as oil, but excepting food and medical supplies. This would at least have made the embargo on Italy as well as Ethiopia a genuine handicap, and would also have encouraged the League to stiffen its sanctions. Provision that Congress might discriminate and impose the embargo only on aggressors was included—unnecessarily, since Congress had the unquestioned right to exert its authority at any time, but to show that the administration cared more for the policy than for its own delegated and discretionary authority to invoke it. This Pittman-McReynolds Bill also prohibited loans to belligerent governments. Isolationists made a strong fight against the Bill, and Secretary Hull appeared before a committee to urge its adoption. The Bill did not pass. On the day that the 1935 Act expired, a hastily enacted resolution extended the Act to May 1, 1937, with an added prohibition of loans and credits to belligerents, and extension of the mandatory arms embargo to any additional states which might become involved in war as a result of applying sanctions against an aggressor. The latter provision served warning that the United States would not only not coöperate with the League, but would also penalize any nation that did. The President signed the new measure, but issued a request that businessmen voluntarily refrain from selling oil and other such non-embargoed materials useful in war to belligerent powers. This was a poor substitute for the embargo on such materials against Italy, and the coöperation with the League powers for collective security which the administration had desired.

Spain was the scene of the next attempt by aggressors to destroy a peaceful government. This struggle took the form of a civil war, for which the Neutrality Act did not provide. The administration did not deviate from the policy of France and Britain and the Non-Intervention Committee of the leading powers. The Committee did not prevent aid by Germany and Italy to the rebel dictator, Franco, but it retreated from the previous rule of international law that a recognized government might buy arms to put down revolt. Only the Soviet Union and Mexico refused to coöperate with this "non-non-intervention" policy and aided the Spanish Republic. It was generally considered that not only the policy of the League powers and the strength of isolationism in this country, but also the powerful campaign in favor of Franco which was conducted by the Roman Catholic Church, most of whose members in the United States were Democrats, led the administration to adopt the policy of embargoing the first government to fight the troops of Hitler. Later, in 1941, the President wrote:

It is useless to argue, with our present knowledge of European and Asiatic affairs, that Spain should have been the place for the democracies of Europe to stop the aggressor nations. . . . The people of the United States and their representatives certainly were not prepared in 1937 to risk the slightest chance of becoming involved in a quarrel in Europe which had all the possibilities of developing into a general European conflict. . . .

It should be borne in mind also that the Rebels in Spain had control over more shipping than did the Loyalists. As a result, if American war materials had been allowed to be sold to the participants in the Spanish conflict, the overwhelming probability was that the Rebel forces would have received greater assistance through American implements of war than would have the Loyalists of Spain.[21]

But many supporters of the Spanish Republic believed that an embargo on the Rebels, and aid to the Republic, the

[329

policy which the United States insisted foreign powers should pursue when it was thrown into civil war in 1861, should be the policy of the government towards the Spanish conflict. Such discrimination between aggressors and their victims would no doubt have been no more acceptable to Congress when applied to civil wars than in international wars, but the administration never proposed discrimination to Congress in the Spanish conflict as it did in other situations.

At first it enforced its policy of embargo on both sides in Spain by extra-legal persuasion. In December, 1936, two exporters nevertheless insisted on using their legal right to sell second-hand airplanes to the Spanish Republic, and consent was reluctantly granted by the State Department. In his Annual Message of January 6, 1937, the President asked that the arms embargo of the Neutrality Act be extended to civil wars. Isolationists were likely to be less sympathetic to the cause of the Spanish Republic than those who believed in collective security, but this time the former found the administration on their side. On January 8, in the first act of the new Congress, a resolution was passed specifically prohibiting the export of implements of war to both sides in Spain, just in time to prevent the shipment of more than one-fourth of one of the airplane orders to the Republic.

The imminent expiration of the Neutrality Act of 1935 produced a new and more intense debate intermittently during the fight over the Judiciary Reorganization Bill. Twenty neutrality measures were introduced. A resolution was finally passed and signed on May 1 which contained minor concessions to the administration. It conferred upon the President discretion as to whether he found that a state of war existed which required the imposition of the arms embargo; but if the embargo was imposed on one belligerent, it had to be imposed on all countries involved in the war. Other commodities useful in war could also be embargoed. No date of expiration was set for the arms and commodities embargo. Another new feature of the Act was limited in its term to May 1, 1939. This was the "cash and carry" plan, which granted the President discretion to prevent the sale of commodities other than arms but useful in war to belligerents unless they paid cash for them in this country before delivery and transported them in ships not owned by the United States. The plan was a compromise between extreme isolationists who desired a mandatory embargo on all materials useful in war, and those who feared that American exports of basic raw materials, such as cotton, oil, and metals, would be ruined.

"Cash and carry" was adopted with a European war in mind: it gave obvious advantages to the powers in control of the seas and would therefore benefit Britain and France more than Germany and Italy. But the next assault on the peace of the world came from the Japanese when they invaded China in July, 1937. In this situation the concessions obtained by the administration were of little value. Japan had a large merchant fleet as well as navy, while China had neither one. Japan also had her own munitions industry, so that under the full operation of the new law she could import raw materials at will under cash and carry, pay for them with her silk and other exports to the United States, carry them home in her own ships and manufacture them herself, thus feeling no effects of the arms embargo. China, on the other hand, could obtain neither arms nor raw materials if the Neutrality Act were invoked. Isolationists demanded that it be invoked nevertheless and that the United States military and naval forces be withdrawn from the Far East. This sentiment was partially appeased by the decisions of the administration to forbid the shipment of arms to either belligerent on government-owned merchant vessels and to

[331]

warn private owners that such cargoes would be carried at their own risk. These restrictions were felt by China more than Japan: the Chinese Ambassador declared that the attitude of his government was one of "deep disappointment." [22] Further than this, the Neutrality Act was not invoked, on the legalistic ground that the belligerents had not declared war. The cruel irony that in order to keep open any supply lines to China it was necessary to permit Japan to obtain much more aid from American sources than China could emphasized for many people the unwisdom of the Neutrality Act.

The Japanese invasion of China and its revelation of the inadequacy of American policy were the immediate causes of the President's first attempt to win popular support for collective security. He chose Chicago, in the heart of the isolationist Midwest, for his important speech of October 5, 1937. The address was a warning to the nation. If aggression were allowed to succeed in other parts of the world, "let no one imagine that America will escape, that America may expect mercy, that this Western Hemisphere will not be attacked."

If those days are not to come to pass—if we are to have a world in which we can breathe freely and live in amity without fear—the peace-loving nations must make a concerted effort to uphold laws and principles on which alone peace can rest secure. . . .
There is no escape through mere isolation or neutrality. . . .
There is a solidarity and interdependence about the modern world, both technically and morally, which makes it impossible for any nation completely to isolate itself from economic and political upheavals in the rest of the world.[23]

Americans might be happy that for the moment they spent far more for bridges and boulevards and dams than for armaments, but they were compelled to look ahead. Ten per cent of the world was breaking down all law, order, and morality, and the remaining 90 per cent was doing nothing about it.

When an epidemic of physical disease starts to spread, the community approves and joins in a quarantine of the patients in order to protect the health of the community against the spread of the disease. . . .

War is a contagion, whether it be declared or undeclared. It can engulf states and peoples remote from the original scene of hostilities. We are determined to keep out of war, yet we cannot insure ourselves against the disastrous effects of war and the dangers of involvement. . . .

Most important of all, the will for peace on the part of peace-loving nations must express itself to the end that nations that may be tempted to violate their agreements and the rights of others will desist from such a course.[24]

The public response to the President's invitation to "quarantine the aggressors" was on the whole unfavorable. The charge was made that he had attempted to distract public attention from the current revelation of Justice Black's former membership in the Ku Klux Klan, and to reassert his leadership after the failure of the court plan by announcing a sensational foreign policy. A strong minority approved collective security and believed that the President had, if anything, understated the dangers of aggression. This minority included important groups of writers, educators, clergymen, and other public leaders, but they were decried as Jeremiahs by "realists," and the public was fairly indifferent.

Practical indifference was also the reaction of the American public when on December 12, 1937, the United States gunboat *Panay* was bombed and sunk by Japanese airplanes under circumstances which made the plea of a mistake incredible. Isolationists made capital of the occasion by demanding the withdrawal of American forces stationed in China. The Ludlow Amendment was almost passed by Congress shortly after the turn of the year. In March, Hitler annexed Austria and immediately began the drive for the destruction of Czechoslovakia. Britain's policy of appeasement under Prime Minister Chamberlain was complemented and re-enforced by the American policy of neutrality: both opened the gates to the aggrandizement of Nazi Germany as well as Italy and Japan. In Britain all hope that appeasement would be abandoned by the Chamberlain government seemed gone with the resignation of Anthony Eden as Foreign Minister in February. In the United States the President was bound by the Neutrality Act, but he worked to obtain support in Congress for stronger policies in limited fields.

The Vinson Act of 1934 had authorized a naval-building program which would bring the Navy up to treaty strength, but Congress did not appropriate sufficient funds to accomplish this purpose before Japan broke down the whole system of treaty limitations on naval strength. On January 29, 1938, the President recommended to Congress an increase by 20 per cent of its appropriations and the expansion of the Navy until it should be capable of protecting the coasts in both oceans at the same time. Debate was sharp. Isolationists accused the administration of having a secret agreement with Britain and of intending to use the Navy as an implement of diplomacy and "aggression" rather than merely of defense. Secretary Hull peremptorily denied that there was any secret arrangement with any foreign power. The debate took place while Hitler annexed Austria and the Japanese opened new campaigns in China. The obvious crumbling of international order and treaties, and the admission by Japan a year earlier that it was building a navy beyond treaty limits, made the wisdom of the President's recommendation clear. Many isolationists voted for the measure even while they denied that the danger of war was sufficient to justify action for collective security. But this ambivalence was also detectable in the policies of Britain and France. The Naval Expansion or "Two Ocean Navy" Act was passed with substantial majorities and signed on May 17.

On June 11 Secretary Hull announced that the government was informally requesting that no airplanes be sold to Japan because of Japanese bombing of civilian populations.

It was apparent that any action which looked to the defense of the Western Hemisphere was acceptable to majority opinion in and out of Congress, even though activities which might reduce the danger of American defenses ever being challenged were still politically impracticable. On August 18, the President made a speech in Kingston, Ontario, in which he extended to Canada the protection of the Monroe Doctrine: "I give to you assurance that the people of the United States will not stand idly by if domination of Canadian soil is threatened by any other Empire." [25]

In September, Hitler dismembered the Czechoslovak Republic. The Munich Accord among Germany, Italy, France, and Great Britain was greeted as a guaranty of "peace for our time," but this final spasm of delusion died rapidly. Time for arming and success in piecemeal conquests had been assured the Axis by the appeasement-neutrality policy of the other powers; now the only question that remained was how far those conquests would be allowed to proceed before the peaceful powers, each one coming to its decision painfully and alone, called a halt. Britain and France drew the line at Poland; Russia and the United States waited until they were attacked; but it was apparent early in 1939 to all but the most blinded advocates of appeasement-isolation-neutrality that another world war was inevitable.

The administration undertook intensive preparations for defense and coöperation with the peaceful nations during the last months of 1938. On March 18, the Mexican government had decreed the expropriation of oil and other properties owned by British and American interests. This most severe test of the Good Neighbor policy was at first met by reprisals against Mexico. Silver purchases by the United States Treasury from Mexico were suspended, and a boycott was imposed against Mexican oil. But Mexico showed by raising her tariffs against American goods, concluding agreements to sell oil in a barter agreement with Germany, and breaking diplomatic relations with Britain that she meant to assert her sovereignty with all the vigor of an equal of the great powers. The suspicions that the Good Neighbor policy was merely a new mask for economic imperialism, and that the United States would not grant Mexico such full sovereignty as Britain and France had exerted when they defaulted their war debts, led all Latin America to watch closely the outcome of Mexico's desperate bid for economic independence.

Mexico did not deny its obligation to pay owners for their properties, but between payment for actual investments and additional payment for the prospective value of unexploited oil properties, Mexico insisted on the former course, while the owners were equally insistent on the latter. The possibility of agreement seemed slight until in November the United States accepted an arrangement for compensation to be paid to American owners of expropriated farm lands on terms not unfavorable to Mexico. This fixed the pattern for similar solution later of the major question of oil properties.

It was particularly important that the United States did not push its claims so aggressively as to lose the support of Mexico or disillusion other Latin American countries with the Good Neighbor policy, because it hoped to obtain agreement on an ambitious plan of hemispheric solidarity at the December meeting of the Pan American Conference in Lima, Peru. At the Conference the proposals of Secretary Hull to bind together the twenty-one republics in a close union for defense were defeated by Argentina. Nevertheless a compromise was reached which became the famous Declaration of Lima. Since the Clark Memorandum of the Hoover administration and subsequent promises and actions of the Roosevelt administration had ended unilateral enforcement of the Monroe Doctrine by the preventive method of intervention with armed force whenever local conditions invited non-American aggression, the only method to secure preventive enforcement of the Monroe Doctrine consistently with the Good Neighbor policy was through multilateral action. The Declaration of Lima was an agreement among the American republics to take such action:

In case the peace, security, or territorial integrity of any American republic is thus threatened by acts of any nature that may impair them, they proclaim their common concern and their determination to make effective their solidarity, coördinating their respective sovereign wills by means of the procedure of consultation established by the conventions in force and by declarations of inter-American conferences, using measures that in each case circumstances may make advisable.[26]

This Declaration indicated the effectiveness of the Good Neighbor policy as a means of achieving joint defense of the hemisphere, and it led to concrete action after the Second World War had begun.

On November 17, a new reciprocal tariff agreement was signed with Canada. On the same day the most important of all the agreements made under the Act of 1934 was concluded with Great Britain. Substantial tariff reductions on important products were conceded by both countries. The agreement signified a drawing together of the two great democracies once again after the ties established during the First World War had been seriously strained by the refusal of the United States to join the League of Nations, the war debts, and other problems.

A loan of twenty-five million dollars was made to China in December by the Export-Import Bank, and the Treasury extended credit arrangements which made it possible for China to purchase substantial quantities of war materials in the United States. For the first time China was given material proof that the United States was not neutral, but identified her own interests with the cause for which China was fighting.

These and other incidents showed increasing orientation of American policy towards support of the non-aggressive countries. At the same time, in notes, public statements, and by the recall of Ambassador Hugh Wilson from Germany on November 14, the refusal of the administration to conciliate aggressor nations was made known. Of the Nazi pogroms which occasioned the recall of Ambassador Wilson, the President publicly declared: "I myself could scarcely believe that such things could occur in a twentieth-century civilization." [27] During the summer the Intergovernmental Committee to assist political and religious refugees from Germany had been established at Evian, France, on the initiative of the United States, but the Hitler government required that a ransom, in the form of purchases of German goods, be paid by the world for the release of hostages. The administration refused to aid Hitler's scheme to "barter human misery for increased exports." [28] Later, a few areas of refuge were opened in the British Dominions and elsewhere. At the time of the Munich crisis, the President addressed two letters to Hitler strongly urging that peaceful negotiations be substituted for force and war. But he did not undertake to pass on the merits of the controversy between Germany and Czechoslovakia.

The administration could have no real influence in restraining aggressor nations so long as it was bound by the Neutrality Act of 1937. The revision of that law in such manner that the economic and political power of the United States should be thrown into the scales against aggression became the dominant purpose of the administration in 1939. The creation of further domestic reforms became secondary to the construction of a sound foreign policy. The two seemed incompatible so long as the administration relied upon the support of conservative Southern Democrats for a stronger foreign policy.

Liberals complained of the "retreat to the right." If the administration retreated, it did so not without powerful rearguard action. It defended the laws and reforms which had been achieved during the period of the Second New Deal against strong assaults, and effectively reduced the opposition in Congress to sniping against the appropriations which would permit existing agencies to carry on work already authorized. Such opposition tactics were sometimes successful, but no significant law of the Second New Deal was repealed, and a few measures were strengthened by amendments.

The inability of the administration to secure revision of the Neutrality Act in order to make the United States the "arsenal of democracy" until after the Second World War had actually begun indicates the necessity to concentrate its efforts on that front and to avoid widening the split in the Democratic Party which had begun in 1937.

As it was, the United States during the six years of the creative period of the New Deal had installed changes in its economic, social, and governmental institutions wider in scope and of deeper significance than during any previous period since the Civil War. A massive body of domestic reform laws had by 1944 withstood the shocks of war and of virtual loss of Democratic majorities in Congress, and they seemed secure against the third Republican effort to put the administration of Franklin Delano Roosevelt out of office: the Tennessee Valley Authority Act, the Glass-Steagall Banking Act, the Gold Reserve Act, the Securities Exchange Act, the Reciprocity Trade Agreements Act, the National Labor Relations Act, the Social Security Act, the Public Utility Holding Company Act, the Wealth Tax Act, the Farm Tenant Act, the Housing Act, the Agricultural Adjustment Act, and the Fair Labor Standards Act.

Not the least mark of the success of the New Deal was that it did not disaffect groups which were restricted by its reforms as much as it increased the loyalty towards democratic institutions of the great majority of the American people who benefited by those reforms. The proof of this came when the transition was made from peace to war and the people of the great Republic more thoroughly than in any previous war in their history were united for victory.

REFERENCE NOTES

CHAPTER I

[1] These and following figures are taken from *Statistical Abstract of the United States: 1940* (Washington: U.S. Government Printing Office, 1941), pp. 310-346, 496, 804.

[2] New York: Vanguard Press, 1931.

[3] *A New Deal* (New York: Macmillan Company), 1932, p. 172.

[4] *Justice*, XIII (June, 1931), 10.

CHAPTER II

[1] *The Public Papers and Addresses of Franklin D. Roosevelt: With a Special Introduction and Explanatory Notes by President Roosevelt* (New York: Random House, 1938), I, 159-206.

[2] *Ibid.*, p. 221.

[3] Franklin D. Roosevelt, "Our Foreign Policy: A Democratic View," *Foreign Affairs*, VI (July, 1928), 573-586.

[4] James A. Farley, *Behind the Ballots: The Personal History of a Politician* (New York: Harcourt, Brace and Company, 1938), p. 61.

[5] *Ibid.*, p. 71.

[6] *Ibid.*, p. 75.

[7] *Ibid.*, p. 81.

[8] *Ibid.*, p. 83.

[9] *The Public Papers . . . of F. D. Roosevelt*, I, 623.

[10] Farley, *op. cit.*, p. 101.

[11] Raymond Moley, *After Seven Years* (New York and London: Harper and Brothers, 1939), pp. 13-14, *et passim*.

[12] *The Public Papers . . . of F. D. Roosevelt*, I, 624-627.

[13] *Ibid.*, pp. 627-639.

[14] *Ibid.*, p. 646.

[15] *Ibid.*, pp. 647-659.

[16] *Ibid.*, pp. 659-669.

[17] *Ibid.*, p. 789.

[18] Moley, *op. cit.*, p. 45.

[19] *The Public Papers . . . of F. D. Roosevelt*, I, 742-756.

[20] Farley, *op. cit.*, p. 171.

[21] *Ibid.*, p. 177.

[22] Moley, *op. cit.*, p. 52.

[23] *The State Papers and Other Public Writings of Herbert Hoover*, ed. William Starr Myers (New York: Doubleday, Doran and Company, Inc., 1934), II, 383.

[24] *Ibid.*, pp. 408-428.

[25] Moley, *op. cit.*, p. 64.

[26] *The Public Papers . . . of F. D. Roosevelt*, I, 844-845.

CHAPTER III

[1] *Statistical Abstract . . . 1934*, p. 730.

[2] Moley, *op. cit.*, pp. 78-79.

[3] William Starr Myers and Walter H. Newton, *The Hoover Administration: A Documented Narrative* (New York and London: Charles Scribner's Sons, 1936), p. 288.

[4] *Ibid.*, pp. 331 et passim.

[5] *The Public Papers . . . of F. D. Roosevelt*, I, 661.

[6] *Ibid.*, p. 663.

[7] Moley, *op. cit.*, p. 119.

[8] *Statistical Abstract . . . 1936*, p. 430.

[9] Myers and Newton, *op. cit.*, p. 337.

[10] *Ibid.*, p. 338.

[11] *Ibid.*, pp. 339-340.

[12] *Statistical Abstract . . . 1940*, p. 167.

[13] Myers and Newton, *op. cit.*, p. 341.

[14] *Ibid.*, pp. 344-345.

[15] Moley, *op. cit.*, p. 143.

[16] Details of these events vary in the following accounts: Myers and Newton, *op. cit.*, pp. 364-366; Moley, *op. cit.*, pp. 144-147; *The Public Papers . . . of F. D. Roosevelt*, I, 870-871.

CHAPTER IV

[1] *The Public Papers . . . of F. D. Roosevelt*, II, 11-16.

[2] Moley, *op. cit.*, p. 151.

[3] *Congressional Record*, Vol. 77, Pt. 1 (73rd Congress: Special Session), pp. 63-65, 67.

[4] *Supra*, p. 40. *The Public Papers . . . of F. D. Roosevelt*, II, 49-54.

[5] *Cong. Record*, Vol. 77, Pt. 1, p. 218.

[6] *The Public Papers . . . of F. D. Roosevelt,* II, 66.

[7] Moley, *op. cit.,* p. 155.

[8] *The Public Papers . . . of F. D. Roosevelt,* II, 56.

[9] *Ibid.,* pp. 34-37.

[10] *Ibid.,* p. 74.

[11] George N. Peek with Samuel Crowther, *Why Quit Our Own* (New York: D. Van Nostrand and Company, 1936), Chaps. II-IV.

[12] *Senate Hearings: Committee on Agriculture and Forestry* (73rd Congress: 1st Session), Vol. 17, pp. 81 *et passim.*

[13] *Ibid.,* pp. 163, 171.

[14] *Cong. Record, loc. cit.,* p. 747.

[15] Moley, *op. cit.,* p. 160.

[16] *New York Times,* Jan. 6, 1933.

[17] *Ibid.,* April 2, 1933.

[18] Moley, *op. cit.,* p. 186.

[19] *House Hearings: Committee on Labor* (73rd Congress: 1st Session), Vol. 4, 18.

[20] *Ibid.,* pp. 3-5, 9.

[21] *Ibid.,* pp. 61-67, 139-158, 886.

[22] Moley, *op. cit.,* p. 187.

[23] *New York Times,* April 12, 1933.

[24] *Cong. Record* (73rd Congress: Special Session), Vol. 77, Pt. 2, pp. 1924, 2065.

[25] *House Hearings, ibid.,* pp. 91-727.
  Cong. Record, ibid., pp. 1188-1189, 1195.

[26] Moley, *op. cit.,* p. 187.

[27] *New York Times,* May 2, 1933.

[28] *New York Herald Tribune,* May 1, 1931.

[29] *New York Times,* Dec. 18, 1931.

[30] *Ibid.,* June 25, 1932.

[31] Moley, *op. cit.,* p. 188.

[32] *House Hearings, loc. cit.*

[33] *New York Times,* May 4, 1933.

[34] *The Public Papers . . . of F. D. Roosevelt,* II, 155-158.

[35] *New York Times,* May 6, 1933.

[36] Moley, *op. cit.,* p. 189.

[37] Moley, *loc. cit.*

[38] *Senate Hearings: Committee on Finance* (73rd Congress: 1st Session), Vol. 13, p. 6.

[39] *House Hearings: Committee on Ways and Means* (73rd Congress: 1st Session), Vol. 18, pp. 68-72.

40 *Ibid.,* p. 142.

41 *Senate Hearings, ibid.,* pp. 288-289, 395 *et passim.*

42 *The Public Papers . . . of F. D. Roosevelt,* II, 246.

43 *United States Statutes at Large* (73rd Congress), Vol. XLVIII, Pt. 1, p. 64.

CHAPTER V

1 *The Public Papers . . . of F. D. Roosevelt,* II, 138.

2 *Loc. cit.*

3 *Ibid.,* p. 167.

4 *Ibid.,* p. 186.

5 Moley, *op. cit.,* p. 213.

6 *Ibid.,* p. 215.

7 *Ibid.,* p. 240.

8 *The Public Papers . . . of F. D. Roosevelt,* II, 264.

9 *Ibid.,* p. 266.

CHAPTER VI

1 *Statistical Abstract . . . 1934,* p. 730.

2 *Ibid., 1936,* p. 298.

3 *The American Yearbook: 1933,* ed. A. B. Hart (New York: American Yearbook Corporation, 1934), p. 360.

4 *Statistical Abstract . . . 1934,* p. 304.

5 *Ibid.,* p. 730.

6 *Ibid.,* p. 284.

7 *The Public Papers . . . of F. D. Roosevelt,* II, 295-303, 308-311.

8 *Statistical Abstract . . . 1936,* p. 323.

9 *Ibid., 1934,* p. 284.

10 Hugh S. Johnson, *The Blue Eagle from Egg to Earth* (Garden City: Doubleday, Doran and Company, Inc., 1935), p. 295.

11 *Statistical Abstract . . . 1940,* p. 346.

12 Peek with Crowther, *op. cit.,* Chs. II-IV.

13 Henry A. Wallace, "Agricultural Conditions," *The American Yearbook: 1933,* p. 446.

14 *Statistical Abstract . . . 1936,* p. 669.
Peek with Crowther, *op. cit.,* pp. 129-130.
The American Yearbook, 1933, pp. 451-452.

15 *Statistical Abstract . . . 1936,* p. 601.

16 *Ibid.,* p. 606.

17 *Ibid.,* p. 298.

CHAPTER VII

[1] *The Public Papers . . . of F. D. Roosevelt*, II, 352. Cf. James Daniel Paris, *Monetary Policies of the United States: 1932–1938* (New York: Columbia University Press, 1938), p. 120.

[2] *Current History*, XXXIX (Jan., 1934), 452.

[3] *Statistical Abstract . . . 1934*, p. 284.

[4] *Current History*, XXXIX (Jan., 1934), 454-455.

[5] *The Public Papers . . . of F. D. Roosevelt*, II, 525.

[6] *Statistical Abstract . . . 1934*, p. 730; *ibid.*, *1935*, p. 748.

[7] *Ibid.*, *1936*, p. 323.

[8] *Ibid.*, p. 298.

CHAPTER VIII

[1] Moley, *op. cit.*, p. 284.

[2] *Loc. cit.*

[3] *The Public Papers . . . of F. D. Roosevelt*, III, 49.

[4] *The New International Year Book: 1934*, ed. F. H. Vizetelly (New York and London: Funk and Wagnalls Company, 1935), pp. 230, 232.

[5] *Ibid.*, p. 230.

[6] *Senate Hearings: Committee on Finance* (73rd Congress: 2nd Session), Vol. 14, pp. 27-29.

[7] *Ibid.*, p. 4.

[8] *The Public Papers . . . of F. D. Roosevelt*, III, 115.

[9] *Senate Hearings, op. cit.*, pp. 57-97 *et passim.*

[10] Moley, *op. cit.*, p. 324.

[11] *The Public Papers . . . of F. D. Roosevelt*, III, 117.

[12] *Loc. cit.*

[13] *Statistical Abstract . . . 1936*, p. 601.

[14] *Ibid.*, p. 298.

[15] *Ibid.*, p. 601.

[16] *The Public Papers . . . of F. D. Roosevelt*, II, 13.

[17] Paris, *op. cit.*, pp. 127-130 *et passim.*

[18] *The Public Papers . . . of F. D. Roosevelt*, III, 55.

[19] *Ibid.*, p. 57.

[20] Johnson, *op. cit.*, p. 272.

[21] *The Public Papers . . . of F. D. Roosevelt*, III, 137.

[22] *Ibid.*, p. 129.

[23] Irving Stone, *Clarence Darrow: For the Defense* (New York: Doubleday, Doran & Co., 1941), pp. 508-509.

[24] *The Public Papers . . . of F. D. Roosevelt*, III, 137.

[25] Johnson, *op. cit.*, pp. 272-273.

[26] National Recovery Review Board, "Report to the President" (mimeographed copy in Columbia University Law Library, New York), I-III.

[27] *Cong. Record* (73rd Congress: 2nd Session), Vol. 78, Pt. 9, pp. 9234-9240; 9320-9328; 9333-9336.

[28] Johnson, *op. cit.*, Chs. XXVIII-XXIX.

[29] *The Public Papers . . . of F. D. Roosevelt*, III, 417-418.

[30] *Statistical Abstract . . . 1936*, p. 766.

[31] *Ibid.*, pp. 298, 323.

[32] *The Public Papers . . . of F. D. Roosevelt*, III, 127.

[33] *Ibid.*, p. 130.

[34] *New International Year Book: 1934*, pp. 673-674.

[35] *Statistical Abstract . . . 1940*, p. 354.

[36] *Cong. Record* (73rd Congress: 2nd Session), Vol. 78, Pt. 4, pp. 3443-3444.

[37] *Senate Hearings: Committee on Education and Labor* (73rd Congress: 2nd Session), Vol. 5, pp. 8-12.

[38] March 26, 1934.

[39] *Senate Hearings, op. cit.*, p. 376.

[40] *Ibid.*, p. 383.

[41] *Ibid.*, p. 407.

[42] *Ibid.*, pp. 497-498.

[43] *New York Herald Tribune*, April 10, 1934.

[44] *New York Times*, April 30, 1934.

[45] *The Public Papers . . . of F. D. Roosevelt*, III, 167.

[46] *New York Times*, March 28, 1934.

[47] *Current History*, XL (May, 1934), p. 201.

[48] *Cong. Record* (73rd Congress: 2nd Sesssion), Vol. 78, Pt. 11, p. 12018.

[49] *Ibid.*, p. 12052.

[50] Moley, *op. cit.*, p. 292 *et passim*.

[51] *The Public Papers . . . of F. D. Roosevelt*, III, 439.

[52] *New International Year Book: 1934*, p. 722.

[53] *Current History*, XLI (Dec., 1934), p. 333.

[54] *The Public Papers . . . of F. D. Roosevelt*, IV, 15.

CHAPTER IX

[1] *Public Papers . . . of F. D. Roosevelt*, II, 545.

[2] New York: Dodd, Mead and Company, 1934.

[3] *Public Papers . . . of F. D. Roosevelt*, III, 240.

[4] *Cong. Record* (73rd Congress: 1st Session), Vol. 77, Pt. 5, p. 4888.

[5] *New York Herald Tribune*, December 15, 1932.

CHAPTER X

[1] *Public Papers . . . of F. D. Roosevelt*, IV, 15-25.

[2] *Senate Hearings: Committee on Finance* (74th Congress: 1st Session), Vol. 15, pp. 922, 1217, *et passim.*

[3] *Public Papers . . . of F. D. Roosevelt*, IV, 324.

[4] *Ibid.*, V, 663-666.

[5] *Public Papers . . . of F. D. Roosevelt*, IV, 152.

[6] *Ibid.*, pp. 149-151.

[7] *Ibid.*, p. 281.

[8] *Ibid.*, p. 274.

[9] Farley, *Behind the Ballots*, p. 242.

[10] *The American Progress*, Vol. I, No. 32 (Mar. 29, 1934), p. 1.

[11] *Ibid.*, Vol. II, No. 3 (Feb. 1, 1935), p. 4.

[12] *Current History*, XLII (Aug., 1935), p. 515.

[13] *The American Progress*, Vol. II, No. 8 (July, 1935), p. 1.

[14] *Public Papers . . . of F. D. Roosevelt*, IV, 271

[15] *Ibid.*, pp. 273-274.

[16] *Ibid.*, pp. 355-356.

[17] *Ibid.*, p. 357.

[18] *Ibid.*, IV, 102.

[19] *Ibid.*, IV, 100.

[20] *Ibid.*, pp. 98-99.

[21] *Current History*, Vol. 42 (Sept., 1935), p. 630.

[22] *Public Papers . . . of F. D. Roosevelt*, IV, 83.

[23] *Ibid.*, p. 81.

[24] *Current History*, Vol. 42 (April, 1935), p. 66.

[25] *Senate Hearings: Committee on Finance* (74th Congress: 1st Session), Vol. 17, p. 14.

[26] *Ibid.*, pp. 127, 769.

[27] *Ibid.*, Vol. 18, p. 2454.

[28] *Ibid.*, Vol. 17, p. 1113.

[29] *Senate Hearings: Subcommittee of Committee on the Judiciary* (74th Congress: 1st Session), Vol. 14.

[30] *House Hearings: Committee on Labor* (74th Congress: 1st Session), Vol. 5, p. 203.

[31] *Ibid.*, p. 200.

[32] *Senate Hearings: Committee on Education and Labor* (74th Congress: 1st Session), Vol. 6, p. 122.

[33] *House Hearings: Committee on Labor* (74th Congress: 1st Session), Vol. 5, p. 174.

CHAPTER XI

[1] *Panama Refining Company* v. *Ryan*, 293 U.S. 388.

[2] *Railroad Retirement Board* v. *Alton Railroad Company*, 295 U.S. 330, p. 368.

[3] *Humphrey's Executor* v. *U.S.*, 295 U.S. 602, p. 629.

[4] *Louisville Bank* v. *Radford*, 295 U.S. 555, p. 602.

[5] *Schechter Corporation* v. *United States*, 295 U.S. 495, p. 548.

[6] *Ibid.*, p. 542.

[7] *Ibid.*, p. 551.

[8] *Public Papers . . . of F. D. Roosevelt*, IV, 215.

[9] *Ibid.*, p. 219.

[10] *Ibid.*, pp. 220-221.

[11] *Ibid.*, pp. 297-298.

[12] *Statistical Abstract . . . 1940*, p. 340.

[13] *Ibid.*, 1936, p. 766; *ibid.*, 1938, p. 782.

[14] *Ibid.*, 1940, p. 322.

[15] *U.S.* v. *Butler*, 297 U.S. 1, pp. 62-63.

[16] *Ibid.*, p. 74.

[17] *Ibid.*, pp. 85-86.

[18] *Ibid.*, pp. 87-88.

[19] *Ashwander* v. *TVA*, 297 U.S. 288.

[20] *Carter* v. *Carter Coal Company*, 298 U.S. 238, p. 332.

[21] *Morehead, Warden*, v. *New York ex rel. Tipaldo*, 298 U.S. 587, p. 611.

[22] *Ibid.*, p. 628.

[23] *Ibid.*, p. 631.

[24] *Ibid.*, p. 632.

[25] *Ibid.*, p. 633. Italics added.

[26] *Ibid.*, p. 635.

[27] *Public Papers . . . of F. D. Roosevelt*, V, 191-192.

CHAPTER XII

[1] *Public Papers . . . of F. D. Roosevelt*, V, 8-18.

[2] *Ibid.*, pp. 102-107.

[3] *New York Times*, March 19, 1936.

[4] *Current History*, XLIV (August, 1936), p. 52.

[5] *Public Papers . . . of F. D. Roosevelt*, V, 233-236.

[6] *Current History*, XLIV (August, 1936), p. 53.

[7] *Ibid.*, p. 53.

[8] Herbert Harris, "That Third Party," *Current History*, XLV (October, 1936), p. 91.

[9] *Ibid.*, p. 96.
[10] *Public Papers . . . of F. D. Roosevelt*, V, 377.
[11] *Ibid.*, p. 316.
[12] *Ibid.*, p. 495.
[13] *Ibid.*, p. 389.
[14] *Ibid.*, pp. 388-389.
[15] *Ibid.*, p. 424.
[16] *Ibid.*, p. 487.
[17] *Ibid.*, pp. 482-483.
[18] *Ibid.*, p. 486.
[19] *Ibid.*, p. 485.
[20] *Ibid.*, pp. 487-488.
[21] *Ibid.*, p. 488.
[22] *Ibid.*, p. 536.
[23] *Ibid.*, p. 549.
[24] *Ibid.*, p. 557.
[25] *Ibid.*, p. 571.
[26] *New York Times*, Oct. 2, 1936.
[27] *Ibid.*, Oct. 8, 1936.
[28] *Ibid.*, Oct. 10, 1936.
[29] *Ibid.*, Oct. 13, 1936.
[30] *Ibid.*, Oct. 14, 1936.
[31] *Ibid.*, Oct. 22, 1936.
[32] *Ibid.*, Oct. 17, 31, 1936.
[33] *Ibid.*, Nov. 1, 1936.
[34] *Ibid.*, July 17, 24, Aug. 3, Sept. 26, Oct. 30, Nov. 1, 1936.
[35] *Ibid.*, Oct. 30, 1936.
[36] *Time*, Oct. 26, 1936, p. 16.
[37] *World Almanac*, 1937, pp. 906 ff.

CHAPTER XIII

[1] *Time*, Nov. 16, 1936, p. 93.
[2] *Public Papers . . . of F. D. Roosevelt*, V, 636.
[3] *Ibid.*, p. 639.
[4] *Ibid.*, pp. 639-640.
[5] *Ibid.*, p. 641.
[6] *Ibid.*, pp. 641-642.
[7] *Public Papers . . . of F. D. Roosevelt* (New York: The Macmillan Company, 1941), 1937, p. 5.
[8] *Ibid.*, p. 52.

[9] *Ibid.*, pp. 53-54.

[10] *Ibid.*, p. 54.

[11] *Ibid.*, p. 55.

[12] *Loc. cit.*

[13] *Ibid.*, p. 59.

[14] *Ibid.*, p. 116.

[15] *Ibid.*, p. 121.

[16] *Ibid.*, p. 126.

[17] *Ibid.*, p. 129.

[18] *Ibid.*, pp. 132-133.

[19] *West Coast Hotel Company* v. *Parrish*, 300 U.S. 379, pp. 399-400.

[20] *National Labor Relations Board* v. *Jones and Laughlin Steel Corporation*, 301 U.S. 1, p. 33.

[21] *Ibid.*, p. 34.

[22] *Ibid.*, p. 42.

[23] *Public Papers . . . of F. D. Roosevelt*, 1937, p. 153.

[24] *Helvering* v. *Davis*, 301 U.S. 619, pp. 644-645.

[25] *New International Year Book, 1937*, p. 751.

[26] *Public Papers . . . of F. D. Roosevelt* (Random House), V. 672-673.

[27] *Cong. Record* (75th Congress: 1st Session), Vol. 81, Pt. 7, p. 7882.

[28] *Public Papers . . . of F. D. Roosevelt* (Macmillan), 1937, 210-211.

[29] *Ibid.*, p. 254.

[30] *Ibid.*, pp. 80-81.

[31] Carey McWilliams, *Ill Fares the Land* (Boston: Little, Brown and Company, 1942), pp. 69, 89, 104, 218-219.

[32] *Public Papers . . . of F. D. Roosevelt*, 1937, 82.

[33] *Ibid.*, p. 84.

[34] *House Hearings: Committee on Ways and Means* (75th Congress: 1st Session), Vol. 25.

[35] *Statistical Abstract . . . 1938*, p. 782; 1939, p. 774.

[36] *Ibid., 1940*, p. 322.

[37] *Ibid.*, p. 340.

CHAPTER XIV

[1] *Public Papers . . . of F. D. Roosevelt*, 1938, 12.

[2] *Ibid.*, p. 227.

[3] *Ibid.*, p. 333.

[4] *World Almanac*, 1939, p. 754.

[5] *Public Papers . . . of F. D. Roosevelt*, 1938, 312.

[6] *Ibid.*, p. 313.

[7] *Ibid.*, p. 364.

[8] *Ibid.*, p. 179.

[9] *Ibid.*, pp. 191-192.

[10] *Ibid.*, p. 37.

[11] *New York Times,* January 11, 1938.

[12] *Public Papers . . . of F. D. Roosevelt,* 1938, 398.

[13] *Ibid.*, pp. 488-489.

[14] *World Almanac,* 1939, pp. 535, 769 ff.

[15] *New York Times,* August 13, 1938.

[16] *Public Papers . . . of F. D. Roosevelt,* 1938, 468-469.

[17] *Ibid.*, p. 464.

[18] *Ibid.*, pp. 466-467.

[19] *Ibid.*, 1939, 7. Italics added.

[20] *Ibid.* (Random House), IV, 346.

[21] *Ibid.* (Macmillan), 1937, 192-193.

[22] Whitney H. Shepardson in collaboration with William O. Scroggs, *The United States in World Affairs, 1937* (New York and London: Harper and Brothers, 1938), p. 205.

[23] *Public Papers . . . of F. D. Roosevelt,* 1937, 408-409.

[24] *Ibid.*, pp. 410-411.

[25] *Ibid.*, 1938, 493.

[26] Shepardson, Scroggs, *U.S. in World Affairs, 1938,* pp. 376-377.

[27] *Public Papers . . . of F. D. Roosevelt,* 1938, 597.

[28] *Ibid.*, p. 174.

INDEX

354]